PLAY THERAPY
WITH
SEXUALLY
ABUSED
CHILDREN

PLAY THERAPY

WITH

SEXUALLY

ABUSED

CHILDREN

A SYNERGISTIC CLINICAL-DEVELOPMENTAL APPROACH

Robert A. Ciottone, PH.D.
John M. Madonna, ED.D.

with historical commentary by
Mary Acunzo, PH.D.

JASON ARONSON INC.
Northvale, New Jersey
London

Production Editor: M'lou Pinkham

This book was set in 11 pt. Berkeley Book by Alpha Graphics of Pittsfield, New Hampshire, and printed and bound by Book-mart Press of North Bergen, New Jersey.

Library of Congress Cataloging-in-Publication Data

Ciottone, Robert A.
    Play therapy with sexually abused children : a synergistic
clinical-developmental approach / by Robert A. Ciottone and John M.
Madonna, with historical commentary by Mary Acunzo.
      p. cm.
    Includes bibliographical references and index.
    ISBN 1-56821-571-1 (alk. paper)
    1. Sexually abused children—Mental health. 2. Play therapy.
I. Madonna, John M. II. Title.
RJ507.S49C54 1996
618.92'858360651—dc20   95-42102

Manufactured in the United States of America. Jason Aronson Inc. offers books and cassettes. For information and catalog write to Jason Aronson Inc., 230 Livingston Street, Northvale, New Jersey 07647.

To Mickey and all the children like him.

Contents

Preface   ix

Acknowledgments   xiii

I   Introduction: Synergistic Play Therapy   1

II   A Boy Named Mickey: Family Dysfunction
and the Impact of Sexual Abuse   5
     The Assessment and Planning Phase   8
     The Foster Care Interface   11
     An Overview of Problems and Goals   17

III   Clinical Antecedents of Synergistic Play Therapy   23

IV   The Conceptual Framework of Synergistic
Play Therapy   37

V   Synergistic Play Therapy with Mickey Begins   53

VI   The Development of Metaphor as a
Therapeutic Vehicle   85

VII   Setting the Stage for Recall of Trauma   117

VIII Overcoming Remaining Defenses: Full Disclosure   137

  IX Accessing the Rage   151

   X Retribution through the Metaphor of Play   163

  XI The Closing Stages of Play Therapy   179

 XII Implications of Synergistic Play Therapy:
      Retrospect and Prospect   203

References   215

Index   221

Preface

This book presents a newly defined approach to play therapy, one that synergistically integrates a metatheoretical, developmental perspective with the clinical work of Haim Ginott. The latter is in itself an integration of several clinical perspectives regarding child treatment that draws upon the constructs and techniques of the psychodynamic tradition, learning theory principles, and Rogerian self-theory. In the approach presented here, which we have termed *Synergistic Play Therapy*, the metatheoretical frame of reference within which these notions are considered is the organismic developmental perspective, originally articulated by Werner (1948, 1957), Werner and Kaplan (1963), and Wapner and Werner (1957), and elaborated by Kaplan and colleagues (1976), Wapner and colleagues (1973), Wapner (1981), Wapner and colleagues (1981), and Cirillo and Kaplan (1983). In that context therapeutic gain is defined as developmental advance of the sort characterized by the orthogenetic principle. That concept, articulated by Werner (1957), holds that all that occurs through development proceeds from a global and diffuse state through increasing differentiation and hierarchic integration.

With reference to play therapy as a means by which to resolve problems that impede or reverse progress in the child's developing "self–world" relationship, the orthogenetic principle establishes an overarching goal. Specifically, the effort becomes one of helping the child differentiate aspects of the experiential fusion that results from the dedifferentiating impact of pathogenic factors (such as the trauma of abuse). Play therapy, therefore, is intended to help the child achieve a differentiated sense of self and an integrated, "healthy" perspective that encourages goal-oriented transactions that reflect the entitlement of rights and the empowerment of developing mastery.

Inherent in this approach is the assumption that the self–world relationship has both structural (part–whole) dimensions and a dynamic (means–ends) aspect, the latter defined by the individual's transactional patterns. These develop in the context of a world constructed by the active imposition of meaning. In other words, each person cognitively, affectively, and valuatively construes the physical, interpersonal, and sociocultural aspects of the environment and transacts with the world thus structured. The way in which a child construes a world that has been in some way neglectful, rejecting, or traumatizing is therefore, by definition, a critical determinant of the prospect for his or her achieving developmental advance. What meaning, for example, does the child give to his or her abuse? What feelings emerge and what relative importance does the child assign to the experience and its implications for self concept and self–world relationships?

Disclosure is a crucial element in play therapy with sexually abused children. In this context *disclosure* does not mean simply a child's sharing information about the abuse, but rather the recall and representation of the trauma and the cognitions, emotions, and valuations associated with it. When disclosure thus defined does occur, psychotherapeutic *working through* becomes a possibility.

The working through sought in play therapy with abused children involves the differentiation and integration of the cognitive, affective, and valuative impact of the trauma. It is then imperative to facilitate the reshaping of the associated behaviors, which have converged to form a pathological constellation of one sort or another, into a pattern that represents developmental advance. With disclosure and working through thus defined, play therapy becomes a powerful modality for achieving psychic integration in the wake of abuse.

Typically, the recall and representation of abuse is extremely difficult; anxiety and consequent defenses combine to form a powerful resistance. The first challenge for the play therapist is therefore to establish a compelling and safe treatment environment such that the damaging effects of the abuse can become manifest. The process of providing that safety goes beyond the need for rapport that exists in all clinical interactions. Here it is necessary to communicate that neither judgment nor censure will befall the child and that no exploitation, coercion, negation of rights, or forceful violations of privacy or dignity will occur, nor will the therapist recoil from or abandon the child when she or he risks the vulnerability of setting defenses aside.

It may seem odd to highlight negatives (i.e., what will not occur) in considering the concept of rapport. Abused children, however, have been traumatized by aberrant forms of "approach behavior." To base beginning attempts at establishing a therapeutic relationship solely on the therapist's willingness to reach out—however caring or supportive the intent—may, paradoxically, lessen the child's psychological availability by encouraging withdrawal and/or constriction. More subtly, a youngster, while masking rage, may respond by increasing his or her reliance upon compensatory behaviors intended to secure and retain caring responses from others.

What of the child whose egocentric construction of the abuse experience leads him or her to a heartfelt but secretive sense of responsibility for it? Or the child whose recollection includes the physical pleasure that may have occurred? When the posture of victim seems a requirement implied by the therapist's manner, children who have construed their experience of abuse in such terms may well retreat further into a secretly maintained sense of eroded worth, feeling it to be disguised only by their success in deceptively presenting the demeanor that the therapist seems predisposed to value. In other words, the child who, despite objective fact, does not feel exploited may assume the role of victim but fail to engage in play or interaction with a genuineness that would allow developmental advance to occur. A contrived, saccharinlike quality may begin to characterize the process. In such instances play therapy will likely deteriorate from providing the potential for psychic integration and developmental advance into what has sometimes been called "making nice," a frequent pretender to the designation "psychotherapy."

Obviously, rapport needs to include the availability of warmth (but not its uninvited imposition) and caring (but with an appreciation of the ways in which the child construes its various forms of expression within a frame of reference colored by the experience of abuse). Typically, qualities of compassion are highly developed among clinicians who seek to respond to the psychological needs of abused children. In fact, it is largely because child clinicians are likely to be deeply touched by the suffering of an abused child that reminders of the need to begin from the child's frame of reference are sometimes necessary. Only in that way can interventions be consistently and effectively geared to the child's affective and valuative constructions. The alternative is likely to be countertherapeutic, that is, interventions reflective solely of the therapist's need to compensate for the horror of abuse by extending global and diffuse caring.

In this book we discuss instances in which a play therapist needs to contain the impulse to frame interventions out of compassion alone. We present an alternative conceptual framework, *Synergistic Play Therapy*, based on the developmental characteristics of the child's perspective. Another and overarching aim of this book is to present Synergistic Play Therapy as a means by which to integrate play therapy technique fashioned after the work of Ginott with an organismic-developmental metatheoretical perspective originally articulated by Heinz Werner, and to derive applications therefrom for play therapy with sexually abused preadolescent children.

The book recounts the case of a boy pseudonymously named Mickey, and discusses theoretical concepts to help the reader understand the psychological damage he suffered as a result of abuse. We give a rationale for developing treatment goals, shaping playroom technique, and framing interventions, and follow it up with transcripts from several sessions and a discussion of the concepts and applications they exemplify. The book concludes with an overview of Synergistic Play Therapy theory and technique and how, in this instance, they formed the basis of an effort to help a boy named Mickey. This book is an elaboration of earlier clinical research regarding the play therapy treatment of a sexually abused child (Ciottone et al. [1992] and Ciottone and Madonna [1992, 1993]).

Acknowledgments

Our thanks and appreciation to Michael Moskowitz and Jason Aronson for helping this work reach the public forum.

* * *

Any litany of tribute and gratitude inevitably errs by its omissions. This one is no exception.

Thanks to the many children who, over the past thirty years, have shared their young lives with me. Thanks also to the parents and other caregivers who allowed me to join with them in their daunting responsibility to seek the fullest development for the youngsters in their charge.

Thanks to my family who taught, modeled, and extended love and good humor, strong values, and gentle sensitivity. Theirs has been an unquestioned readiness to reach out and respond with caring that is always present, never maudlin, and often couched in laughter. Thanks to my own children, Greg, Kim, and Jon, and to my granddaughter, Heather; to my parents, Anthony B. Ciottone and June McCarl Ciottone; to George and Phyllis Ciottone; to Judy Marino, my wife of many years; to Rosaria Barrancho Ciottoni; to Nick and Rose Comerci; to Carlo V. Ciottoni; to Bertha and

George McGilton; to Peggy Ann and George McCarl; and to all whose names, through the union of Irish and Italian families, would require many more pages to list. Thanks to every one of them for having shaped my life.

Thanks to the gifted teachers I have had the honor to study with. Particular thanks to Drs. Helen Peixotto, Arthur Orgel, Norman Harway, Robert Goldstein, and Seymour Wapner.

Thanks to the very talented colleagues and friends from whom I have learned so much. Special thanks to Drs. Jerry B. Saffer, Sherrill "Ted" Conna, Martin Young, and Robert C. McMillan. Thanks to Ms. Xu Xiang. A very special acknowledgment to Craig Feldman, Ph.D., a gifted child clinician whose life was tragically ended by leukemia while he was still a young man. Thanks to Judith Israel, MSN, who served as family therapist in the case presented.

Thanks also to the many interns and graduate students whose insightful questions and energetic dedication have provided stimulation that has been invaluable for me. Graduate students at Clark University over the past twenty-five years are due a special note of thanks in that regard.

—*Robert A. Ciottone*

* * *

I wish to thank my wife, Karen, whose encouragement and patience made my efforts possible. Also, I would like to thank my children, Matthew, Kara, Jeff, Katie, and Iris, for teaching me much about how childhood should be.

—*John Madonna*

* * *

Finally, we both want to thank Kim Josefek, whose computer wizardry rescued us at a big moment, and the graduate students from Clark University's Department of Psychology for their efforts in this regard: Johanna Sagarin, Michelle Mamberg, and Stephen Young.

Introduction: Synergistic Play Therapy

The intensity of feelings, thoughts, and needs attendant upon a child's developing relationship with the world is seldom matched in adult life. Like a splash of color on a new canvas, the impact of early experience upon a youngster's frame of reference remains undiminished in its salience.

In human development the importance of being heard and understood is unquestioned. A child's attempt to share the effort of making sense of ongoing experience, however, is often muted in its hearing by the filter of adult perspective. To some extent such communication fails when adults become rusty in the expressive modes of childhood, particularly with regard to the communicative function of play. Indeed, as Erikson (1963) stated, "To play it out is the most natural and self healing process in childhood."

Treatment of psychological problems requires communication, no less in work with children than with adults. As Ginott (1959) has noted, "A child's play is his talk and toys are his words." Play therapists, therefore, must not abandon the perspective of an adult, but restore to it fluency in the language of play and with it an active awareness of what it was like when precedent and context were yet to take on the complexity that would mollify impact. It is, in other words, the play therapist's challenge to view self–world relationships from the cognitive, emotional, and valuative vantage point of the child as well as the adult. Accordingly, the purpose of this book is to outline, illustrate, and discuss one means for doing so. Specifically, we present a conceptual framework, along with derivative techniques, for what we have termed *Synergistic Play Therapy*, a powerful treatment method that can be used with youngsters approximately 5 through 10 years old.

Drawing upon a unique resource, the authors have extensively studied a completely videotaped record of a two-and-one-half-year course of Synergistic Play Therapy conducted by R. Ciottone with a sexually abused boy who was 7½ years old at the beginning of treatment. Therapy transcripts from key stages of treatment are presented with a description of the accompanying "choreography" of playroom interactions. Although comments interspersed with those sessions have particular reference to work with children suffering the effects of abuse, the approach is also discussed in terms of its general application in play therapy. The concepts and techniques are in fact applicable to youngsters presenting a variety of psychological problems.

The play therapy concepts and techniques of Ginott are the pivotal framework for the approach presented here. The approach includes theoretical constructs drawn from psychodynamics, learning theory, and cognitive development, with internal consistency maintained through implied recognition of the organismic developmental notion of psychological levels of organization. Indeed, that aspect of the organismic developmental perspective represents a metatheoretical frame of reference for the effort outlined here. Clinical data that emerge in psychotherapeutic interaction can be understood in terms analogous, for example, to hierarchically ordered concepts of bodily structure. A hand might be conceptualized as a configuration of cells, as histological microsystems, and/or as a gross anatomical structure. Likewise, to organize psychological data at one level of organization does not diminish the conceptual utility of another, but rather implies "nested constructs" with interventions conceptualized at one level (e.g., psychodynamic) having the potential to reverberate through others (e.g., cognitive, behavioral, familial).

The principles of organismic developmental "metatheory" included here are those derived originally from the work of Heinz Werner and furthered by Seymour Wapner, Bernard Kaplan, and others. In that context development refers not to chronology or "stages" but to the ordering of phenomena from more primitive to more advanced, or from relatively global and undifferentiated to relatively differentiated and hierarchically integrated. Like all that occurs through development, therefore, a child's self–world relationships, the ways in which she or he understands them, and the transactional patterns of behavior that result are orderable on a continuum from more primitive to more advanced, both in their structural (part–whole) and dynamic (means–ends) aspects. The principles associated with that framework have found application in many areas of psychology and it is our view that they also provide a rich metatheoretical context within which to conceptualize and monitor the progress of play therapy.

Although we seek clarity in theoretical reasoning, it is also our intention to emphasize playroom technique. How, for example, might a therapist manage being the object of a child's aggressive play or angry acting out? What, after all, are appropriate limits and how can they be established and enforced? Should feeding or gift giving be part of the process? What toys and how many of them should be available in a playroom? To what extent is it helpful for a therapist to participate in play with the child? How might a therapist phrase comments in order to achieve and maintain therapeutic rapport?

Obviously, answers to such questions depend upon the theoretical perspective of the therapist, but it is our view that those formulations need to be made explicit. Through case illustration and discussion we will attempt to make them explicit and in the process make clear both the part–whole and means–ends relationships that define Synergistic Play Therapy.

A Boy Named Mickey: Family Dysfunction and the Impact of Sexual Abuse

By the time he had logged only seven short years of life, Mickey wanted to die. He had twice tried to hang himself, but had been discovered and punished for his trouble. Sometime later he barely escaped injury when he crept into a parked car and set it on fire. Retrospectively, it can be said that he was probably "red flagging" the abuse that was later disclosed and that had continued undiscovered during the Department of Social Services' (DSS) repeated investigations of physical abuse and neglect complaints. Tragically, Mickey's actions do not defy understanding when the dysfunction of his family and the failure of protective societal systems are considered.

Mickey had determined very early that he could rely only on himself. He had accepted the notion of required self-sufficiency, not in a depressed or self-pitying way, but as a kind of unquestioned premise. Feelings of sadness and a sense of despair eventually caught up with him, not because he was unable to rely upon the concern and help of others, but because he sometimes reached the limits of his own resourcefulness.

Mickey was, however, also possessed of a decisiveness beyond his years and of a "don't look back" philosophy by which he simply accepted as necessary the most extreme consequences of his acting upon any option he chose, even when he saw it as the only one available. Whatever other purpose his suicidal behavior might have had, Mickey had considered death an option.

An extraordinary capacity for empathy combined with strong feelings of responsibility more than qualified Mickey for the description of "parentified child" with regard to his sister and four brothers. Although he was the second of five, his sister, one year older, was significantly less capable and further hampered by learning disabilities. Like the three younger boys, Carol looked upon Mickey as a big brother. With each episode of violence, Mickey felt their pain as well as his own. Most frequently he comforted them by relying on his ability to cajole them into smiles with jokes and good humor and to reassure them, at least for a while, with his firm "take charge" attitude. Each new episode of abuse, however, increased the burden of his feeling that he had again failed to protect his sister and brothers.

Chaos had long characterized Mickey's immediate and extended family. Alcoholism, drug abuse, incest, and various other forms of dysfunction frequently led to the temporary disbanding of the various nuclear groupings that made up the larger family. Despite those regularly occurring disruptions and the fuzzy boundaries of both the individuals and the subsystems they formed, a family identity and a kind of pride in it persisted.

Mickey's paternal grandmother held the implicit place of authority in the family and seldom related to anyone outside it. Although her clan was scattered across a large urban area, with children from time to time being placed in and taken out of foster care, the grandmother's presence at the center of the diffuse and shifting family mass maintained within it a paradoxical coherence. Her admonition that "the family takes care of its own trouble" and the resulting disaffection by family members with others of their ranks (however battered or however young) who disclosed "troubles" to authorities became perhaps the most prominent manifestation of that coherence.

Mickey's father never held a job for long nor had he ever shown evidence of maturity or sound judgment. More ominously, he had been arrested for exposing himself in a local park and he had fathered at least one child in his many sexual contacts with the wives and daughters of relatives. One of the eleven abuse and neglect complaints investigated by the DSS in the fourteen months following its first awareness of the family led to substantiation of a charge that Mickey had been beaten and denied food by his father and an aunt.

The pattern of dysfunction presented by Mickey's mother was at once more extreme and less consistent. Investigations of abuse and neglect complaints brought to light instances of her beating the children or failing to provide for them, typically after abusing alcohol or cocaine. She was also characterized, however, as being warm and caring until she turned to her addictions to escape from feeling overwhelmed. It was reportedly during an episode of cocaine use that her son attempted to hang himself.

It is noteworthy that on an earlier occasion, after his mother had cut her wrists in a fit of despair exacerbated by alcohol, Mickey had summoned help for her. On another occasion Mickey had stopped his mother from putting her head in an oven filled with gas. The likelihood that Mickey was trying to rally his mother to respond to him as he had to her adds another possible dimension to his own suicide attempts.

On at least one occasion, substantiated during an investigation, and probably more frequently, Mickey had seen his mother sexually involved with one of the boyfriends who regularly came to the home during his father's frequent absences. When Mickey was referred for psychological diagnostic testing, his having witnessed the sexual activity of adults was seen as the basis for the indications of anger and conflict regarding sexuality that were evident in his protocols. Tragically, ongoing abuse was not identified either in the test data or in the repeated home investigations. Ironically, the obvious problems of the home had apparently been so florid that they distracted attention from consideration of less obvious patterns of victimization.

Gonorrhea of the throat was diagnosed in Mickey's 8-month-old cousin and reported by the hospital emergency room to the DSS. Further investigation revealed that the 3-year-old brother and 2-year-old sister of that child had been similarly infected. Several cousins, including Mickey and his sister, were visiting in the home when the social worker came to interview those children and their mother. As the 3-year-old told of his abuse by two uncles, another cousin, 7-year-old Mark, spontaneously interjected, "Hey, Uncle Buddy and Uncle Freddy did that to us too." The expanded investigation that followed substantiated abuse of fifteen children in the extended family.

Disclosure led to the children's again being placed in various foster homes. That process in itself was colored by an extra measure of fear for the children ever since one of their cousins, a 2-year-old, had been killed in a foster home house fire some years earlier. Mickey, however, was placed initially in the home of Ted, a paternal uncle, and his wife, Millie, together with Mark and Mickey's 6-year-old brother, Phil, another of the abuse victims.

Buddy and Freddy were paternal uncles and in fact visited Ted's home on occasion, even while the investigation proceeded. Unlike other family members, however, Ted was considered both determined and able to safeguard the children from the abuse that had been alleged, even though at that point he was unconvinced that his brothers had in fact assaulted the children of the extended family, including his own.

From all that is known, the children were protected from further assault by their uncles during this period. Mark, however, for having disclosed the abuse, was the object of subtle but powerful censure by the family, orchestrated by the cousins' paternal grandmother. By involving "outsiders" he had, in the family's view, violated the principle that "the family takes care of its own troubles."

Mickey was referred for treatment planning and case management to a social worker from the child abuse unit of an urban mental health center. She in turn requested evaluation of the potential utility of play therapy for him, his sister Carol, and his cousins Mark and Phil.

THE ASSESSMENT AND PLANNING PHASE

Each of the four children was seen for about twenty minutes in a playroom setting to gauge how they used play as communication, how they managed the attendant stimulation, and their tolerance and responsiveness to reflections or observations about their play. An attempt was also made to gain impressions regarding the children's readiness to address the continuing legacy of hurt associated with their abuse and the disruption of their living circumstances.

Consistent with his role as would-be protector of the others, Mickey asked to be seen first. He wanted, it seemed clear, to check things out.

In the playroom Mickey maintained a posture that was more cautious than guarded. His demeanor was friendly, but he kept his distance. He took the initiative in seeking out and using toys, but seemed to modulate his involvement with them so as not to compromise his vigilance.

In his play and in his manner Mickey had a way of combining an engaging boyishness on the one hand with an unspoken sense on the other that was reminiscent of the weariness and resignation of an adult who has taken as a premise that trust must always remain tentative. A self-conscious smile tinged with a wry quality beyond his years gave way rapidly to a furrowed brow and a no-nonsense tone whenever he felt that control of the situation was slipping from him. At no time, however, did Mickey test limits or seek to exercise control unreasonably; he seemed only to want to assure himself that events would not take him by surprise or deny him the option of disengagement.

Mickey also proved responsive to reflections about his play and was attuned to its metaphorical implications. At one point, for example, when a construction of playthings fell, Mickey responded to the observation "It looks like you know something about things going wrong" by saying "I sure do, lots of things."

When Carol was seen for the brief playroom evaluation, she presented a much less organized pattern of behavior and a more strident tone. She raced from one toy to the next, alternately issuing demands and warnings. With Carol, metaphorical probes were quite unnecessary to determine the accessibility of material related to the abuse: she spontaneously and angrily stated that "Nobody better try to rape me or I'll kill them or I'll get my brother."

Mark proved the most disorganized of the children. His disheveled appearance mirrored the confusion of his thinking and the impulsivity of his actions. A high level of tension and anxiety was abundantly evident in Mark's motoric and vocal patterns and in his inability to stem the flow of oral and nasal fluids that moistened and stained his face and, every few minutes, his shirtsleeve. From the statements he made and from his play, it was clear that Mark was as much troubled by the family's subtle rejection, and by their emotional neglect in the wake of his impulsive disclosure, as he was by the abuse itself.

When Phil entered the playroom, he stood passively with his hands in his pockets and, in an expressionless, matter-of-fact way, asked, "Are you going to rape me now?" He went on to explain that "You were with my brother and with my cousins one at a time so you must have raped them and now it must be my turn." The unquestioned premise from which Phil quietly reasoned thundered with the enormity of the atrocity that had been visited on these youngsters. After only seven years in this world, Phil had taken as one of its givens the assumption that a child's being alone in a room with an adult male, even for a short time, meant that the child would be raped.

Play therapy seemed an appropriate modality for all of the children. Each had a slightly different understanding of what had occurred and of its reasons and implications, but the impact for each had been colored by egocentric thinking that left a legacy of assumed responsibility for their own victimization. Self–world relationships for each had been brutalized and distorted. Fears had become so frequently and consistently realized that little hope, save that sustained by denial, had survived. Each child had used play sequences in eloquent communication, and in fact seemed to take comfort in the buffer it provided from experiences that were fearsome even in recall, but which they were nevertheless driven to address. That same need led each child in different ways to be responsive to interventions that had to do with thoughts and feelings about the abuse and about the upheavals that followed in the wake of its disclosure, even when those interventions were couched in metaphorical terms geared ostensibly to the implications of play sequences.

Family systems issues clearly needed to be addressed throughout the extended family, but nuclear groupings were so fractured as to be barely definable in their form, much less in their function. With the possible exception of Ted and Millie and their children, family therapy seemed more an intermediate or long-range goal than a current method.

By strongly embracing a fundamentalist religion, Ted and his wife had become an exception to the chaos that characterized the other family members. The adjustment they achieved thereby, however, had a brittle quality that seemed to militate against any approach that might threaten the delicate balance that sustained them. Moreover, they made it clear from the outset that they could care for Mickey only until alternate foster placement became available. In addition, they were planning a move of considerable distance in a few months and long-term family treatment would not be possible. It was therefore decided to initiate individual play therapy for each of the four children with concurrent parent counseling provided to Ted and Millie for as long as they were in the area.

The mental health center in which treatment was to take place served also as a clinical training site. Since Mark and Phil would be leaving with their parents in a matter of months, they were assigned to interns with a treatment plan based on short-term goals and with the anticipation that a transfer would eventually be made to service providers in the area to which their parents planned to move. Because Carol had reacted with such a strong sense of alarm at the time of the playroom evaluation, it seemed appropriate that she be seen by a woman.

The sex of the therapist is an issue often overdone in clinical planning; a skilled therapist of either sex should be able to work with children of both sexes on most issues, perhaps by translating the basis for discomfort into therapeutically beneficial interventions. In this instance, however, the abuse Carol had suffered at the hands of adult men, and her reaction to it, seemed likely to introduce problems into any treatment provided by a man that would require more time to work through than would be justified by the eventual benefit of that process. The interns who agreed to see Phil and Mark were women, but Carol's needs clearly pointed to a relatively long-term treatment plan and her continuing availability seemed assured by the stability of the foster home in which she was placed. She was therefore assigned to a woman on the staff of the center.

Play therapy with Mickey was to take place weekly with Dr. Robert Ciottone. With Mickey's agreement, reviewed periodically with him, and with written permission from the Department of Social Services and from his biological mother, all sessions took place in front of a one-way mirror and all were videotaped. Mickey had the option of visiting the observation/ camera room behind the mirror at any time, and in fact did so with some frequency throughout treatment. During the first year the interns treating Mark and Phil and the staff member treating Carol observed Mickey's play therapy. Discussions among the therapists provided an unusual opportunity to coordinate treatment. During the second and third years other interns observed as a training exercise and coordination with Carol's therapist continued. Transcripts presented in later chapters are drawn directly from the videotapes.

THE FOSTER CARE INTERFACE

During the course of treatment Mickey's living circumstances changed six times. In fact, play therapy as an effort to resolve problems associated with the abuse essentially ended after about a year and a half, but the process continued as an exercise in providing Mickey with some object constancy. Until his prospects for some stability of placement became clear, Mickey often underscored the importance of extending treatment that would have terminated under better conditions by remarks such as "This is about the only thing I can count on happening."

Mickey's remarks were not attributable simply to transference phenomena: in his wanderings through the foster care system, he seemed to have the Midas touch in reverse. During his stay at Ted and Millie's home,

Mickey joined the other children in appearances before the grand jury seeking to indict his uncles, but his particularly damning testimony earned him a share of the lingering family disdain previously reserved for Mark.

Two months later Mickey was sent to a foster home that was expected to continue as a placement for an extended period of time. One month after he arrived, however, his foster father died. Several weeks later his foster mother, a stern but fair woman whom Mickey had come to respect, left, grief stricken, to spend a month with her family in France. He was then transferred for short-term foster care to a home with several biological children who openly resented his arrival. Mickey nonetheless formed a close relationship with Sally, the foster mother, a warm but chronically frantic woman whose view of life was punctuated by inevitable crises.

Mickey returned to his previous placement when the foster mother returned from France. Several weeks later, in the context of a play therapy session, he disclosed that he was being sexually accosted by another foster child in that home, an 11-year-old girl who was herself an abuse victim. Mickey indicated that she was entering his bedroom each night, masturbating him and threatening him with harm if he told anyone. Although the situation was one in which the distinction between perpetrator and victim becomes meaningless, Mickey acknowledged that it came under our agreement that confidentiality would not cover anything that threatened his safety. When the DSS was advised of the situation, the girl was moved to another placement, but shortly thereafter the widowed foster mother decided that she could no longer provide foster care.

Mickey's next move was back to the foster home that had served as short-term placement during the absence of the first foster mother. Like the first, it was intended to be a continuing site. Two weeks after Mickey arrived, however, the foster father left the home, having decided, after a long period of conflict, to seek a divorce. The biological children of the family, who had resented Mickey's joining their number, blamed him for their father's departure.

Shortly thereafter, Sally, overwhelmed and more frantic in managing crises than she had been previously, decided that she could no longer provide foster care. She had, however, developed a fondness for Mickey that led her to insist that he remain until the DSS found him a foster home that would in fact be stable. Despite periodic crises that threatened to require emergency placement, Mickey remained in Sally's home for eight months.

From the time of their initial removal from the home, Mickey, Carol, and their three younger brothers were brought together periodically in the offices of the DSS so they could see each other and meet with their mother. More often than not, however, the mother did not appear. During the first year following disclosure of the abuse, she continued to use alcohol and drugs despite several hospitalizations for addiction. Occasionally she showed up at Sally's to see Mickey. Although told by the DSS to send the mother away with the instruction to attend the scheduled meetings, Sally allowed her to see Mickey when she arrived sober.

For Mickey, unpredictability became predictable; he did not see his mother when he expected to and he did see her when he did not expect to. His emotional dilemma was compounded by guilt when he saw his siblings. Their foster parents followed DSS guidelines and they envied and resented his seeing their mother.

For about two months during Mickey's stay at Sally's, when his mother's stated intentions of rehabilitating herself seemed particularly ill-fated, his father began to press demands for custody. The DSS imposed a set of requirements by which the father might demonstrate his capacity for responsible parenting, much as had been done for Mickey's mother. Though his behavior pattern gave even less reason to assume success in that effort than had Mickey's mother's, legal constraints under which the DSS operated required that he be given a chance to demonstrate parental competence.

Mickey's father showed up once at the mental health center and twice at the offices of the DSS to meet with the children, each time accompanied by his new girlfriend. She soon became disillusioned with him, however, in part because she recognized his insensitivity in expecting and demanding that the children relate to her in a warm, familiar way from the outset. During his third and unaccompanied visit to the DSS, Mickey's father lost control. He had to be led out by several office staff with the children witness to the spectacle. After that incident, he made no further effort to seek custody.

Characteristically, Mickey responded to his father's behavior in a parentified way. At times he enjoyed the picture outlined by his father's promises, but seemed to recognize that it would likely amount to little more than a fantasy within which he might take occasional respite, but upon which he could base few hopes. He regarded his father with a kind of embarrassed understanding and a private hurt that he attempted to disguise with a thin smile. His manner left no doubt, however, that he would not tolerate any demeaning rebuke of his father.

The search for long-term foster care had been delayed by the father's aborted petition for custody, and Mickey remained in Sally's home during that period. At the same time, unexpectedly, the mother began to make significant gains in her own rehabilitation. She completed a relatively intensive inpatient detoxification program, secured a job and an apartment upon discharge, embarked on an outpatient program of psychotherapy, and attended all scheduled meetings with the children. With much anguish, she eventually released the three youngest children for an open adoption that would allow her to maintain contact with them, but she reaffirmed her intention to establish a home in which to raise Mickey and Carol. In her view the two oldest had been most burdened by memories of brutality and horror. Recognizing both the problems involved and her own limitations, she felt she could be most effective by devoting herself to Mickey and Carol while assuring herself of the well-being of the others in an indirect but vigilant way.

As Carol had been in a strong, stable foster home from the start, the additional waiting for her mother to meet custody requirements simply extended her stay there and at the school she had been attending. For Mickey, however, it meant another move of both home and school.

Partly to compensate Mickey for the foster home difficulties he had endured and partly because few alternatives were available, DSS placed him in an affluent suburb more than an hour from the urban center in which he had lived. Previously transported by taxi from school to the play therapy sessions, Mickey was now driven in by a social worker each week. His new foster father, a professional who worked in the city, picked him up at the center for the return ride.

At first, the relative ease of transportation and the affluence of the new foster home seemed to be changes in which Mickey could take comfort. The school experience also seemed a positive one, with teachers taking an interest in Mickey and willing to confer with the treatment team. That level of responsiveness was unlike the other schools he had attended in which Mickey was seen as transient and less behaviorally troublesome than others in typically overcrowded classrooms with much acting out.

To be sure, Mickey tried the tolerance and understanding of his new teachers when he realized how different his experience was from that of the other children. Perhaps to offset the potential for ridicule and/or to hasten peer acceptance, Mickey began regaling groups that gathered around him in the schoolyard with explicit accounts of sexuality to which he had been witness, including to his own abuse. When teachers responded to the resulting flurry of parental phone calls by asking Mickey to share his stories with his therapist instead, he did so and expressed surprise and appreciation of the understanding and nonpunitive tone of the request.

Despite the benefits of his new placement, Mickey's "reverse Midas" fortunes again emerged. The home included two teenaged foster children and three biological children, one an adolescent, one in her early 20s, and a boy who was just 20. Apparently without his parents' knowledge, the 20-year-old had become involved in substance abuse and began to resent the presence of foster children in the home. As the youngest but not the least assertive child in the home, Mickey became the target first of verbal barbs and eventually of physical battering.

Although he did not at first disclose the physical abuse in play therapy, after each session Mickey began to call Sally from the lobby of the center while he waited for his new foster father. Mickey had agreed to an extended family relationship with Sally and in fact had come to refer to her as "aunt."

In his telephone calls to Sally, Mickey frequently asked whether he might visit for weekends, as he had sometimes done since moving. Shortly thereafter, Mickey presented a play sequence in therapy that prompted the therapist to observe that it seemed getting away was important to him. Mickey responded by explaining the physical punishment to which he was increasingly subject in his foster home. Not coincidentally, the session in which Mickey spoke about his physical abuse at the hands of the 20-year-old was one in which the social worker, with Mickey's knowledge and permission, had stayed to observe.

When the DSS pursued the issue of Mickey's treatment in the home, the foster parents became frightened, defensive, and fearful that their names would appear on a list of child abusers. Despite assurances that no such steps were considered, they retained an attorney through whom all communication with the Department and with the center was channeled. Their treatment of Mickey became formal and mechanical at best.

During Mickey's stay in the suburban foster home, his mother continued to make impressive strides toward rehabilitating herself and re-establishing a home that could receive Mickey and Carol. She had come close to overcoming the prognosis that most had seen as guarded at best, but still had some time left in the agreed-upon period during which she was to demonstrate her stability. In light of the problems with Mickey's foster placement, however, a decision was made to return the two children to her care.

The mother had established an apartment with a "significant other," Jack, a gruff but caring divorced man with grown children. As part of the rehabilitation program and in anticipation of their establishing a family unit, they had participated in a series of meetings, several of which included Mickey and Carol. In that context they had seemed both sensitive to and realistic about the challenge they were facing. Despite some initial wariness, both children responded positively to Jack's rough-hewn sincerity. Warmth was evident between the children and their mother, who related to each other in a manner reminiscent of comrades in past wars. Mickey even seemed to relinquish his accustomed parental role to his mother.

Play therapy continued for some five months after Mickey's return, but it was essentially a continuation of the effort to ease transitions that had become the focus and raison d'être of treatment after the first year and a half. Direct sequelae of his abuse were no longer evident in Mickey's presentation during the last year of therapy, but the obvious need for object constancy had continued and intensified.

When the children returned to their mother, family therapy was initiated with another therapist, but neither child was defined as an "identified patient." During the time of overlap between the two treatment modalities, Mickey went to lengths to preserve the distinction, setting an agenda for his participation in each according to what he deemed "my things" and "family things."

Because he had grown older, and because it is the predictable pattern in play therapy in any case, communication became more explicitly conversational and less reliant on the modality of play. That progression notwithstanding, Mickey chose not to speak of the disease and eventual death of one of Jack's grown daughters because, he later explained, "that's a family thing." The boundaries he imposed reflected some of the rigidity by which he had earlier preserved the integrity of some domains of life space even while others were being decimated. Mickey's ability to do so, even in the face of tragedy, seemed one reflection of his having resolved conflicts resulting from the experience of abuse at a time when egocentricity characterized his thinking.

Toward the end of therapy, Mickey no longer felt a sense of causal ownership of tragedy as "my thing." In that way and in many others he signaled his readiness to end therapy, an option made more viable by his living circumstances finally having stabilized. Predictably, ambivalence about termination came to the fore and Mickey requested a kind of "taper down" schedule by which the intervals between the final six sessions were lengthened.

By mutual agreement, several of the last sessions were spent viewing the videotapes of early meetings. Again ambivalence was evident; Mickey alternately wanted to listen to them and to put them aside, particularly when his own pain over the abuse was unmistakable in his play. He also asked to invite his mother and Carol to the next-to-last session so they might see the tapes. When they did attend, it seemed important to Mickey that his mother in particular hear sequences that reflected his rage. When her own pain and guilt came forth in response to such sequences, it seemed equally important to Mickey to comfort and forgive her.

The final session was subdued. Both child and therapist agreed they had been many places together and would remain that way in each other's memory. They also agreed that probably they would often recall their time together, perhaps even at the same moment, so they would be together both in the remembering and in the memory. They agreed that they meant much to each other but that it was right that they end their meetings.

Family therapy continued, as did progress for the reconstituted family unit. At times Mickey sent messages through the family therapist to say that all was well.

AN OVERVIEW OF PROBLEMS AND GOALS

Mickey had been brutalized. The atrocities to which he had been subjected—anal intercourse, oral sex, forced sexual contact with his sister for the entertainment of the perpetrators, seeing his sister abused and hearing her cries to him for help—prompt a response that fuses rage, pity, horror, helplessness, and a storm of emotions that no language captures.

Human reactions notwithstanding, however, it becomes the therapist's formidable challenge to differentiate problems in psychological terms so as to formulate a treatment plan that gives direction and coherence to the need to respond in a helpful way. Moreover, that initially distasteful task must be accomplished without compromising, or being compromised by, the sense of compassion and empathy that sustains the effort. It is in fact the differentiation of problems that allows a child to use play therapy as a means by which to move beyond the formless and pervasive fusion of external pressure and internal conflict toward an integration of experience that represents further developmental advance.

For Mickey, abuse was not an event but an unrelenting process. In a concrete sense he was victimized many times over a relatively long period. As with all victims of trauma, however, the psychological sequelae of his victimization extended its impact across temporal as well as experiential dimensions. Distortion of his developing self concept and the upheaval of his life circumstances were the two areas in which Mickey had suffered most dramatically.

Though Mickey's earlier suicide attempts might be understood retrospectively in part as having been an effort to draw attention to his abuse and/or to rally his mother, they reflect also the erosion and decay that had occurred in his view of his own worth. Whatever other motivation he may have had, Mickey considered destroying the self that was him.

In one way or another, most theoretical construct systems consider children's self concepts to coalesce around the messages they receive about themselves from others. Mickey's experience told him he was an instrument to be used. In one sense, therefore, his apparent willingness to sacrifice himself in order to "flag" the abuse, perhaps on behalf of his sister, or to prod his mother into fulfilling her parental role, was consistent with a sense of self as having worth only in subordination to others' needs. Feeling himself to be a person of intrinsic worth with needs equal in importance to those of others thus became a basic therapeutic goal for Mickey.

For many children who have been victims of abuse, a complication in the effort to address the damage to self concept may occur in an unexpected form. Tragically, some children who are sexually exploited in ways presented to them as ostensibly nonthreatening have seldom known affection that was as comforting and pleasurable. With disclosure or discovery of the abuse, the concern and support of professionals for the child as victim may leave him or her more inclined toward self-depreciation because of memories that include the sense of pleasure that was experienced. In such instances a therapist's need to relate in an understanding and nonjudgmental way dramatizes the importance of rooting perspective in the child's frame of reference, and conversely highlights the danger of relying solely on human compassion and rescue needs.

In Mickey's case, in no way did the abuse "feel good." The need to set aside pre-established hierarchies of horror in assessing the impact of the abuse upon his self concept did, however, take another form that might not have been predicted. As a parentified child who had taken the responsibility of looking after his older but less capable sister very seriously, Mickey felt most strongly a sense of failure in his role of protector. Not only had he failed to shield her from abuse, he witnessed his sister's abuse and listened to her cries, unable to help. Worse, he had been forced into sexual contact with her for the entertainment of his uncles.

Although he had repeatedly been subjected to extremes of abuse individually, Mickey's feeling that he had failed his sister was by far the most damaging assault upon his self concept. In effect, how he construed the abuse circumstances gave rise to a more difficult variation of the frequently evident assumption of responsibility by child abuse victims, who assume, through developmentally primitive egocentric thinking, that they have caused what they do not otherwise understand.

In other words, Mickey had no doubt that he had failed his sister. A further goal of treatment, therefore, needed to involve the fostering of a perspective that recognized external causality, an acceptance of his limitations in the face of it, and feelings about himself based on recognition of his love for his sister rather than on his inability to do all that he wanted to for her. In a related vein, Mickey's feeling of failure underscored the importance of addressing both the legacy of aggression likely to flow from the frustration of his protective needs and the intropunitive expression of those aggressive impulses, particularly in view of his history of suicidal behavior.

Like most victims of child abuse, Mickey showed some evidence of disruption in his developing body image. In his play he periodically made reference to sexual organs or functions. When he did so in direct reference to himself, and to a lesser extent when he spoke about doll figures in the playroom, Mickey tried to objectify his statements almost as if he were speaking about separate parts unconnected in form or function to anything. In effect, he attempted to deny their ownership by, or certainly their integration with, the concept of person. Frequently, however, he was unable to sustain that defensive distance and lapsed instead into highly animated, emotionally charged celebration of body parts in song and play that carried with it the connotation that he was bad and blameworthy. In addition to fostering in play therapy the development of conflict-free sexuality in a general sense, therefore, it became evident that treatment needed to address the integration of body image in a concrete sense, particularly with regard to the bodily parts and functions from which Mickey tried to distance himself, as if from the abuse itself and its implication of blame.

With regard to body image, it is important to note that many sexually abused children fear that they might be pregnant, boys no less than girls. Mickey initially indicated that he harbored that fear himself, but subsequently it became clear that he did not. Therapists need to consider, however, that a child may be left with that fear as a result of any abuse experience, whatever its nature and regardless of the sex of the child or the time that has passed since the abuse.

Disruption of life circumstances was the second general problem area addressed in Mickey's treatment. Although his family life had been problematic at best, it was all he knew. In noting that older children who are removed from abusive circumstances and placed in safe alternative care often run away and return to the abusive setting, John Romano, during psychiatric grand rounds at the University of Rochester (New York) School of Medicine in 1968, likened the well-intentioned disruption of the mother–child bond to "shaking the pillars of heaven." For Mickey, the heavens kept falling down upon him. Not only did his family dissolve when the abuse was disclosed, but one foster care home after another proved disastrous, and his frequent moves were like faint but cruel echoes of his initial loss of family. He had lost his mother and, for a long period, any hope of being reunited with her. Although the DSS periodically brought the siblings together, he had lost the brothers and sister with whom he had formed a quasi-parental as well as fraternal bond. He lost his school, neighborhood, friends, and familiar routines—in short, all he had known.

Child therapists need to remind themselves often of the importance that the concrete aspects of a context hold for a child and of the impact of their abrupt loss. Attending understandably to the more abstract dimensions of a child's experience, and of the need to change them when they are punishing or depriving, can result in overlooking the impact of loss that seems trivial from an adult perspective. The ambivalence conveyed by the child's muffled sigh of relief may then seem puzzling to caregivers who have in fact remedied an untenable situation by bringing about a change of context. The puzzle becomes understandable, however, when the child's ongoing experience is considered.

Knowing what will be seen looking around a room when first awakening brings with it some reassurance, even if the day ahead brings punishment. Objects take on great importance, like predictable landmarks in harsh terrain. A chair, a broken step, a patch of grass, or a picture on the wall can, sadly, become sources of comfort that nonetheless leave a patchwork of empty places in a child's experience when a move is necessitated by larger considerations.

In a related way that makes the point, one child said, upon successful completion of therapy, "I'm happy now because things are good. But in a way I'm mad at you. You took away my best friend. I used to cry every night into my pillow and my pillow got to be my best friend that way. Now I don't cry at night and that's good. But I lost my friend the pillow."

The "object constancy" function of play therapy becomes vitally important for children whose lives are disrupted by a change of context, and so it needed to be for Mickey. His world turned upside down on a regular basis. The play therapy sessions became one of the few predictable parts of his experience, a fact he stated simply by saying, "This is all I can count on." At one point during the play therapy Mickey dramatically and graphically made that point. After a session he asked that he and the therapist adjourn for a moment to the copy machine in the adjoining office. There he composed a picture of his hand cradled in the therapist's. He made several copies and quietly, but with obvious pleasure, gave one to the therapist, showed copies to others in the area, and took the remaining ones home with him.

Mickey took obvious comfort in the continued availability of the same playthings, even when new ones were added and previous ones fell into disuse. In fact, problems associated strictly with the abuse per se were essentially resolved after about a year and a half of play therapy, but treatment was continued with explicit discussion of the need to do so ". . . until where to live got straightened out."

III

Clinical Antecedents
of Synergistic Play Therapy

Despite the abundance of literature regarding play therapy, only a few comprehensively address what actually transpires in the playroom (e.g., Corder 1990, Haworth 1990, Moustakas 1955), particularly with regard to the treatment of sexually abused children. Playroom inquiry and evaluation of abuse of children have been discussed at length (e.g., Anderson and Berliner 1983, Brassard et al. 1983, Gardner 1994, MacFarlane et al. 1986), as have the sociological aspects of the problem (e.g., Finkelhor 1979, 1982, Finkelhor and Araji 1983, Groth 1978, Lindholm 1984). Relatively few works have focused on the analysis of actual play therapy sessions (e.g., Haworth 1964, 1990, Moustakas 1955); other sources have provided an overview of various approaches used in play therapy (Schaefer 1976, 1988, Schaefer and O'Connor 1983, Sgroi 1982).

Synergistic Play Therapy, elaborated here, represents an integration of relevant antecedent treatment approaches, with developmental theory and the evolving perspective of practicing clinicians. Accordingly, extensive microanalysis of specific interactions between therapist and child is presented so the relationship between theory and technique is made clear.

Psychotherapeutic work with children initially grew out of the psychoanalytic tradition in Europe. Sigmund Freud's case of "Little Hans"

(1909) was the first recorded explanation of childhood dynamics through their expression in play. Somewhat later, it became widely recognized by child clinicians that their efforts would require considerations different from those upon which adult treatment was based (A. Freud 1928, 1929, 1964, 1965, Hug-Hellmuth 1920, 1921, Klein 1927, 1955, 1959, 1960, 1975a,b).

Not only was Hug-Hellmuth credited with being the first theorist to make special considerations for the treatment of children, but she has also been cited as the first clinician to use toys with any regularity in that process. Although a staunch advocate of Freudian theory who employed the principles of adult psychoanalysis in her work with children, she pointed out the limitations of doing so. First, she noted that children do not come to treatment of their own accord, nor do they typically have a desire to change, that is, to give up the "naughtiness" that results from current tensions in which they are immersed, not simply from past conflict. To help children overcome their resistance to the therapy process, she allowed them to bring their own playthings to treatment sessions and sometimes joined in play with them.

The contributions of Hug-Hellmuth notwithstanding, the major psychoanalytic theorists credited with the establishment of child analysis were Melanie Klein and Anna Freud. Although they both used play in their work with children, their approaches and their conceptualization differed, particularly with regard to issues such as free association, transference, and interpretative interventions. Klein's treatment of children was based on the fundamental assumption that children's play, just like the free associations of adults, provides access to the unconscious (Hinshelwood 1994). In describing her play technique, Klein (1955) stated:

> This approach corresponds to a fundamental principle of psychoanalysis—free association. In interpreting not only the child's words, but also his activities with his toys, I applied this basic principle of the mind to the child whose play and varied activities, in fact his whole behavior, are means of expressing what the adult expresses predominantly by words. [pp. 223–224]

Klein (1975a) maintained that the therapist needs to avoid suggesting direction to, or imposing connotation upon, the child's play so that those forms of expression can be analogous to the verbal free association of adults in treatment. The choice of toys within the session was therefore to be left completely to the child, as was his use of them. Additionally,

Klein's procedure often included keeping the child's toys in a locked drawer to ensure that only she and the child would have access to them (1955). This procedure was characterized as a parallel to adult treatment with regard to confidentiality, that is, only the therapist and patient would have access to the toys and their meaning would be thereby safeguarded much as are the statements of adults in treatment.

In criticizing Klein's approach, Anna Freud (1965) maintained that equating play with verbal free association was theoretically untenable. Throughout her professional life, Freud resisted all attempts to view play as being similar to verbal interaction with adults on the premise that certain key conditions for free association could not be met in treatment with children. For one, she noted that adults typically make their own decision to begin treatment. Consequently, there is often the recognition that a problem exists; with it there emerges a beginning capacity for insight. Children on the other hand seldom enter treatment of their own volition. Rather, they do so because an adult authority figure, usually the parent, decides upon it. As a result, the child often assumes an oppositional posture. Further, because the child may not recognize that a problem exists, there is little possibility for insight, at least as it is defined in adult treatment. In advancing her position, Freud (1965) stated:

> It is one disadvantage that some of these modes of [play] behavior produce mainly symbolic material and that this introduces into child analysis the elements of doubt, uncertainty, arbitrariness which are inseparable from symbolic interpretation in general. Another disadvantage lies in the fact that, under the pressure of the unconscious, the child acts instead of talks, and this unfortunately introduces limits into the analytic situation. [pp.29–30]

As Anna Freud implied, free association, by its very definition, is not constrained in any way. A patient may, without censure, say anything that comes into her or his mind. Play, however, cannot be allowed to proceed under these same conditions. When aggressive or sexual impulses are activated in children, it would not necessarily be beneficial, or even realistic in commonsense terms, for them to be acted out in a literal way without limits being imposed. Destructive impulses overtly directed toward oneself or the therapist, for example, cannot be allowed for obvious safety reasons.

Even if such action sequences were allowed to proceed but were thwarted in their final expression, enduring damage to the child's relationship with the therapist is likely to result. Such behavior is thus counter-therapeutic in its impact. Symbolic expressions and/or the substitutive use of playthings, however, can be retracted, reframed, and expressed differently at a later point. Developmental advance, rather than developmental regression or rigidification of pathological processes, can thus occur.

With reference to the historical dialogue between Freud and Klein on this point, play as conceptualized in the context of the Synergistic approach proposed herein bears some correspondence to free association in adult treatment. The parallel, however, is less than complete; play in the Synergistic approach indeed takes on some of the characteristics of free association, including spontaneity, unencumbered choice of expressive direction, and freedom to include—or exclude—any array of real-life referents in any combination, recalled, fantasized, wished for, or feared. In the Synergistic approach, the similarity between free association and play, however, resides primarily in the metaphorical rather than in the literal dimension of the play.

Another pivotal theme focused upon by early clinical theorists had to do with the notion of similarity between the ways in which play and dreams might be conceptualized. Anna Freud (1965) pointed out the imprecision and arbitrariness of play, given its symbolic nature. Klein (1927) on the other hand emphasized the utility of symbolism in play, comparing it with the dream work that is often a key aspect of adult treatment. She described children as acting out their wishes as well as their experiences through the symbolism of play much as occurs in dreams. Klein (1927) stated:

> In their play, children represent symbolically their phantasies, wishes and experiences. Here they are employing the same language, the same archaic, phylogenetically acquired mode of expression as we are familiar with from dreams. . . . [T]he underlying sources and thoughts are revealed to us if we interpret them just like dreams. [p. 32]

Indicating that it is not the symbolism of the individual acts of play alone that provides data for interpretations, Klein (1975b) stated:

> [We] must not be content to pick out the meaning of the separate symbols in the play, striking as they often are, but must take into consideration all the mechanisms and methods of representation. . . . Children have shown again and again how many different meanings a single toy or a single bit of play can have, and that we can only infer and interpret their meaning when we consider their wider connections and the whole analytic situation in which they are set. [p. 8]

Yet another issue discussed at length by these pioneers in the psychological treatment of children had to do with the nature and function of transference in play therapy. As noted by Klein (1955), transference refers to

> the main discovery of [Sigmund] Freud, that the patient transfers his early experiences and his feelings and thoughts in relation first to his parents and then to other people [e.g., the psychoanalyst]. [p. 224]

Although Klein and Anna Freud agreed that transference with children differed from that with adults, their theoretical explanations were quite dissimilar. Anna Freud (1926, 1928) maintained that the whole nature of a child's transference is different from that of an adult, whereas Klein (1975b) simply claimed that the time it takes for a transference to develop is different for a child than for an adult. Specifically, Klein maintained that transference develops immediately in children in contrast to the many sessions often required for adults to bring that dynamic to the treatment relationship. The rapid development of transference in children was cited by Klein as her rationale for making interpretative interventions in the very beginning stages of treatment.

Rather than viewing transference as immediately and intrinsically present in play therapy, Anna Freud (1926) argued that its development needed to be an early goal of treatment to be achieved by careful effort on the part of the therapist. Consequently, she viewed play as a means toward the achievement of transference rather than as simply the manifestation of what was already present. For her, play, in that sense, was "preparatory" to transference.

Parenthetically, it is interesting to note that the differences between these two clinical theorists roughly parallel a longstanding distinction in the philosophical roots of epistemology. The difference between perspectives can perhaps be seen as tracing back on the one hand to the tabula rasa proposed by Aristotle (i.e., that the "mind" was a blank slate upon which experience was to impose meaning) and on the other hand to the notion of "innate ideas" proposed by Plato (i.e., the "mind" as a matrix through which experience was filtered and by which it gained meaning).

Because Anna Freud adopted the position that play was the vehicle by which transference came to impose meaning upon the child's previously "blank screen" with regard to his sense of the play therapy experience, she sought to prepare the child for treatment in a way analogous to the effort made with adults,

. . . producing in him an insight into his illness, arousing confidence in the analysis and the analyst, and transforming the decision to be analyzed from an outward one to an inner one. [A. Freud 1928, p. 4]

Anna Freud (1928) maintained that children were unable to experience a "transference neurosis" as do adults in treatment, but she continued to emphasize the importance of establishing a positive transferential rapport at the outset of play therapy.

Although Anna Freud and Melanie Klein relied heavily on the use of children's play in their treatment, they used the technique quite differently. Klein focused on the representational quality of play, using the symbolism of a child's play to provide her with clues and representations of unconscious desires, fears, and so on. Anna Freud argued that relying solely on inferences about the latent content of play could be misleading.

In Klein's psychoanalytic play technique, the interpretations of children's play were central and were used the same way for children as for adults: to produce insight into the unconscious. She claimed that interpretations that ". . . penetrate [the] level of the mind which is being activated by anxiety" and are made at the "right time" will be effective in alleviating the symptoms such as anxiety (Klein 1975b, p. 30). Through such interpretations, Klein set out to accomplish two important objectives of psychoanalytic treatment: ". . . the exploration of the unconscious as the main task of the psychoanalytic procedure, and the analysis of the transference as the means of achieving this" (Klein 1955, p. 224).

In maintaining that interpretations could be made immediately in the treatment, Klein (1975b) emphasized her sense of the importance of the therapist speaking in the images and symbols that the child employed in play. She cited as an example a young patient who pointed to a swing and said, "'Look how it dangles and bumps' and so when I answered, 'That's how Daddy's and Mommy's thing-ummies bumped together,' he took it in at once" (1975b, p. 32). Klein credited the success of this interpretation with the use of language that the child had previously presented in a session.

In criticizing Klein's constant interpretations of children's play, Anna Freud (1964) stated:

[Klein] translates, as she goes along, the actions undertaken by the child . . . into corresponding thought; that is to say, she tries to find, beneath everything done in play, its underlying symbolic function. [p. 34]

For Anna Freud, not all aspects of children's play were symbolic. She felt that children often acted out scenarios that occurred during the day and did not necessarily signify aspects of their unconscious.

Likewise, in Synergistic Play Therapy, not every vignette in the treatment process is considered to be pregnant with deep meaning; some are simply diversions. Alternatively, they may be at times an effort to recoup from the aftereffects of having addressed emotionally charged, conflict-ridden issues, either directly or through some metaphorically expressed approximation of their meaning. The vehicle that provides respite is understood to be the representation in play of conflict-free spheres of experience within which the child feels comforted and reassured. In effect, the child may be seen in the Synergistic Play Therapy approach as perhaps gathering strength before again addressing the problem-laden concerns to which he will be inevitably and inexorably drawn.

A focus on process rather than on content characterized Anna Freud's use of interpretation as a therapeutic intervention. Specifically, she was interested in a child's style of play (e.g., dramatic or inhibited), which she considered to provide valuable information regarding the child's defenses. In other words, her comments were more likely to take a form such as "I can tell that's something you don't want to say because you're afraid you will be punished if you say the wrong thing" than one predicated on the more primitive inferential implications of the child's play upon which Klein might focus, such as "You're afraid you will be eaten up if you play with the mommy and daddy dolls that way."

The symbolic nature of the play, although useful in formulating interpretive comments, was for Anna Freud secondary to the defenses inferred from the child's style of play. Klein's interpretations, on the contrary, were primarily based on the substantive content of the play and its corresponding symbolism.

Synergistic Play Therapy emphasizes the process dimension as well as the content of a child's activities. Accordingly, interventions often take the form of commentary on the child's inferred feeling associated with a play sequence. Secondarily, inferences drawn from the content of play, or from the dialogue accompanying it, serve as the conceptual basis of inquiry and reflection. The therapist's willingness to challenge or accept the child's rejection of those interpretations is based on a sense of timing with regard to the child's defensive posture as well as on the underlying transference relationship.

Of the child therapists who took a direction different from the psychoanalytic tradition, Virginia May Axline was among the most influential. Having worked with Carl Rogers, Axline (1947) developed an approach to child therapy predicated on assumptions similar to those that served as premises for nondirective treatment with adults. Her application of these principles was later taken further by Guerney (1976, 1983).

Initially, Axline began with the notion that every person has the inherent ability to achieve self actualization. From this point of view, given the right conditions, an individual would be able to develop a self concept in a mature, independent, and enriching way. This premise implies that a therapist needs to provide an all-accepting and understanding atmosphere in which progress toward self actualization can proceed. In other words, Axline argued that, given the appropriate setting, children too can reach their true potential.

The setting that Axline viewed as most fit for this purpose was a playroom in which the child had free rein. A few limitations would provide the appropriate sense of reality and security within which the young child might develop toward her or his ultimate potential. Playing with the child upon request, and making only nonjudgmental comments in the process, was seen by Axline as necessary to develop the child's sense of security.

One major difference between nondirective and psychoanalytic approaches in play therapy lies in the way historical data are conceptualized in terms of their role in treatment. A historical approach is basic to the psychoanalytic method, that is, examining past experience in relation to current functioning. Self theory (Maslow 1954, Moustakas 1953, 1959, 1966, 1973, Rogers 1948, 1951, 1961) and the technique of nondirective therapy derived from it are, however, based on the notion that the dynamic interplay of current psychological and environmental forces produces changing configurations of one's personality. Since this process is constant, and since new ingredients can be continually integrated in this striving for self actualization, historical forces remain largely irrelevant in terms of conceptualizations from which therapeutic technique is derived.

Play therapy of a nondirective sort is seen as fostering self-realization in a child by creating favorable conditions for such to occur. The notion of unconditional positive regard as a sine qua non of development is basic to the tenets of self theory and to the nondirective therapy technique deriving from it. The principles of Synergistic Play Therapy likewise espouse the importance of the therapist's conveying to the child a nonjudgmental attitude as well as respect and unconditional positive regard independent from, and unaffected by, the child's feelings, impulses, or fantasies. That goal, however, is approximated by emphasis upon the "agent–act" distinction, that is, the notion that only actions (commissions, omissions) are subject to evaluation but the intrinsic worth and dignity of the child is never questioned, either explicitly or by implication. Interventions are framed accordingly with evaluative attributions addressed to a child's "products" rather than to his or her "personhood" (e.g., "That was an angry thing to do" rather than "You are an angry boy").

The role of the therapist in nondirective therapy is limited largely to reflection of the child's own expressed emotionalized attitudes. Axline (1947), for example, stated:

> Emphasis . . . is placed upon the reflection of the expressed feelings back to the children, and complete acceptance of any feeling the child might express. There is value in catharsis—the outpouring of feelings—but the addition of reflection of feeling and acceptance is the added element that helps to clarify the feelings and helps the child to develop insight. [p. 146]

In Axlinian technique, interpretation is avoided and instead reflection of the client's communication is the basis of interventions. Much of a child's play, however, is nonverbal and requires some degree of tentative interpretation, even if reflection is the therapist's goal. The therapist's reliance upon interpretation, as the term is used in classical approaches, thus hinges on his or her willingness to accept the child's negation of the attempted reflection (i.e., the raising of play communication to a verbal level) rather than to consider the response to be an example of resistance.

In Synergistic Play Therapy the therapist's readiness to accept correction by the child regarding the inferred meaning of a play sequence is determined by the stage of treatment. Early in the treatment process there is little, if any, challenge to the child's rejection of the therapist's reflection or interpretation of the child's play. Instead, through multiple reframings, an effort is made to arrive at a statement of meaning that is closest to the therapist's inference about the child's experience and one that the child can accept. At the same time, in the early stages of treatment, the therapist grants the child the final say and is willing to offer "Oh, I was wrong about that . . . what you meant was. . . ."

As the process continues, the therapist and child have typically shared, often through metaphor, a growing awareness and acknowledgment of the child's accustomed defenses, the reasons for them, and the ways in which they operate. At that phase of treatment the therapist is increasingly inclined to hold to spoken inferences despite their encountering some degree of resistance in the child (e.g., "That's something you don't like to say, but I can tell that you really do feel . . .").

Aside from the value ascribed to interpretation in the more classical sense, Synergistic Play Therapy largely accepts, as guidelines rather than as rigid requirements, the eight principles articulated by Axline (1947) for play therapy to proceed:

1. The therapist must develop a warm, friendly relationship with the child, in which good rapport is established as soon as possible.
2. The therapist accepts the child as he or she is.
3. The therapist establishes a feeling of permissiveness in the relationship so that the child feels free to express his or her feelings completely.
4. The therapist is alert to the feelings the child is expressing and reflects those feelings back to the child in such a manner that he or she gains insight into his or her behavior.
5. The therapist maintains a deep respect for the child's ability to solve his or her own problems if given an opportunity to do so. The responsibility to make choices and institute change is the child's.
6. The therapist does not attempt to direct the child's actions or conversation in any manner. The child leads the way; the therapist follows.
7. The therapist does not attempt to hurry the therapy along. It is a gradual process and is recognized as such by the therapist.
8. The therapist establishes only those limitations that are necessary to anchor the therapy to the world of reality and to make the child aware of his or her responsibility in the relationship.

Still other approaches to the incorporation of play in therapy with children rest primarily upon the principles of learning theory. The acquisition of new and adaptive behaviors and the extinction of counterproductive behaviors are sought, in some of these approaches, through direct reinforcement by the therapist (Azrin and Nunn 1977, Bandura 1977, Yates 1970). Generalization of newly acquired behaviors beyond the playroom may be attempted as well, through systematic stimulus and/or response generalization (e.g., Goldfried and Davison 1976, Marlatt and Gordon 1980, 1985). Desensitization of phobic reactions in children often takes such form (Madonna 1990, Young 1989).

In other instances play may be used to modify the response gradient through paradoxical prescription. In one example that has been termed *ordeal therapy*, that modification is accomplished, perhaps metaphorically through the use of toys and play sequences, by pairing the dysfunctional behavior with a noxious stimulus, that is, a prescribed contingent ritual or circumstance under which the behavior is allowed (Madonna and Ciottone 1984). In related treatment strategies, particularly those that address highly circumscribed problematic behaviors, systematic relaxation and light trance hypnosis may be incorporated into the play treatment (Young 1991).

Social learning theory (Bandura and Walters 1963) also represents a behavioral framework within which play therapy can be conceptualized. From this theoretical perspective, modeling of adaptive behavior, prob-lem-solving skills, and interpersonal sensitivity is considered to be a pri-mary agent of change. With sexually abused children a strong effort would be made to model in the playroom behaviors and attitudes that preclude pathogenically rigid reliance upon the dimension of "victim–victimizer," particularly in child–adult interactions (e.g., Acunzo et al. 1991).

By implication, positive rapport is of particular importance in social learning approaches; it is the rapport that allows and motivates the dys-functional child to model the behavior of the therapist. Likewise, rapport needs to be an important component in group play therapy. It is essential that the therapist foster a positive rapport among all of the children in that circumstance. When the therapist succeeds in doing so, an interperson-ally successful child included in a group play treatment program better serves as a "model" whom less successful youngsters will be inspired to emulate (Ciottone and Madonna 1984).

The work of Haim Ginott has been in many ways a benchmark in the theory and practice of play therapy (Ginott 1957, 1958, 1959, 1960, 1961a,b, 1975). Although his writings were not voluminous, as a teacher and clinician he successfully integrated many aspects of psychodynamic concepts, self theory, and learning theory principles in an approach that speaks in very practical terms to playroom technique.

One aspect of Ginott's approach that has particular relevance to the treatment of sexually abused children is the emphasis he places on the issue of respect for boundaries. A therapist operating from Ginott's framework does not, for example, presume a child's readiness to accept even those gestures intended to be helpful. Instead, an offer is made to respond to a child's request for assistance if that request is made explicit (e.g., "If you would like me to help you move those toys, I will help" or "If you need help getting that coat unbuckled, let me know and I will help you").

Children who have been sexually abused have suffered a traumatic violation of boundaries. Because they have been exploited, the development of rapport with them is often a gradual and tentative process. Understandably, abuse victims frequently approach treatment with a wariness born of their battered capacity to trust adults. Any uninvited intrusion upon their space or their prerogatives can have an impact very different from the therapist's intent, regardless of how benevolent or benign that intent may be. For example, a gesture by the therapist intended to be helpful to a child struggling with his or her clothes would likely have a more troublesome meaning for a child who has been sexually abused than it might for another youngster.

Other young victims of abuse sexual abuse may rely on counterphobic defenses and seem unconcerned about boundaries in the context of play therapy. At times they may seek to abrogate them fully. In such instances abused children relate with an immediate and excessive familiarity, often inviting inappropriate access to self. Obviously a therapist declines such "invitations." Less obvious, but of equal importance, is the therapist's continuing use of interventions that reaffirm and reinforce the message that boundaries will be respected, notwithstanding the child's seeming lack of concern about them or the apparent impulse to abandon them.

Play therapists using Ginott's approach also remain alert to the shifting locus of interpersonal boundaries and to the need to provide the child adequate personal space. Often, the increasing proximity of metaphorical play to its referents in traumatic experience, and/or in undifferentiated feelings of conflict related to that experience, results in the child's requiring greater personal margins.

The need for boundaries to be expanded for the child to avoid feeling overwhelmed, and to preclude countertherapeutic dedifferentiation, might well be triggered by the therapist's ongoing comments. As the therapist reflects on the child's play in terms that are increasingly conflict-proximate, the child may signal the need for expanded boundaries because of troublesome associations and the threatening emotions and impulses they invite. Without that buffer by which to preserve a sense of safety and reassurance, the child might well suspend participation in the therapeutic process and instead engage in a defensive retreat more enduring than the intermittent respite from intensity that children often seek.

The effort to adjust interpersonal boundaries in response to a child's changing need for personal space may take the form of the therapist's varying the literal, physical distance between himself and the child. Alternatively, in dialogue with the child, or in thinking aloud about the child's play and its apparent communicative import, a therapist may shift verbal references between second and third person expressions (e.g., "Sometimes you feel . . ." or "Sometimes a guy might feel . . ."). In yet another approach the therapist may make attributions to a group in which the child can choose to claim membership, at least for the moment (e.g., "Some kids wish they could . . ."). It is important to recall, however, that in all interactions the therapist maintains a nonjudgmental, accepting attitude in tone and demeanor, independent of where on the continuum of interpersonal proximity communication is occurring.

As rapport develops, and as the prospect of addressing conflict becomes less fearsome, children tend to draw in their boundaries. Greater interpersonal proximity then becomes possible, both literally and in the form of verbal expression. Changes along that dimension do not occur simply as an arithmetic progression over time, however. Instead, shifts tend to happen with some frequency, both over the course of a number of sessions and, in a short-lived way, even within the context of a single meeting.

Notwithstanding growing trust on the part of the child, the Synergistic Approach urges the therapist to remain respectful of the child's boundaries and alert to the cues that signal even a momentary need for their expansion. In keeping with Ginott's approach, it is often nonverbal cues upon which the therapist must rely in monitoring such variations in the child's need for personal space. They include increased motoric tension, a change in the tempo of speech, or a shift in the frequency and duration of eye contact or gaze aversion.

Limit setting is the primary means in play therapy by which the therapist acknowledges the integrity of boundaries and communicates a continuing respect for them. Ginott has listed six reasons for limits to be maintained in play therapy (Ginott 1961b, pp. 149–150):

1) Limits direct catharsis into symbolic channels, i.e., unacceptable impulses can be sublimated into actions that are consistent with societal expectations.

2) Limits enable the therapist to maintain attitudes of acceptance, empathy, and regard for the child client throughout the therapy contacts, i.e., assures that the therapist will remain within his own tolerance of disruptive behavior.

3) Limits assure the physical safety of the children and the therapist in the playroom setting, i.e., the children must not physically attack themselves or the therapist.

4) Limits strengthen ego controls, i.e., unaccepted impulses are accepted and controlled without excessive guilt and gratification is delayed.

5) Some limits are set for reasons of law, ethics, and social accept-ability, e.g., sexual play or urinating on the floor is not acceptable behavior.

6) Some limits are set because of budgetary considerations, e.g., expensive toys are not destroyed.

When imposing a limit, a therapist operating from Ginott's perspec-tive would be quick to introduce a substitute means by which the child might express him- or herself. In that process the therapist fosters differ-entiation of thought, feeling, and action and thereby resolves a frequently occurring conflict suffered by children whose experience remains global and diffuse. For example, if a sexually abused child reacts to the fear of further violation by counterphobically accosting another youngster and is told simply, "Don't do that!" he might well hear the admonition as having to do as much with the feeling and impulse that he is experiencing as it does with the action he has taken. In such a circumstance a child might well respond by thinking, in effect, "I still feel that way. I can't change my feelings or keep ideas from coming into my mind. I am guilty of being dis-obedient and bad."

The use of substitutes encouraged by Ginott can resolve that dilemma for the child while teaching him or her a skill that fosters the generaliza-tion of therapeutic gain from the playroom to other sectors of life. In a playroom interaction, for example, a child's impulsive attempt to assault the therapist literally, or even symbolically (e.g., pointing an index finger at the therapist with thumb raised in a mock shooting gesture), might be countered by the comment "I know how you feel. You're angry at me. It's okay to feel angry. But I'm not for hitting [shooting]. This can stand for me [offering the child a Bobo doll or some other soft plaything that has vaguely human or at least nondescript form]." At times the therapist might even hold the object in front of herself or himself so as to dramatize the impact of the sequence.

Because a substitute can be discarded or redefined in its symbolism, the child can, when the feeling of the moment subsides, re-establish posi-tive interaction with the therapist more comfortably and with less residual guilt. The therapeutic strategy of introducing substitutes while differenti-ating internal experience from external action also provides a means by which the child can represent transference phenomena in play, that is, a toy that can stand for an important figure in the child's life permits expres-sion of otherwise forbidden feelings and impulses and renders them sa-lient in the therapy process through the metaphor of play.

IV

The Conceptual Framework
of Synergistic Play Therapy

The play therapy approach of Haim Ginott, one of the main perspectives upon which Synergistic Play Therapy is based, includes constructs drawn from several theoretical systems. From a psychodynamic approach, for example, the notions of conflict, defenses, transference, and mastery are included in a central way. The concept of hierarchically ordered strivings is also a basic one.

In terms of how interventions are framed, Piagetian principles are pivotal, such as the notion of a progression in cognitive development from sensorimotor through concrete thinking and increasing levels of abstraction and formal operations (1951). From self theory there is drawn the notion of a primary impetus or biological imperative in the direction of growth and development toward self actualization through self awareness. Principles of learning through association and/or reinforcement are included in this theoretical perspective as well as, for example, in the emphasis upon helping the child experience the playroom as a safe context within which to approach anxiety-provoking issues through the gradualized approximations of symbolic play and verbal metaphor.

Sophisticated clinicians will recognize that attributing techniques to different construct systems in a way that implies mutually exclusive designation is in fact an oversimplification; though language may differ, several orientations subsume ideas that are at least closely related to those identified with alternate approaches. Although most discussions of play therapy center on the ways in which one or another of these theoretical systems organizes clinical data, we will attempt instead to intertwine elaboration of our theoretical perspective with suggestions for playroom technique by considering the data related to Mickey's treatment.

At the outset it is important to highlight some of the organismic-developmental metatheoretical concepts we have sought to integrate with our adaptation of Ginott's approach. The orthogenetic principle, for example, holds that developmental advance involves progress from a more primitive level of fusion toward differentiation and hierarchic integration. Conversely, dedifferentiation with regression toward primitivity may occur in the wake of troubling experiences.

Differentiation does not always imply hierarchic integration (i.e., subordination of the parts to the whole of experience in a coherent fashion). Instead, differentiation and isolation may eventuate, a sidetracking by which some aspect of experience is indeed differentiated from the diffusion and globality that had previously precluded a sense of its separateness, but by which it remains unintegrated and experientially alone in its differentiated state. Dissociative states or feelings of depersonalization are analogs of such differentiation and isolation.

Another pathological sidetracking that can occur is that of differentiation and conflict, a developmental state that implies differentiation of some aspect of experience but with an even less benign failure of differentiation and hierarchic integration; not only does separateness continue, but it does so in a way that generates tension, which in itself poses the ongoing threat of dedifferentiation when even relatively minor pressures are encountered. In effect, ego resources are strained to a point that renders otherwise manageable degrees of stress potentially dedifferentiating in their impact.

In either case—differentiation and isolation or differentiation and conflict—transactional patterns by which self–world relationships are shaped and maintained are restricted. Specifically, an impaired sense of self and/or a distorted perception of the world can lead to the determination that few instrumentalities are available or effective for achieving one's goals or the favor of others.

A related principle drawn from organismic developmental metatheory is the notion that behavior is goal directed and reflective of the meaning the individual imposes upon ongoing experience. Although the self–world relationship the individual thus constructs is considered a holistically indivisible unit of analysis in that conceptual context, each of its components can be understood in its several aspects. Specifically, the individual comes to regard various aspects of his or her environment in its physical (objects and places), interpersonal (people) and sociocultural (rules, customs, and expectations) aspects in ways that can be characterized as cognitive (knowing), affective (feeling) and valuative (attaching relative levels of importance or unimportance). The means or instrumentalities that individuals see as available and effective (or unavailable and ineffective) for transacting with the world thus construed are therefore the result of the ways in which they cognitively, affectively, and valuatively construe their relationship with the physical, interpersonal, and sociocultural aspects of their environment.

Given those premises, the therapist's task becomes one of helping a child achieve developmental advance in self–world relationships (i.e., increasingly differentiated and hierarchically integrated cognitive, affective, and valuative constructions of the physical, interpersonal, and sociocultural aspects of the environment) and develop correspondingly more advanced instrumentalities for transacting with the world thus structured. In doing so, the therapist has access to a kind of 3" × 3" schema that can serve as a guideline for framing interventions:

WAYS OF STRUCTURING ASPECTS OF THE WORLD ENVIRONMENT

Cognitive (*knowing*)   Physical (*objects and places*)

Affective (*feeling*)   Interpersonal (*people*)

Valuative (*assigning   Sociocultural (*rules, customs,
relative importance or   or expectations*)
unimportance*)

Consider the following examples of interventions in play therapy drawn from the suggested framework:

"Maybe you have some feelings about having to take care of your sister" (affective construction of sociocultural and interpersonal aspects of the environment).

"I can tell you know about scary dark places" (cognitive construction of a physical aspect of the environment).

"I wonder what the most important rule would be for those dolls to know about if they were real kids and they went to your school" (valuative construction of a sociocultural aspect of the environment).

"You know something about angry people all right" (cognitive construction of the interpersonal environment).

"I bet you have some special friends" (valuative construction of an aspect of the interpersonal environment).

Through the use of playthings and/or verbal metaphor, the self–world relationship frame of reference can also provide a basis for helping the child develop instrumentalities that increase a sense of agency (i.e., feeling it possible to act upon the world rather than feel that being acted upon is the only possibility). When a child constructs a scene with dolls or puppets, or even with figures drawn on a chalkboard or easel, for example, the therapist might wonder aloud whether the characters in the drama could try one or another alternate course of action if they knew or felt or valued differently some aspect of what they confronted.

One of the most effective ways for a play therapist to encourage a child's developmental progress is to use play and playthings as metaphor. Through reflection of play sequences, a therapist can venture reflections and interpretation that carry with them alternative constructions that a child might employ in the way she or he construes and transacts with a world that has seemed rejecting, neglectful, or traumatizing. At the same time, both the child and the therapist have the concrete here-and-now referent of the play sequence and the toys in which to take recourse when direct consideration of the metaphorical referents seems likely to be overwhelming or otherwise counterproductive.

Often dialogue based on reflection of play sequences becomes a process of speaking at two levels simultaneously, with both the child and the therapist aware of the parallel referents, but with only one being acknowledged in words. In such instances it is not unusual for a knowing smile to be passed between therapist and child as an acknowledgment of the metaphor and an unspoken agreement to maintain it.

Sometimes a brief intervention can serve as a probe regarding the child's willingness to approach the referent of a play metaphor directly. One example was noted earlier when, during the evaluation, an assembly of playthings Mickey had produced fell and he responded to the comment "You know about things going wrong" by saying "I sure do, lots of things."

Children use the metaphorical dimension of play in a variety of ways. Cathartic expression is an obvious and frequent example, but metaphor may also become the vehicle a child uses to venture communication of some construction that she or he fears may elicit a negative judgment from the therapist. In such instances the refuge of apparent reference only to the concrete playthings promises to circumscribe the child's perceived risk. Alternatively, a child may employ the metaphorical potential of play to rehearse alternative transactional patterns.

Occasionally a child may employ play metaphors in an effort to determine how best to construe the therapist and the unfolding process. A dramatic example occurred early in the play therapy with Mickey. Having set up and populated a top-access dollhouse, he proceeded to cover the structure with newsprint, such that the paper draped down over the sides. He then proceeded to circle the dollhouse, occasionally lifting the newsprint to peek in the windows and doors. In the context of discussion about "peeking," he asked whether the therapist would join him in that activity.

As an abused child, Mickey was metaphorically asking the therapist whether he was one of those adult males who had no regard for privacy and was willing to impose himself on others. Obviously, the therapist declined Mickey's invitation, saying instead, "If you want me to know what's in there, you can tell me." The response from Mickey was a relieved smile and a quantum step forward in the development of trust.

With regard to specific techniques and the basis for them, several assumptions adopted in this approach to play therapy are particularly relevant. For purposes of discussion they can be presented as premises with conceptual implications and derivative techniques.

One such is the notion that *children use play as a means of communication*. From that very straightforward premise derives the idea that the therapist needs to make available toys that facilitate communication in the area of concern.

As simple as it sounds, this is often a neglected principle. Too often, play therapists succumb to the temptation to engage in some enjoyable regression and choose toys that are personally appealing rather than ones that have relevance and rationale within the treatment plan (Ginott 1975). In a related vein it should be noted that therapists often overstock a playroom with an array of toys that distract and/or overstimulate a child such that the agenda for the session becomes a function of the stimulus pull of playroom trappings rather than of the child's psychological needs. In the Synergistic approach to play therapy, no toy is made available that does not have at least potential value as a vehicle for communication of issues considered relevant within the working conceptualization of the child's needs.

Typically, basic playroom equipment includes some doll and/or puppet figures, structures that can represent home or school, drawing or painting equipment (with the character of those materials—e.g., finger paints, watercolors, markers—perhaps chosen with an eye to the child's need for more or less organization and control or for flexibility and freedom of expression), and a larger stuffed or inflatable doll that can be used for displacement. Frequently there is good reason to include playthings that encourage gross motor movement, toys that lend themselves to aggressive expression, water, toy vehicles, various hats or disguises that allow a child the opportunity to seek, in an assumed role, the safety necessary for expression that might otherwise be inhibited. The point, however, is that every toy or plaything should be thought about in terms of the goals and objectives of the treatment plan for the particular child. If there is no reason for a plaything other than the impression that "any kid would like that," it will probably serve no constructive purpose with regard to treatment goals and therefore has no place in the playroom.

Another premise from which playroom technique is derived in this approach is the idea that **with good rapport and a trusting relationship, issues of conflict and concern will emerge, at times tentatively and at times with a long-lived intensity**. From that premise comes the contention that the therapist does not have to force issues, but instead can allow the child to determine the timing for addressing concerns and the extent of their focus each time they appear.

When therapists have a very definite agenda, they sometimes infuse it with a kind of urgency that leads them to pounce on crucial issues the moment they emerge. Paradoxically, and particularly with reference to sexually abused children, the effect may be for those issues to recede in their accessibility because of how the child construes the therapist's eagerness to focus on them. Alternatively, if, as Meadow (1981) suggests, the therapist succeeds first in developing a therapeutic context distinguished from other aspects of the child's experience by its psychological safety, the child will be more open to the therapist's reflecting play themes in ways that address those issues, at first brushing them lightly with nonspecific metaphor and eventually with increasing approximations to direct reference.

In a related vein, there is also implied in this premise the need to respect the limits of a child's tolerance for specific issues at any given time (Spotnitz et al. 1976a,b). In other words, the therapist should not run roughshod over a child's clear signals that he or she has had enough for now but instead allow the focus to shift away from a certain issue with confidence that it will re-emerge.

A corollary to the notion that a child's sense of timing ought to be respected is the requirement that the end of each play therapy session be preannounced: "Five more minutes and it's time to go." Therapists are accustomed to the frequently evident pattern of adults presenting loaded material in the waning minutes of the therapy session. The same ambivalence that prompts adults to wait until the end of the hour can lead a child to delay presentation of troublesome concerns until there is little time left. Although adults tend to track the time of the therapy session, children are less able or likely to do so, even when the playroom has a clock. Preannouncing the approach of the hour's end often triggers a flurry of emotionally charged interactions.

Providing a five-minute warning has the additional advantage of minimizing the likelihood that a child will conclude that whatever she or he did just prior to the end of the session prompted the therapist to bring the proceedings to a close. Children often infer causality from the contiguity of events in a way that Sullivan (1953) called "parataxic reasoning," a process further encouraged by the developmentally primitive tendency of a child to explain in egocentric terms events that are not otherwise easily understood. Feelings of rejection, and/or a renewed determination to withhold material that seems to the child to be offensive to the therapist, may result when a child has not been alerted to the approaching end of the session, no matter what occurs between the preannouncement and the subsequent statement that "Now our time is up."

Yet another premise in the Synergistic approach to play therapy is that *the therapist seeks to maintain rather than blur the child-adult distinction, yet does so in a way that reassures the child rather than threatens him or her with the unavoidable power dimension*.

This is a tricky line to walk, but in this approach the emphasis is upon remaining the adult. Participatory play is not part of the process, nor is there an effort to relate to the child in childlike ways. Instead, the therapist maintains the adult posture but attempts in the process to avoid structuring interactions as a power or demand experience for the child. Consistent with that effort, the therapist remains an observer of the child's play rather than a participant in it, and provides ongoing commentary of reflection and interpretation of the play, framing the interventions in ways intended to foster developmental advance.

Nonparticipation in play is a guideline, not a requirement locked in concrete. Unless the child requires the therapist's participation to carry out a sequence that has obvious therapeutic importance, however, assuming the role of observer/commentator is likely to prove a more effective way to achieve treatment goals; the potential for play to stimulate regression and/or competitive impulses in the therapist, even momentarily, can compromise the therapist's alertness to opportunities for effective intervention.

Although children periodically seek to cajole a therapist into more active play, most are responsive to a straightforward explanation: "I understand that you want me to play, but I'd rather watch and think about what you're doing and talk about what you're doing. For me, it's a whole lot easier to understand what you're trying to tell me and how you are feeling and how I can help you when I spend all of my time thinking about what's happening in your play. It's kind of hard for me to do that when I'm playing and I want to help you as best I can. So you play and I'll think about it with you while you play."

When a therapist participates in play with a child, there should be a good reason. There were, in fact, several instances during play therapy with Mickey that therapist participation was deemed helpful and appropriate. At one point, for example, Mickey took a play telephone and gave another one to the therapist. He then proceeded to playact a call to the police station in which he reported his own abuse and asked for protection.

At another point in play therapy Mickey became animated and almost exuberant in apparent reaction to voicing his rage toward the perpetrators of his abuse. To punish them symbolically, he asked that the therapist throw a doll that he decided represented the perpetrators so that he could "wind up and belt them." Such instances are less participation in a child's play than they are a kind of facilitating of his or her use of play as a means of communication. The distinction can be elusive, but is often an important one to consider.

As a child moves toward preadolescence and away from symbolic play as a means of communication, some activity, often of a board game variety, may serve as an interpersonal buffer during what is primarily verbal conversation with a therapist. Such interactions obviously require the therapist's active participation. That circumstance, however, approaches the perimeter of what has been defined as play therapy in this discussion.

Conceptualizing play therapy in the way suggested here also requires recognition that *the therapist must remain mindful of the power dimension when reflecting the inferred meaning of a play sequence*. In that connection it is helpful to phrase inquiries indirectly rather than as explicit questions because, from a child's perspective, even a casual question from an adult carries with it the implicit demand for a response. However unintentioned that demand may be, children simply do not feel the same option not to respond that is reserved for an adult without feeling defiant and/or guilty.

Rather than asking a child "What do you think about that?" or "How did you feel about that?" inquiries might be phrased as if the therapist were musing aloud: "I wonder what [Mickey] thought about that" or "A guy sure could have some feelings about something like that" or "Maybe that's something you know about."

By casting interventions in such terms, the therapist extends to the child the option of responding or remaining silent without feeling that she or he is running contrary to an implicit demand. When that issue is an obviously salient one, the option of disagreeing with the implied premise of a statement can be further legitimized with the option of a nonresponse: "Maybe that's something that's really important to you . . . or maybe it's not."

By phrasing inquiries indirectly, the therapist is spared the subtle but frequent discomfort, borne of a sense of obligation, associated with eliciting some kind of response from a determinedly silent or withdrawn child. In such instances a therapist might voice an additional observation, one the child can use to affirm the accuracy of the first without losing face by acquiescing to a demand that she or he abandon the posture of silence, and without becoming engaged in a tug-of-war with the therapist.

A sequence that seems to go nowhere might begin with a minimally inferential reflection of an aggressive play vignette carefully framed in terms intended to avoid a judgmental tone but to allow instead nonthreatening communication about such issues. For example, "Maybe [Susan] knows about angry feelings." At times, however, there may only be a pause; the child does not respond in any way that might lend itself to being reframed in words. In other words, a therapist might feel there is no way to continue the interaction by acknowledging or reflecting the child's having fully or partially affirmed or rejected the therapist's initial intervention.

In such instances the therapist might give meaning to the silence by a kind of thinking out loud: "[Susan] didn't say anything so it must be that she does know about angry feelings because I know that [Susan] is not the kind of girl who would let people think wrong things about her."

Often such interventions will lead to head nods affirming or negating what the therapist has ventured. In such instances the therapist must accept

without challenge what the child has indicated by saying, for example—
and preferably with dramatic emphasis: "Oh, I was right about that! [Su-
san] does know about those things. I'll bet she knows about a lot of other
stuff too" or "Oh my, I was wrong! [Susan] doesn't know about that stuff."

At times, by gesture, the child may negate what the therapist has
wondered aloud, but do so with obvious ambivalence. In such interactions
the therapist might amend the intervention, voicing it in a way that allows
that ambivalence to be expressed: "Oh my, I was wrong. [Susan] doesn't
know about that stuff . . . except maybe kind of." If the child again dis-
owns the notion, rapport building—and the child's need to feel empowered in the context of the therapy—requires that the therapist accept the
child's last indication. When it is clear to the therapist that the initial intervention was accurate and that the child's negation of it reflects a defense
that has to remain intact for the time being or that the child is focused on
the process of interaction and feeling empowered within it, the contention
can be accepted in words that allow the child to amend the communication in later interactions ("Oh, I see, that's how you feel now"). At the very
least, communication is occurring and the child has learned that, in the
playroom, he or she has prerogatives that will be respected.

In work with children, no less than with adults, a therapeutic contract needs to be negotiated to make explicit the purpose of meetings as
well as the ground rules governing the process. Obviously, that process
is accomplished in the language of a child and it occurs over time. With
regard to the power dimension of play therapy, frequent reference may be
made to the contract when questions emerge that require structuring or
limit setting by the therapist.

The typical playroom contract with a child includes discussion at the
outset regarding limits as well freedoms (Ginott and Lebo 1961, 1963). In
addition to presenting the notion that "this is a special place where people
can say whatever they want and do what they want," therapists should
explain that privacy remains intact so long as no one's safety is in jeopardy. In short, the rule is that no one can hurt himself or herself or anyone
else. Additions to the contract involving interaction with the child's parents may be negotiated with the child by explaining that "sometimes it is
hard to be a kid but sometimes it's hard to be a parent too, so maybe I (or
another therapist) will meet with your parents to help them figure out parent
worries." With such an amendment, it is important to reaffirm the child's
right to privacy for anything that does not jeopardize safety.

Elaboration of the aspect of the contract that has more direct bearing on behavioral limits often takes the form of the therapist's having to prohibit an action that has the potential of leading to physical harm or to a loss of impulse control. Instances of the latter, in fact, might seem so frightening and/or so irretrievable to the child as to be clearly and profoundly countertherapeutic. In either instance, how limit setting is framed and presented should take at least two issues into account. First, the child could construe the intervention solely in power terms that represent an abrogation of previously implied prerogatives. Second, the child could perceive the therapist's effort in this regard as a challenge that invites interpersonal struggle.

The phrase "the rule is . . ." often helps maintain a level playing field in the playroom when it becomes necessary for the therapist to or prohibit a behavior. In effect, the implication is that the rule applies equally to both child and therapist. A further implication may be that the requirement was put in place previously by an authority that acted independently, and in fact before the child even appeared on the scene. Thus framed, the prohibition is not one imposed by the therapist arbitrarily, punitively, or as a statement of the child's lack of perceived worth. Instead it represents a previously unarticulated but enduring characteristic of the circumstance. To reinforce that notion, reaffirm the child's perceived worth, and encourage the developmentally advanced use of substitutes in the acceptable rechannelization of impulse, the therapist should, in the wake of such an intervention, immediately suggest a substitute: "That makes you angry, I understand. But the rule is, the chalkboard isn't for hammering. This [an inflatable doll or perhaps an overstuffed sofa] can stand for whoever you want it to. You can hit it to show how angry you feel."

In such instances the therapist can help the child adjust to the use of substitutes by providing an affectively toned commentary as the child ventures use of the substitute: "Oh, I see. You're not just angry, you're *very* angry! You're not just very angry, you're *very, very* angry! Now I understand even better."

In this approach to play therapy it is assumed that irreversible or irretrievable acts by a child are most often likely to prove countertherapeutic. If, for example, a child symbolically vents anger at some adult by smashing or decapitating a wooden doll, he or she may well experience a cathartic sense of relief for the moment. The child's next thought, however, may be to rehearse some strategy for restoring the relationship with that adult, but the doll's head is on one side of the room and the smashed body on another and not much can be accomplished in the thematic play metaphor that had been initiated.

In addition to their obvious implication for choosing playroom stores, therefore, such sequences may prompt a therapist to invoke "the rule is . . ." phraseology to further amend the play therapy contract. Specifically, a therapist might suggest the use of a Play-doh doll (which can be restored) or a drawing on an easel (which can be redrawn) as vehicles to express extremes of rage since "the rule is, the dolls are not for smashing." Such interventions are not necessarily made for safety or privacy concerns, but to encourage the use of substitutes, avoid irreversible acts, and foster therapeutic gain.

Symbolically irreversible acts are as likely as those of a physical nature to prove counterproductive. A child who points a gun at a therapist may feel he has committed an irreversible act when transference leads at some later point to a need to express love. For that reason substitutes are recommended for these instances as well: "The rule is, I'm not for shooting. But this [a doll or an inflatable] can stand for me. Show me how you feel."

Again, it is helpful for the therapist to comment on the child's actions by introducing the substitute object and by using affectively toned words that reflect the intensity of the child's feelings while communicating a nonjudgmental acceptance of them. In doing so the therapist also helps the child develop the more flexible instrumentality of language for transacting with the interpersonal aspect of his or her surroundings. Within the context of the therapy process, such interventions make it more possible for the child in subsequent play sequences to shift the form and emphasis of communications without being constrained by the inflexibility of antecedent concrete action.

Some of the most trying sessions for a play therapist are those inevitable instances when a child acts out a frenzy of oppositionality. Children who are habitually predisposed toward such behavior may be poorly served by the approach outlined here and may require a treatment plan that begins with a behaviorally oriented strategy to help them gain the necessary control to benefit from a playroom approach. Any child may at times be overwhelmed with an agenda of oppositionality, perhaps prompted by the interaction of transference with current life circumstances or with the surfacing legacy of the past.

At times a child may simply persist in a behavior that has been identified as not in keeping with what "the rule is." The therapist must remain consistent and require compliance with the rule while identifying the affective urgency that underlies the impulse as well as its cognitive and valuative parameters, and while making substitutes available: "I understand. You feel very angry about what you saw and you want to smash that dollhouse to show how important those feelings are to you. But the rule is, the dollhouse is not for smashing. This [perhaps some clay] can stand for whatever you want it to. Show how you feel with this."

When the child persists in a threat or an effort to continue the proscribed action, it may become necessary to remove the opportunity to do so, perhaps by taking away an object or a plaything. Should this become necessary, it is important that the therapist precede the action and accompany it with commentary that is nonjudgmental in tone and that intends in its content to affirm and ally with that aspect of the child's ongoing experience of self that would prefer to find a less disruptive means of managing in the face of strong feeling: "You're having a hard time controlling things now. I understand. Sometimes it's really hard. For now I'll take this away because you're having a tough time and then we'll bring it back later." At that point it is sometimes effective to suggest the substitute again.

Most frequently, crises of control and defiance subside when the therapist avoids entering into a struggle or communicating in tone or gesture that the oppositionality was taken in a personal way or as the basis for devaluing the child. Sometimes, however, the defiance may escalate such that the child begins to storm around the room throwing toys or otherwise attempting mayhem. A physical attack on the therapist may occur, perhaps in the form of objects being thrown. Consistent with the notion that irreversible acts are countertherapeutic, the therapist must disallow the behavior, even if it requires physical restraint of the child.

When a child must be physically restrained, the therapist is faced with the formidable but important challenge of continuing to speak in a manner that remains calm in tone, measured in tempo, and reassuring in content. The therapist's remarks might resemble the following: "You're having a hard time controlling yourself now. I know that can be a scary feeling. I'll help you control yourself for a while because I know it is hard right now and that can be scary . . ." and so on.

Providing calm reassurance in that manner while holding a child who is attempting to hit, kick, spit, and scream four-letter-word epithets is the kind of experience that can lead the most dedicated therapist to consider another profession, but happily it does not occur often. Moreover, when a therapist does accompany physical restraint with verbal reassurance, the child's struggle usually becomes one of diminishing resistance. Loss of control is frightening to a child, and the therapist's efforts in this regard, so long as they are perceived as affiliative rather than adversarial, are apt to be experienced as reassuring. Assuming no disruption of life circumstances or current victimization, recurrent patterns of escalating defiance that require physical restraint indicate that the therapist reconsider diagnostic impressions, treatment recommendations, the child's readiness to make use of play therapy, or at least the stimulus value of playroom stores for that child.

There is yet another implication for play therapists regarding the power dimension inherent in any adult–child interaction: that is the way in which even a helping gesture might be construed by a child as an unwelcome or at least an unauthorized intrusion. The help a therapist offers a sexually abused child who is struggling to unfasten his or her coat might be experienced very differently from what the therapist intends. An adult's willingness to simply reach out and take some action with regard to the child's clothes could easily trigger a developmentally regressed construction of his or her relationship with the therapist, one in which dedifferentiation recalls the experience of victimization rather than one that promises relief from its emotional sequelae.

Particularly with children who have a history of abuse, but also in play therapy generally, it is extremely important that explicit permission be sought before the child's space or person is intruded upon. In the example given above, the therapist should preface any gesture with a statement such as: "If you'd like me to help you, just tell me and I will" or "Maybe you'd like some help." Except when the child's safety is at risk, the therapist should wait for the child to grant permission. In its description this guideline might seem unnecessarily formal and distancing, but in practice it conveys a respect for the child's rights and typically builds a stronger and warmer rapport.

Subtler versions of the same circumstance may emerge when a child is struggling to accomplish some goal with playthings, such as seeking to balance a set of objects atop each other. Again in a spirit of helpfulness, a therapist might reach out spontaneously to align one of the objects. From the child's perspective, however, that gesture could be experienced as another example of an adult's willingness to invade the child's sphere of activity. Although its impact would obviously be slight, even that interaction could work against the effort to help the child appreciate the possibilities of a more developmentally advanced self–world relationship. It is generally useful to state the offer to help during playroom interactions before presuming to do so.

To be mindful of a child's psychological space is as important as being attentive to his or her person, physical space, or sphere of activity. One way to measure degrees of intimacy vis-à-vis psychological space is the form of speech used in making attributions to the child through reflection and/ or interpretation. To say, for example, "That's something that could really get a *guy* feeling sad" is less immediate in its impact then musing aloud, "I'll bet *Mickey* really felt sad about that." The most intimately stated form (and therefore the one that has the greatest potential to be experienced as empathically comforting or threatening) is to address the child directly: "I'll bet *you* felt really sad about that."

In the Synergistic approach to play therapy it is incumbent on the therapist to monitor, on a moment-to-moment basis, the child's readiness to accept and/or to benefit from one or another level of sharing. The yardsticks to measure that dimension include not only the physical distance between therapist and child, but also the degree to which attributions couched in reflections and interpretations reach into the core of the child's experience, and even the form of speech used in making those efforts.

With regard to the dimension of physical intimacy, some children— particularly those who have been sexually abused—may adopt what has been characterized as a *counterphobic* posture: in an effort to master the anxiety associated with a feared circumstance, they may seek it out. In an unarticulated way that defensive process seems predicated on the notion that some level of mastery can be achieved by at least choosing the time and place for confronting the fear. In the context of play therapy that flawed strategy may prompt a child to continually seek to extend the boundaries in terms of physical contact with a therapist. And, out of a compassionate urge to comfort a victimized child, the therapist might respond and unwittingly contribute to the anxiety that enhances the potential for dedifferentiation.

Responding to the manifest form of a child's counterphobic impulse will in all likelihood increase the child's anxiety level and prompt an effort to achieve yet more physical intimacy. It is not unknown for play therapy to deteriorate into hour-long thumb-sucking sessions with the child sitting on the therapist's lap. In addition to leaving the well-intentioned but misguided therapist in an almost inescapable quandary, the failed treatment effort obviously fosters developmental regression rather than advance and leads to little if any promise that the regression will serve any productive purpose. In the Synergistic approach to play therapy, *the therapist must monitor the degree of intimacy that is required, encouraged or allowed*.

In some instances hunger for intimacy, and fear of it, may manifest itself in a child's seeking to be fed in a literal way. A request of that sort may strike a chord with therapists, who by definition want to nourish children, albeit symbolically, and who—particularly with abused children—may want to compensate in some measure for their suffering.

When therapy seems to be going particularly slowly, a therapist might be tempted to seize upon the child's request to be fed as providing an opportunity to feel that at least some contribution is being made to the child's well-being. With a few important exceptions, however, acceding to the request in literal terms rather than by reframing it to reflect more encompassing needs leads to little more than short-term satisfaction and to a precedent that becomes a focal but nonproductive redefinition of the therapy contract.

Sharing food to mark noteworthy events such as holidays or birthdays may add to the process of therapy, but there is danger in its being overemphasized. When food is shared, the therapist might reflect on the symbolism of child and therapist uniting in the process. In other words, when both take in parts of one food, it becomes more possible to feel somehow united outside of the play therapy session as well as within it. That aspect of the potential meaning of food sharing in play therapy can be particularly useful to highlight at the time of termination, but its value will be significantly compromised if it has become too frequent.

Another danger of food sharing as a regular part of therapy is its implicit invitation to the child to generate requests that eventually must be denied. However needy a child whose problems warrant play therapy may be, those needs cannot be met literally.

For similar reasons gift giving may also lead to short-term satisfaction, but typically fails to advance treatment goals. In addition, young children tend to lose or break objects and may feel guilty if a gift from the therapist meets such a fate. Finally, children may need to pass through a phase of expressing anger toward the therapist as a transference figure. By assuming the role of gift giver, the therapist may hinder that necessary process.

V

Synergistic Play Therapy with Mickey Begins

A complete recounting of the first play therapy session with Mickey follows. As the initial session, it was preceded only by the short, individual playroom screening conducted several weeks earlier of Mickey, his sister, and his two cousins. This first session includes concrete illustrations of many of the issues discussed in previous chapters, particularly with regard to development of a therapeutic contract. In this and subsequent chapters a complete session transcript is provided together with a portrayal of the "choreography" of the action so that some visual picture might emerge for the reader. Discussion of theoretical concepts and treatment strategies is intertwined with the transcription of dialogue and choreography to provide an overview of the process and its rationale.

> *Therapist:* (*Pointing*) Do you know what kind of mirror that is? That's the kind you can see through from both sides . . . and there's a camera over there and other people are going to watch through the camera. Would you like to see it?

As this opening illustrates, helping the child become familiar with the physical environment of the playroom is the first order of business. When observation is to occur, however, it is especially important to remind the youngster of it at the very outset, to renew the consent given before the playroom was entered, and to allay anxiety by allowing the child to explore the apparatus to be used and to meet the people involved. In the absence of such familiarization a youngster might easily project fear, the prospect of judgment and reprisal, or other products of fantasy onto the unknown dimension of the playroom experience about to begin.

With sexually abused children in particular, upon whom adults have intruded without regard for rights of privacy, reassurance through familiarity with the setting is a central issue. Previously exploited children could verbally consent to the prospect of being observed because they feel they have no option to do otherwise. Later, however, they may feel uncertain about the limits of what they have consented to. Preparatory exploration of the physical environment and a direct meeting with the observers—and developing a sense of their roles as helping professionals respectful of the child's rights—may well allay such fears, much in the manner that Werner and Kaplan (1963), Burke (1973), and Cirillo and Kaplan (1983) have highlighted in speaking about the mastery to be achieved by naming the unknown.

> *Mickey:* Yeah. (*Both walk to the observation room and talk with the several people there. One of those present is Mickey's social worker. She explains to Mickey that she and the others could watch and feel a part of things without being right in the room*)
>
> *T:* (*Returning to the playroom*) Shall we let her do that, Mickey?
>
> *M:* (*Nodding agreement*) Mm-hmm.
>
> *T:* Okay, we'll have Diane and the others watch us, but we'll have them promise that whatever we talk about, only we will know about it. This is a special place. We can talk about things here that we don't talk about anywhere else. And maybe Diane will listen and some other people who work here but that's all. (*Mickey draws and erases on the chalkboard*) You know something about chalkboards. This isn't the first time you've messed around with chalkboards. I can tell you've got some experience with that.

Two messages of import are being shared with the child in this interaction: first, the notion of confidentiality is being emphasized as a defining characteristic of all that is to follow; second, empowerment is beginning to occur through the paracommunication that the therapist perceives Mickey as someone who has experience, capabilities, and skills that will be respected. Attributions such as "You know something about that" or "I can tell you have some experience with that" prompts elaboration of focal issues without conveying the implicit demand inherent in the unavoidable power dimension of the adult–child relationship. At the same time it conveys respect for the child's resourcefulness and knowledge.

M: (*Inspecting the available pieces of chalk*) No black?
T: No, but there's different colors there. But you like black, huh?
M: Yeah.
T: I wonder if that's your favorite color?
M: Mm-hmm . . . and blue and purple.
T: I wonder what Mickey's favorite color in the whole world is.
M: (*After pondering for several seconds*) Gray.
T: Gray. Gray is your favorite color. I wonder if gray is a happy color or a sad color or what kind of color it is.
M: I don't know.

This exchange regarding color represents the therapist's effort to understand not only the obvious implication with regard to affective experience but also to indicate to the child that symbolic/metaphorical meaning will be grist for the interactional mill of play therapy.

T: Can't tell sometimes . . . sometimes those things are hard to tell. (*Pause*) Mickey, you know what else about this place, you know what else is special about it?
M: (*Continuing to attend to the chalkboard*) Nope.
T: (*Standing about six feet from Mickey and continuing to avoid any position behind him or outside his line of sight*) What else is special about it is that you and I can talk about whatever we want to talk about, even stuff we wouldn't talk about anywhere else . . . and it'll just stay in this place.

Because Mickey had sustained anal assault by adult men, the therapist is careful not to stir the affective memories associated with that experience at this point lest the playroom take on a threatening quality rather than one that connotes safety. Hence, physical position becomes an important consideration, particularly in the context of discussing "stuff we wouldn't talk about anywhere else."

M: (*Glancing quickly at the therapist and then back to the chalkboard*) What color is this?
T: You take a guess.
M: Yellow.

T: Yellow, that's what it is. (*As Mickey picks up markers near the chalk*) You know what you can use those on? (*Pointing to the paper on the easel*) Those you can use over here too, if you want. (*Noticing the top-access dollhouse partially constructed on a low table, Mickey begins to rearrange the partitions that constitute its interior walls to form rooms*) You can make a house out of this. There's some stuff over there if you want to. (*As Mickey brings articles of furniture and play figures to the house, the therapist demonstrates how the interior partitions can be placed or rearranged*) You want to bring some of that stuff over, don't you?

M: I want to make an apartment out of it.

T: You want to make an apartment out of it. Apartments are important things to make.

In the process of conveying acceptance of the child's choice among available playthings, the therapist encourages developmental advance through differentiation by reflecting Mickey's statement in the form of a valuative construction of the physical aspect of the environment.

M: (*Apparently recalling the dollhouse from the screening session that took place in another area*) Did you take this from a different room?

T: Yes, that's from a different room. I bet you remember that from before. I think you used this stuff before in a different room. (*As Mickey fumbles and drops articles that he is carrying toward the dollhouse*) If you would like some help, you can ask me and I'll help you, Mickey. It will be up to you if you want some help carrying that.

As in this interaction, it is important for a therapist to overcome the impulse to be spontaneously helpful when a youngster is encountering difficulty with some aspect of the physical environment of the playroom or the toys in it. Particularly with children who have been abused, it is crucial to first ask their permission before intruding upon their space, despite the well-meaning basis of a helping gesture. That restraint becomes yet more important if the child's struggle is with some aspect of his or her clothing.

M: (*As he carries more furniture to the dollhouse, Mickey glances fleetingly at the therapist*) If I don't get some soda later I can get some candy.

T: (*Standing a distance from the dollhouse as Mickey hurriedly carries playthings to it and referring to information Mickey had shared before entering the playroom regarding his social worker's gift to him*) You mean with the fifty cents that Karen gave you?

M: Yeah.

T: Wow, you're a lucky guy.

M: Yeah.

T: You're a lucky guy.

M: She always buys me something.

T: Yeah. (*Pause*) But maybe there are some ways you're not so lucky, I don't know.

While accepting without challenge the child's assertion of his good fortune, the therapist gently invites him to also focus on aspects of experience that have been less fortunate. By the therapist's acceptance of the former in such instances, a youngster may well feel less marked in negative terms by attending to the latter.

M: My mother gives me money.

T: Your mother gives you money? Mmmh!

M: (*With a tone of pride in his voice*) Sometimes even a dollar!

T: A dollar!

M: Two dollars!

T: Two dollars!?!

M: (*With increasing emphasis*) Three dollars!

T: (*Matching Mickey's tone of emphasis*) Three dollars!?!

M: It only goes up to three dollars.

T: That's a lot of money!

M: (*Continuing to pile and drop playthings within the dollhouse*) And at my foster mother's . . . the guy who lives downstairs gives me candy all the time too.

T: The guy used to buy you candy all the time?

M: He does.

T: I wonder what guy you mean.

M: The guy who lives downstairs from my foster mother.

T: (*Having misunderstood Mickey's words*) The guy who lives downstairs from your father and mother.

M: (*With emphasis*) My FOSTER mother!

T: (*While helping Mickey reassemble the walls of the dollhouse that had fallen*) Your FOSTER mother. The guy who lives downstairs from your foster mother. He buys you candy all the time? Is he a nice guy?

M: (*In an affirming tone*) Uh-huh.

T: He's a nice guy. (*Pause. Then, as Mickey again sets about arranging the dollhouse in a determined way*) You know, Mickey, it looks to me like you have some ideas about how you like apartments to be. Apartments are something you know about.

M: I do. I know about apartments since I was 3.

T: (*Remaining a distance from Mickey on the other side of the table that holds the dollhouse, and, though Mickey continues to avoid eye contact, staying always in his potential line of sight*) You've known about apartments since you were 3!?! That's a long time! (*Pause*) You know how you like apartments to be. Maybe you even know how you like apartments not to be. You probably have some ideas about that, too . . . or maybe you don't.

Using the approach of highlighting and conveying respect for Mickey's knowledge and experience, the therapist once again invites the child to further differentiate his affective and valuative construction of his surroundings, specifically along lines that reflect the context of his exploitation and loss of family structure. In doing so he explicitly extends to Mickey the previously implied option of negating the therapist's premise and/or of declining to pursue this topic.

M: I always do.

T: (*As Mickey picks up a doll figure, its clothes fall off and he tries, without success, to restore them.*) Sometimes the clothes come off the people.

By phrasing his reflection in the general case, the therapist provides Mickey a context for recalling his own abuse. Additionally, the groundwork has been thus laid for an implicit "process" contract according to which therapist and child will eventually communicate at two levels known to both but with the safety of the immediate concrete referent preserved. Thus metaphor as a therapeutic tool begins to take shape.

M: (*In a muffled tone*) I know.

T: Maybe you know about that too.

M: Uh-huh.

Here Mickey acknowledges application of the statement beyond the general case as one that has relevance to his own experience.

T: That's something you know about too. (*As Mickey persists in his struggle to get the clothes back on the doll figure*) It's important to you to get that back on. I can see.

M: (*Failing to get the doll's pants back on, Mickey bends it into a sitting position and speaks in a strikingly plaintive and hesitant voice that seems at once thin and on the edge of tears*) He's got to go to the bathroom.

T: He's got to go to the bathroom. (*As Mickey again lifts the figure after having placed it for a moment on the toilet in the dollhouse*) All finished in the bathroom already?

M: What?

T: All finished in the bathroom? (*As Mickey again places the figure on the toilet*) Oop, back in the bathroom.

M: (*Pointing to a bathtub in another area of the dollhouse*) There's something over there that goes here.

T: Boy, I wonder what that could be?

M: A tub . . . and some cabinets.

T: A tub. You know about tubs too. That's stuff you know about.

M: (*Seeming almost beguiled as he ponders the kitchen furniture, Mickey rests his head on the palm of his hand, which he has placed against his cheek. Eventually he picks up the stove*) There's the kitchen . . . and the stove. You have to be very, very careful with the stove.

T: Stoves you have to be very careful about. I wonder how come you have to be so careful about them?

M: You can die.

T: You can die!?! How can you die?

M: (*Picking up another play object, Mickey changes the topic*) Is this a sink?

T: I think it looks like it can be whatever you want it to be. It could be a sink. (*Pause*) A sink is a good thing for it to be. (*Pause*) I wonder how people can die from a stove. . . . I don't understand that.

M: You can get burned.

T: You can get burned.

M: By a stove.

T: By a stove.

Although the therapist chose not to pursue the obvious basis for Mickey's observation about stoves—that the child had witnessed his mother's attempted suicide—the process illustrates the power of playthings to stimulate memory. Nevertheless, in keeping with the principle that matters of importance will re-emerge and need not be pounced upon, the therapist allows this memory to elude explicit articulation at this early point.

M: (*Picking up a female doll figure and bending it into a sitting position*) She has to go to the bathroom.

T: She has to go to the bathroom too?

M: I think it would be better to.

T: Everybody goes to the bathroom. (*Pause*) Going to the bathroom is something you think about.

The therapist again reflects Mickey's statement in terms of the general case and, in the process, legitimatizes Mickey's focus on bathroom issues and matters of privacy thereby implied.

M: Yup. (*Pause. Then, as he continues to position the doll figure in the bathroom of the dollhouse*) I have to go to the bathroom too.

T: You have to go to the bathroom now?

M: (*Gesturing toward a closet*) What's in there, toys?

It may be that, by dropping what seemed to be a request to go to the bathroom, Mickey was simply adding support to the interpretive hypothesis ventured above, that is, he was noting that he has privacy issues as well.

T: (*Opening the cabinet door*) I thought that there might be some more of the [dollhouse] furniture in there but here's what's in there . . . teacups.

M: Shall we go get more toys?

T: No, we'll play with these things. These are our things to play with. (*As Mickey's demeanor registers disappointment*) There are certain rules. (*Mickey groans in a subdued way*) Rules are no fun . . . sometimes. There are some rules about what we can play with and what we can't.

At this juncture the therapeutic contract is further shaped by invoking the reality that limits, previously characterized as different from those of most situations, are nevertheless defined by certain rules. By attributing those defining limits to rules rather than to prohibitions imposed by the ad hoc decision of the therapist, counterproductive struggles are minimized.

At times, an exchange such as this will lead to the child's expressing disbelief that the therapist is unable to veto previously established rules, or to the child's feeling angry because the therapist is seen as unwilling to do so. Although that was not the direction of Mickey's reaction, such responses can provide fertile ground for considering with a child whether she or he has known others who failed to satisfy strongly felt wishes.

M: (*Walks around the dollhouse toward the therapist while picking up and examining various pieces of play furniture. He eventually stands directly in front of the therapist with his back toward him. Mickey then takes a wooden toy bed and props it up against a door of the dollhouse from the inside*) What is this, a door block?

T: It could be a door block . . . or it could be a bed. (*As Mickey continues to position the bed against the door*) You'd rather have a door blocker. (*Pause*) Blocking doors is important to you.

In this intervention the therapist addresses what is essentially a developmentally primitive fusion implied by Mickey's question in which the notion of "bed," or, more specifically, the affect associated with that concept, prompts a need, experienced as equivalent, to enforce a "door block," presumably to stave off threat associated with a bed. By first encouraging differentiation of the two notions and then articulating the valuative construction of a door block inherent in Mickey's words and actions—"You'd rather have a door blocker . . . blocking doors is important to you"—the therapist seeks to foster developmental advance around a construction of threatening memories. He then acknowledges Mickey's attempt to develop an effective instrumentality by which to ensure his safety.

> M: I don't like anybody peeking in my room.

In this response Mickey confirms that his reaction was indeed prompted by a need for safety from the danger that has become fused for him with the notion of "bed" or "bedroom." Further, he demonstrates the therapeutic benefit of achieving developmental advance by seizing, with an assertive tone, the mastery over threatening affect that articulation of the differentiated need allows.

> T: (*Walking away from Mickey to the opposite side of the low table, holding the dollhouse such that he is directly in Mickey's line of sight*) You don't want anybody peeking in there because peeking in is not good. (*As Mickey remains intently focused on propping the bed against the door with an urgency that is accompanied by some fumbling*) You want to make sure you've got it blocked there so nobody can peek. (*Pause*) I wonder who would peek in your room?
> M: (*Shrugging*) I don't know.
> T: It's hard to tell sometimes who's going to peek.
> M: Your mom can peek.
> T: Your mom can peek. It's okay if your mom peeks.
> M: But nobody else.

Here Mickey continues the effort to articulate differentiated aspects of experience that previously had for him a regressive, dedifferentiating impact. As an abuse victim, he was deprived of the most basic limit-setting power, that having to do with access to his person. With the therapist providing him both safety and assistance in the articulation process through reflection of words, play, and nonverbal communication, Mickey's tenta-

tive venture into reclaiming the power to determine limits gathers a strength
that becomes evident in his increasingly assertive choice of words and tone
of voice.

> T: Nobody else should peek . . . just mothers. That's the way you think it
> should be. (*Pause*) I wonder if sometimes other people peek even though
> they're not supposed to. Do people peek even when they're not sup-
> posed to?
> M: (*Continuing to position the dollhouse furniture and avoiding eye contact*) Do
> people peek in my room?
> T: I wonder if they peek in your room.
> M: Nope.
> T: They don't peek in your room.
> M: (*With a somewhat emphatic tone*) I lock my door.
> T: (*Matching Mickey's tone*) You make sure that door is locked.
> M: And every day when I take a nap it's locked.

Although the therapist was, of course, aware of the extensive abuse
Mickey had suffered, he frames indirect inquiries in ways that are not
predicated on that awareness. Instead, the therapist's comments are based
on the recognition that Mickey may need to approach disclosure in a
gradualized way.

> T: (*Mickey walks quickly, again positioning himself directly in front of the thera-
> pist and facing away toward the top-access dollhouse on the low table. As he
> does so, Mickey busies himself with the figures in the bathroom area. The
> therapist moves to the other side of the table, again assuming a position directly
> in Mickey's line of sight*) Whenever you take a nap you make sure that
> door is locked.
> M: (*As one of the partitions from the internal structure of the dollhouse topples*)
> What happened to the door? The door fell over.
> T: You want to make sure no peeking goes on.
> M: My sister never peeks.
> T: (*Having mistaken Mickey's words*) Your sister peeks?
> M: (*Once again Mickey walks around the table on which the dollhouse rests such
> that he is standing in front of the therapist and facing away. The therapist
> again moves to a point within Mickey's line of sight*) No, she'd never, or I'd
> tell my mother.
> T: (*As Mickey rearranges the bedroom furniture*) It's hard to decide how you
> want the bedrooms to be. You know that you don't want any peeking
> going on but it's hard to decide what you do want going on.

M: (*Positioning one of the wooden beds*) Mom and dad's bed.

T: Mom and dad's bed. (*Pause*) There's mom and dad's bed.

M: (*Mickey seeks out and retrieves the adult male doll figure*) Where's the dad now?

T: (*As Mickey grasps the male doll figure*) There's the dad.

M: (*Mickey holds one female doll figure in one hand and a second adult female doll in the other; he inspects both with a puzzled look on his face and speaks with a tone of plaintiveness*) They're the same.

In this comment Mickey displays an apparent regression to a dedifferentiated concept of "mother" probably owing less to the impact of abuse per se than to the accompanying trauma of being separated from the family and, more specifically, from the mother he has known. His rapid and often concurrent involvement thereafter with a succession of maternal figures in the persons of social workers and foster mothers has apparently contributed to the sense of fusion and, in turn, to what seemed to be feelings of unrequited loss reflected in his tone of voice.

This vignette illustrates the importance that the therapist remain mindful of the child's phenomenological perspective. To proceed solely from a typically adult preconception in which only the actual abuse defines the trauma would fail to appreciate the profound feeling of loss that a child may experience having been removed from his accustomed context. For the child, the sequelae of disclosure, brought to bear in an effort to shield and protect him or her, often entail an equal or greater amount of suffering that may be overlooked by human service providers relieved at having spared the child further sexual insult.

T: They look the same.

M: I can make either one of them the mom.

T: Sometimes it's hard to tell who's your mother. It's hard to tell who the mother is . . . they look the same sometimes. (*Pause*) That can get a guy pretty confused I think. (*Pause*) Maybe pretty upset.

M: (*Apparently uncertain as to which of the two available female dolls to pair with the father doll, Mickey eventually makes a choice by placing the designated couple together in a bed in one room and putting the other female doll in the larger room of the dollhouse. He then tests the strength of the partitions forming the rooms by grasping them*) This goes here. That goes there.

T: It's okay for moms to peek . . . but sometimes you can't tell who the mom is.

M: My mom can always peek.

T: Your mom can always peek.

M: (*Working intently to set up the furniture in the large room of the dollhouse*) No watching TV yet.

T: TV is not on yet.

M: (*Picking up a piece of doll furniture*) What is this for?

T: That can be whatever you want it to be. (*Pause*) You decide.

By encouraging the child to use his imagination to structure the circumstance, the therapist is employing a kind of projective technique in which the identity of playthings, their relationship to each other, their functions, their potential, and other of their defining characteristics are presented as ambiguous and in need of structuring. Empowering the child to make those determinations typically yields greater insight and more access to a youngster's constructions, concerns, and conflicts than would be the case if the therapist responded to the child's inquiry by offering one or even a range of object and function definitions. Moreover, this interaction contributes to the development of the therapeutic contract in that it implicitly establishes during this first session a pattern that will characterize the process that is to follow.

M: I don't know. (*Examining another piece of furniture, which he takes from one room and places in another*) This belongs in the kids' room.

T: I wonder how many kids live in this place.

M: One, two, three, four . . . my mom has five!

T: Your mom has five kids. That's a lot of kids.

M: (*Picking up doll figures*) One, two, three, four, five.

T: Five. (*Referring to the clothes falling off several of the dolls as Mickey picks them up*) They keep getting their clothes off. (*As the therapist maintains his distance from Mickey standing across the low table that holds the dollhouse and facing him*) It's hard to keep their clothes on sometimes.

With the emergence of this obviously charged sequence, the therapist's tack of avoiding being physically behind Mickey or even out of his line of sight takes on yet greater importance. Indeed, Mickey may well have avoided these references entirely had he felt threatened by the therapist's proximity and/or by any diminished sense of control.

M: He don't got no pants on at all.

T: No pants on at all?

M: None.

T: I wonder where his pants went. (*Mickey looks away from the dollhouse and toward a chair in the corner of the room where the doll equipment had been previously stored*) I don't see them over there.

M: (*Mickey shrugs and turns back to the dollhouse. He then picks up a female doll figure and places her on a couch in what has become the living room area*) This one here, I think she can sleep on the couch.

T: Ah, somebody's got to sleep on the couch.

M: (*Placing a square piece of furniture in front of the door in one of the smaller rooms*) This goes right there.

T: Is that another barricade? (*Pause*) A block?

M: (*Shrugging his shoulders*) Some kind of block. (*Pause*) That's the TV.

T: I see.

M: (*Referring to the doll figures he has placed in the small room*) They're sitting up watching TV in their bedroom.

T: Sometimes people watch TV in bedrooms.

M: (*Continuing to adjust the placement of the doll figures*) He can sit and I'll check the mom out.

T: The mom and the dad are sitting and watching television in the bedroom.

M: Yeah, that's good . . . that's good. They can see from right there.

T: They can see from their bed . . . they can see the television there.

M: (*Picking up the child doll figures and placing them in what has become another bedroom*) These ones are going to bed, going night-nights.

T: Everybody goes night-nights.

M: Okay.

T: Going night-nights is important.

The exchange at this juncture might seem to call for direct inquiry by the therapist concerning the child's knowledge of and/or feelings about bedroom activities other than TV watching. However, to pursue such issues upon their first emergence more vigorously, particularly with a sexually abused child as in this instance, is likely to trigger an intensification of the defenses that are slowly relaxing as the play scene is constructed. Despite the compelling opportunity to pursue issues of central importance quickly, it is nevertheless more in the interest of progress for the therapist to allow a more complete picture to unfold at a pace that the child determines.

In this first session the therapist's forbearance carries with it further communicative import. Specifically, the child experiences that she or he will be able to mention potentially troubling circumstances without being required each time to carry every comment to its most emotionally charged end.

M: (*Looking at some toys on the table outside the walls of the dollhouse*) Is that more stuff? (*Answering his own question*) No, it's not. (*Returning to the bedroom side of the dollhouse*) Is there another kid over there?

T: Is there another kid over here? (*Scanning the dollhouse*) Yeah, there's another kid. (*Handing Mickey the doll figure*) You want another kid? Here's the other kid.

M: I didn't want that one.

T: Oh, you wanted a boy kid and that's a girl kid.

M: (*Seemingly distracted as he puzzles over two pieces of toy furniture that he has picked up*) I wonder . . . hmmm . . . now I know. (*Mickey puts the pieces down*) Like that . . . or go like this. (*At this point the therapist rests his hand on an easel he is standing next to. The newsprint paper draped over it produces a rustling sound*) Is she playing peek-a-boo?

Mickey's sensitivity to the possibility of voyeuristic intrusion is apparent here in his spontaneous association to an unexpected sound.

T: Is somebody playing peek-a-boo? (*Referring to a social worker behind the one-way mirror*) Diane's watching us. (*Pause*) It's okay that Diane's peeking . . . or maybe it's not. (*Pause*) Is that the same as peeking in a bedroom or is that different?

M: (*Momentarily stopping his activity with the doll figures and looking up at the therapist*) Same.

Despite the therapist's implying by his question that a differentiation might be identified, Mickey clings to a sense of fusion with regard to the issue of peeking, thus reflecting the continuing impact of that notion for him and its power to maintain developmental regression at an undifferentiated level. A simple explanation of differences by the therapist at this point would likely have little impact except perhaps to elicit the anger that occurs when defenses not yet ready to be completely relaxed are directly challenged in their viability. Such an approach could also leave Mickey with the feeling that the therapist has little empathic appreciation of the child's experiential framework or the effect of his abuse upon it.

T: It's the same. (*Pause*) I wonder how it's the same.

M: I think it's the same.

T: I wonder how it could be the same.

M: (*Lifting the doll table and placing it within what has become the kitchen area*) Table.

T: Peeking is peeking as far as you're concerned. That's all there is to it. When people peek, they peek.

M: (*Ostensibly unengaged at this point in interaction regarding the topic addressed by the therapist, Mickey moves doll furniture from the livingroom to the kitchen area, naming each piece under his breath as he does so*) This is a chair, that's a chair . . . these are the same.

T: Those two chairs are the same.

M: There's got to be a chair for each so they can sit and eat.

T: Sitting and eating are important, too, in an apartment. A lot of things happen in an apartment that are very important. (*As an internal partition of the dollhouse tumbles*) Sometimes apartments don't stay the way you want them to be.

The issue of "peeking" was apparently too emotionally charged a notion for Mickey to consider possible shades of difference that might apply. With more innocuous playthings, however, he ventured a differentiated perspective in a more leisurely fashion. In doing so, he presented the therapist with an opportunity to offer a valuative construct regarding apartments. The serendipitous occurrence of partitions falling down allowed further elaboration of that issue by the therapist. From the response that follows, it became apparent that Mickey found it both compelling and metaphorically relevant.

M: They fall apart on you.

T: They fall apart sometimes. (*Pause*) Homes have a way of falling apart. (*Pause*) That's not a happy time when a home falls apart. It's a very sad time.

M: It is.

T: It is. (*Pause*) You know.

In this exchange therapist and child begin speaking in the language of metaphor, taking as a reference point at the outset the concrete here-and-now playthings and the scene of home they represent—"They fall apart on you." Discussion then proceeds in a more explicit way to the general case, referencing a more focused but unspecified abstraction—"Homes have a way of falling apart." Eventually dialogue reaches indirectly into the child's acknowledged and articulated feelings about his own experience—"That's not a happy time when a home falls apart. It's a very sad time." Mickey's response is unequivocal—"It is."

As this sequence illustrates, significant sharing of awareness and expression regarding very painful issues can occur even in a first session with a highly defended young abuse sexual abuse victim. When the therapist reflects the child's comments and play in terms of metaphor that recognizes both as relevant to personal experience, but is not so immediate as to threaten the child, it becomes essentially a successfully achieved balancing act on a fulcrum between the poles of direct personal reference and distant play analog. It is this process, consistently enacted, that allows developmental advance to occur with regard to treatment goals.

> T: It's not happy for you. (*Pause*) It sounds like you know about homes falling apart. That's something you know about.
>
> M: (*Continuing to arrange doll furniture and avoiding eye contact*) I know about houses on fire.
>
> T: You know about houses on fire too? You know about a lot of stuff. Sounds like some of the stuff is not very happy stuff. (*Pause*) I wonder what you know about houses falling apart . . . homes falling apart. (*Pause*) You know it's not very happy when it happens, you told me that. (*Pause*) I wonder what else you know.
>
> M: (*As an internal partition falls*) This house keeps falling apart.
>
> T: (*Reaching over to steady a partition*) This house keeps falling apart.
>
> M: It's not staying the way I want it to be.
>
> T: It's not staying the way you want it to be. (*Pause*) I wonder how come houses fall apart.
>
> M: The only time I know about houses falling apart is when there's a fire.
>
> T: The only time you know is when there's a fire?
>
> M: (*Holding and staring intently at an adult female doll figure, then speaking in a forlorn tone*) She's dying.
>
> T: She's dying. (*Pause*) That's pretty sad. (*After Mickey places the doll in the stove*) She died in the stove? I wonder why she got into the stove.
>
> M: (*Walking around the dollhouse looking into each room*) She opened it up and somebody pulled her in.
>
> T: Somebody pulled her into the stove? Goodness, gracious! (*Pause*) I wonder who that could have been?

It can be inferred that Mickey's association may have to do with a memory of having summoned help for his mother when she attempted suicide by placing her head in a stove. That he attributes the cause of that event to an external source and thereby denies intentionality on the part of the figure in the stove suggests that he has maintained this recollection as relatively differentiated but as a source of conflict. As such, it compels him to embellish it in recall with dimensions that represent a denial of the wish of the maternal figure to die and thus abandon him.

A formulation of this sort typically does not lead to a direct intervention, particularly early in the treatment process. Instead it may serve as a theoretical construct by which the therapist can conceptualize these data. Flexibility needs to be maintained in such formulations, however, so as to accommodate subsequent data that, in a hypothetico-deductive manner, may lead to more refined understanding as the treatment process unfolds.

M: (*Ignoring the therapist's "wondering" and placing a final object into the dollhouse*) The house is all set up.

T: The house is all set up.

M: (*Placing an additional partition in the house*) Now can I find something else to put in here that would be nice?

T: (*Scanning the playroom along with Mickey*) You'd like to look for something else, but we don't have anything else. (*Pause . . . then pointing to an easel and paints*) I have an idea, maybe you can draw the kind of stuff you'd like to see in the house.

M: Mmm-hm.

T: Or you could draw a picture of people doing stuff in he house.

M: (*With apparent enthusiasm as he walks toward the easel*) Mm-hmm! (*Lifting the sheet of newsprint away from the easel and inspecting it*) Is this paper big enough to go around?

T: (*Walking toward the easel where Mickey is reaching to remove the paper*) Oh, you want to take the paper off.

M: Yeah, I want to make it so you can't see the inside, so it will have a roof.

T: (*As Mickey carefully but energetically removes the newsprint from the easel and quickly places it over the top of the dollhouse*) Roofs are important things too. (*Pause*) There are a lot of important things about an apartment.

By offering this valuative construction of the physical environment, the therapist encourages developmental advance and implicitly invites Mickey to elaborate the scene that he has begun to construct. In view of the preceding indication that difficult feelings have been evoked in Mickey in relation to the apartment, the therapist's comment seeks also to encourage Mickey to articulate the underlying conflict.

M: (*Struggling to drape the paper over the top of the dollhouse*) Can you help me?

T: (*Reaching to steady the paper from slipping off the top*) You want me to help you?

M: (*Recognizing that the piece of paper fails to cover the entire top-access dollhouse*) I have to get another one, right?

T: It looks that way.

M: (*As he tries to adjust the paper*) Do you have a little tape to tape this thing?

T: (*Checking the desk drawers*) Tape is something I don't have.

M: (*Succeeding in stabilizing the paper on top of the dollhouse*) Oh, it's good.

T: It's good like that.

M: (*Walking back to the easel and tearing another sheet of paper from it*) All I need is one more piece.

T: (*Helping secure the easel as Mickey tears the paper from it*) I can see you're the kind of guy who likes to have things the way they should be. An apartment should have a roof so you want it to have a roof. That kind of stuff is important to you—that things ought to be the way they should be.

Mickey's persistent effort to cover the dollhouse may have various meanings. In one sense he could be seen as attempting to put a lid on things in the face of finding that in this first session he and the therapist have already alluded to issues that are emotionally charged for him. At the same time his actions seem to represent a need to continue the process of constructing the scene, perhaps so that explication of his experience can continue but in a bounded way that does not threaten to become uncontrolled.

M: (*Quickly carrying the paper to the dollhouse and smiling as he drapes it over the top*) Now it's got a roof.

T: Now you feel better . . . it has a roof.

M: (*Mickey first nods his agreement, then drops to the floor and, on his hands and knees, looks into the dollhouse through the windows and doors*) I can peek through the window.

T: YOU want to do some peeking! I thought only moms could peek. (*Mickey giggles*) Ohhhh . . . Mickey wants to do some peeking too!

M: Peek-a-boo!

T: Sometimes when you do some peeking it makes it not so scary that other people peek.

Without pursuing it in an elaborated way at this preliminary point in treatment, the therapist here makes explicit Mickey's recourse to identification with the feared object as a way of seeking to allay anxiety. With abuse victims in particular, pathological identification as a defense needs to be effectively addressed later in treatment since it is through the operation of that defense that child victims can subsequently become adult perpetrators.

M: (*Lifting the draped newsprint paper roof slightly and, on his hands and knees, peering in*) I can't see because the roof fell so I go like this.

T: Mmm . . . you want to peek under the roof too.

M: (*Pushing his face into the large doorway of the dollhouse and gazing into it*) Peek-a-boo! (*Mickey crawls around the dollhouse and looks into each of the windows and doors*) I'm going to peek through the bathroom.

Though Mickey is apparently acting out one aspect of his abuse experience—that of uninvited voyeuristic intrusion—he does so in a playful, coy, almost seductive way that has a counterphobic quality to it. In other words, he may be trying to entice the therapist to engage in the behavior that he fears from adult men in an effort to allay his anxiety by demonstrating to himself that such behavior does not emerge here even when invited. At the same time he may actually be attempting to re-experience some thrilling aspect of the forbidden behavior with men. In other words, Mickey's actions could be seen to represent what has been termed *identification with the aggressor*, a defense that he demonstrates by engaging in the voyeurism.

Either conceptualization serves to alert the therapist at this point to avoid any action that might be construed by Mickey as a willingness to disregard boundaries of privacy by engaging in, or even playacting, intrusive behavior. Parenthetically, this instance highlights the importance of a therapists pausing to consider possible unintended implications of participatory play that might otherwise seem appropriate when viewed solely from the perspective of attempting to advance rapport.

T: Mickey wants to peek in the bathroom too.
M: (*Speaking in a singsongy tone and with a self-conscious smile*) I can't see anyone in the bathroom.
T: I wonder what Mickey sees when he peeks.
M: (*With a coy facial expression and tone*) Can I go to the bathroom? (*Mickey then quickly grasps a piece of flat, rounded toy furniture*) Oh, I wonder what I can use this for.
T: Peeking makes you think you want to go to the bathroom. There's something about peeking that makes you think about the bathroom. It's hard to tell what it is.

By his intervention the therapist is identifying an instance of fusion in Mickey's experience of symbolic violation of rights and bathroom functions, perhaps mediated by the sphincter tension that accompanies both and/or by the possibility that some instances of his own violation might have occurred in a bathroom setting. In any case the accompanying emotions are likely to have a regressive impact on Mickey because of the recall of trauma and violation. Further, those emotions are also likely to blur, at least for the moment, the parameters of a more advanced developmental perspective.

> M: (*Placing the rounded piece of furniture into the dollhouse*) I'd rather leave it in the kids' room. (*Rising and beginning to leave the room*) Okay, I'm going to use the bathroom.
> T: (*Following Mickey out the door*) I wonder if you know where the bathroom is.
> M: Yeah.
> T: (*Mickey went to a restroom adjacent to an office distant from the playroom. The therapist did not accompany him but waited in the corridor near the door of the playroom. After several minutes Mickey returned and both he and the therapist re-enter*) I was wondering about something. I was wondering about how come you didn't close the door to the bathroom when peeking is something that you don't like. I was just wondering about that.

It should be noted that the therapist, from his vantage point outside the playroom door, could see that the bathroom door had been left ajar, although he could not see into the bathroom.

> M: (*Looking directly at the therapist and speaking in a slightly frightened and/or guilty tone*) I did close the door, didn't I?

Mickey demonstrated obvious feelings of alarm, presumably related to the therapist's noting his having succumbed to an impulse to behave in a potentially inappropriate way with regard to bathroom privacy. The therapist does not push the issue by restating the fact that the door was left open. Instead he notes, in a very matter of fact way, that Mickey and he had different thoughts about the circumstance. That tack serves to reduce from a counterproductive level Mickey's fear that he has been caught in an action that will lead to censure or worse. At the same time a precedent is established during this first session, indicating that variations in perspective will be acceptable and that the treatment process will not become a judgmental exercise centered on identifying the departure of Mickey's behavior from some absolute norm that defines right and wrong.

> T: Oh, I thought it was open and you thought it was closed. (*After a pause and then speaking as Mickey fiddles with felt-edged markers on the desk*) Would you like to use those?

M: Yes. (*Mickey then returns to the dollhouse and lifts one of the two sheets covering it*) I'm going to color the inside of the roof. (*Spreading the paper on the floor*) I'm going to color it right here.

T: (*Suggesting the desk top rather than the floor*) How about putting it up here and you color it using these things.

M: (*Spreading the paper across the desk top*) It's a clean piece of paper.

T: It's a clean piece of paper. (*Handing Mickey the felt-edged markers*) And here are the markers.

M: Thank you.

T: (*As Mickey takes one marker and uncaps it*) I'll put these over here.

M: I'm going to draw steps on it.

T: You've got some idea about what you're drawing on that.

M: (*Taking a different color marker*) Is blue good? Can you use blue very good?

T: You could use the blue if you want.

M: (*In a very thin, tentative voice as he smells the ink of the marker*) It smells like the kind I used to have.

T: It smells like the kind you used to have.

M: Yeah.

T: Back in the old days.

M: It is the kind I used to have.

T: I wonder where that was.

M: Back in the old storage.

T: (*Mistaking Mickey's words*) Back in the old school?

M: Storage.

T: In the old storage. I wonder . . . (*Pause*) That must have been a long time ago.

M: It was. (*Pause*) Twice. Twice is enough!

Olfactory stimulation that may occur in the course of play often triggers memories spontaneously and with little benefit of context. Typically those recollections are very primitive and undifferentiated at their first emergence. Though a youngster's comments may seem unexpected and disconnected, it is important for a therapist to remain open to their presentation and to respond in ways that maintain the series of associations that has been triggered. Too often therapists, intent on the verbal content and the contextual sequence of interactions, respond with surprise and or/ incredulity that stems the unfolding associations rather than furthers them.

T: Twice is too much sometimes.

M: Twice is always too much.

T: Twice is always too much. (*Pause*) I wonder what happened twice that
   was too much.

M: (*Pause . . . then speaking in a disheartened tone*) Too much.

T: (*Reflecting Mickey's tone*) Too much.

M: Are you a doctor and a psychiatrist?

T: I'm a psychologist type of doctor.

Having stepped back from the almost trancelike series of associations
ostensibly triggered by the smell of the markers, Mickey may have become
aware of having shared some very basic affect-laden associations that, were
they to be pursued, might involve vulnerability on his part. In that connection he seemed to seek assurance that the therapist was qualified to
accompany him in exploring threatening domains of experience.

M: (*Gesturing toward the picture he is drawing*) I'm going to draw everything
   orange.

T: I wonder if you know what that means.

M: What?

T: What do you think a psychologist does?

M: Youu talk to them.

T: You talk to them.

M: (*Noticing ink from the markers on his hands*) Oh, I have got ink all over me.

T: (*Pause*) It's kind of like being a talking doctor instead of a needle doctor.
   Those kind of doctors talk to kids. (*Pause*) I wonder why those kind of
   doctors talk to kids.

M: Because of what goes on.

T: Because of what goes on. (*Pause*) Different stuff goes on.

M: (*Continuing to orient his posture, gaze, and apparent attention toward the
   drawing he has focused on throughout this process*) A lot of times different
   and the same stuff goes on.

T: Sometimes the same stuff goes on?

M: A lot of times.

T: Even in different places?

M: Yup.

T: Even in different places, sometimes the same stuff goes on.

As Mickey does here, children sometimes approach disclosure by first
engaging in a discussion about some aspect of the abuse that remains, for
the time, unspecified. Although the sequence may end without the topic's
being made explicit, the awareness of both child and therapist regarding
the focus of their cryptic interchange facilitates later emergence of the issue

in a more articulated way, either verbally or through symbolic play. Additionally, the tone of an exchange such as occurred here between the therapist and Mickey develops a kind of synchrony that strengthens rapport and the trust that builds upon it.

> M: (*Scanning the room*) Is there a sink in here? (*Noticing the dart board on the wall*) Can I use the darts?
> T: You'd like to use the darts.
> M: Yup.
> T: (*Pause*) You'd like to not think about what goes on. You'd like a change. You'd like to think about something else. We can talk about something else.

Acknowledging Mickey's need to resist further elaboration at this time, the therapist in this first session continues to develop the therapeutic contract by demonstrating that he will not hold Mickey's feet to the fire but will allow him instead to make determinations about when, for how long, and with what detail issues of concern will be addressed. The therapist thus avoids inducing guilt in the child for the avoidance that he might otherwise feel is furtive and/or against the therapist's will.

> M: (*Mickey throws the Velcro-tipped darts against the board; several of the missiles stick to the felt surface while others fall*) Oooh!
> T: It seems to me that you know something about throwing darts too. That's something else you know about. There's a lot of stuff Mickey knows about.
> M: A lot of stuff!
> T: A lot of stuff. Not just a lot, a VERY lot.
> M: (*Continuing to throw darts*) I even know how to beat people up.
> T: Even how to beat people up? Oh my goodness!
> M: I beat my foster sister up.
> T: You beat up your foster sister? (*Mickey turns toward the therapist and with a facial expression of pride and delight nods affirmatively*) I wonder how come you beat up your foster sister?
> M: But I never beat up my real sister.
> T: Not your real sister, just your foster sister. (*Pause*) I wonder why Mickey beat up his foster sister. I wonder why he did that. Mickey's not the kind of guy to do anything unless he's got good reason.
> M: (*Referring to the darts he has continued to throw*) Two down.
> T: Two down. (*Pause*) Mickey's not telling me why he beat up his foster sister.

M: (*In a tone that rises toward the end with a quality of schoolyard irony and dare*) That's right.

T: That's right, that's something he doesn't want to tell me right now.

M: (*Referring to the darts*) There's supposed to be three red ones.

T: Three red darts.

M: Huh? (*Continuing to throw the darts and commenting on his success with them*) Oh, positively hot!

T: There's something about talking about the things that go on that makes Mickey think about beating people up.

Rather than challenging Mickey's resistance toward elaborating the events to which allusion was made but about which specificity was avoided, the therapist invites Mickey to consider the sequence of his associations and to ponder the relationship between topics. This approach often leads to an increasingly differentiated perspective at a configurational level while leaving intact the temporary prohibitions the child has constructed around the discrete elements that constitute the configuration of concerns. In this instance, however, the strategy proves nonproductive in that Mickey simply holds to a pattern of avoidance that embraces the relationships among issues as well as each in itself.

M: Huh?

T: First we talked about the things that go on and then you tell me about beating people up.

M: Okay.

T: I'm wondering about what makes you think about beating people up.

M: (*Ostensibly preoccupied again with the darts, Mickey mumbles inaudibly to himself as he throws them and some fall from the target*) Okay, aagh! (*Moving quickly back toward the sheets of paper and the Magic Markers across the room*) Okay, I'm coming through.

T: You're ready to do this again.

M: (*Beginning immediately to color the large sheets in a hurried, unsystematic way*) How long do I have to stay here?

T: Sometimes throwing darts and talking about beating people up makes a guy feel ready to do things again.

M: (*Completing one phase of the coloring*) That's done. Now I use yellow. (*Coloring furiously again with another marker*) I'm going to make this orange and yellow and another color too. This is a yellow screen.

T: Orange and yellow.

M: I'm going to make this orange and yellow and another color too.

T: (*As Mickey uncaps a third Magic Marker*) Now comes blue.

M: (*Mickey's pace slows markedly as he adds blue strokes to the sheet he is coloring*) Now green.

T: (*Referring to the many long, vertical strokes Mickey has made on the paper with the markers*) I wonder what those lines stand for. Those lines could stand for anything you want them to stand for. I wonder what they stand for. (*Pause*) Sometimes . . . sometimes colors can stand for how a guy feels. Sometimes you can use colors to show how you feel.

This intervention is an example of the value in the therapist's taking every opportunity to note potential instrumentalities for self-expression in the context of play. Here color is related to feelings, and in fact Mickey quickly adopts the metaphor in a specific and candidly self-disclosing way.

M: That's what I do sometimes.

T: That's what Mickey does sometimes. (*Pause*) Sometimes Mickey uses colors to show how he feels.

M: I'm sad.

T: Feels sad . . .

M: (*Walking around the paper looking for more markers*) I need orange.

T: I wonder what kind of feeling orange shows.

M: (*Placing the cap back on a marker*) I know how to make it fit.

T: Mmm.

M: It can be sad or happy.

T: It can be sad or happy.

M: (*Referring to the size of the paper compared to the top of the dollhouse that he originally set out to cover*) Do you think this will cover the whole thing? To do this right?

T: You can do it however you want. (*As Mickey places the paper over the open top of the dollhouse with the colored side facing inward into the house*) Maybe those colors show how it feels in the apartment because now those colors are the roof of the apartment. (*As Mickey drops to his knees and begins again to peek into the windows of the dollhouse*) Mickey's peeking again.

M: Yeah, to see how it is.

T: To see how it looks.

M: Mmm! The color is in the dining room and half of the . . .

T: Does it show how it feels in the apartment, I wonder?

M: (*Plaintively*) Yup.

T: (*In a subdued tone similar to Mickey's last comment*) Yes, it does.

M: (*Taking another sheet of paper and spreading it on the desk where he had colored the first*) I just got to do a little with blue.

T: (*As Mickey colors the second sheet*) There's the blue. (*When the cap of the marker falls to the floor and rolls away*) Would you like me to get it for you?

Again, this is an example of how important it is that a therapist not presume to reach into the child's space or sphere of activity without being invited to do so; a well-intended gesture of helpfulness could be construed as a willingness to ignore the child's rights and prerogatives. It should be noted as well that a previous invitation by the child for the therapist to act in such a way needs to be considered as permission for that instance only, not blanket permission for all such instances thereafter. In fact, Mickey had previously responded to a similar offer by the therapist in the affirmative but here declines the gesture.

M: No, thank you.

T: No, thank you. (*Pause*) Mickey's the kind of guy who doesn't like people doing things for him because when people do things for you, you kind of owe them something. Mickey doesn't want to owe people something.

M: Mm.

T: You don't want to owe people anything. (*Pause*) Or maybe that's not why.

M: Nah.

T: Maybe that's not something you worry about. (*As Mickey's pace of drawing increases*) There's more lines that show feelings. I wonder what they show this time. (*Pause*) It's hard to tell what they show.

M: (*Continuing his intent drawing and demeanor*) This one is going to be all colored in this time.

T: All colored in this time. No fooling around . . . all colored in.

M: Except I may not color in some. (*Placing the second sheet on the dollhouse and removing the first*) Now I got to get the other one so that the other one will show a lot.

T: This is really going to show a lot!

M: (*After shuffling with the paper, Mickey succeeds in placing it on top of the dollhouse*) There! (*Dropping to his knees, Mickey begins peeking in the window again*) I can peek.

T: Mickey's peeking again.

M: Ah, that's good. (*Spreading the first sheet of paper again on the desk where he colors it further*) Yes! The blue.

T: Yes, the blue.

M: The blue and orange.

T: Because blue and orange show . . .

If not overused, this technique of letting an incomplete sentence hang is effective for encouraging further differentiation of the child's perspective.

M: That you're sad.

T: That you're sad. I see. (*Pause*) It must be that the people in that apartment feel sad. (*Pause*) I wonder what they feel sad about.

M: (*Continuing to avoid eye contact as he has throughout this sequence*) One side blue and one side orange. Right here is orange and that other part is blue.

T: I wonder what people do when they're sad like that.

In his preceding few remarks Mickey had given the impression that he was not participating in the further elaboration of affective experience being encouraged by the therapist. His subsequent response, however, shows that he, like many children in play therapy, had remained alert to the topic even while seeming to attend to other issues. Without missing any beat of its cadence, Mickey was able to rejoin the dialogue that the therapist had persisted in maintaining as a soliloquy of musings.

M: They cry but they hold their tears.

T: They cry but they hold their tears?

M: (*Placing both hands to his eyes as though to catch tears*) That's what I do, I go (*Mickey mimics the sound of a soft cry*)

T: That's like crying inside.

M: Huh?

T: That's like crying inside.

M: (*Lifting his hands from the bottom of his face quickly to his eyes*) I pull my tears up.

T: I see. (*Pause*) You don't want those tears coming out. (*Pause*) I wonder how come. I wonder how come you do that with your tears.

M: (*Shrugging his shoulders, then selecting another marker and again coloring*) I just need to do it once more. Then I'll have a sad, sad, sad, sad house.

Perhaps unable to respond in words because of the intensity of associated affect, Mickey turns to play to demonstrate his feelings to the therapist. His reference may allude to the sadness associated with events that occurred within his home. He also might be recalling the very dissolution of that home, an event that occurred in the wake of the abuse being made known to societal agents by child victims who allowed tears to be seen. In effect, he may be struggling with his sense that expression of the sort the therapist is now encouraging has in the past led to further suffering for him rather than relief. Although it remains in the domain of hypothesis, this exchange may be an example of the importance of beginning with the child's frame of reference, not the frame of reference made urgent for clinicians by their own revulsion at a child's exploitation.

> T: (As Mickey brings the sheet of paper back to the dollhouse and places it on the roof) A sad, sad, sad, sad house. (Pause) There must be a lot of crying inside that people do in that house. (Mickey drops to his knees and again peeks in the windows) Mickey's peeking again.
> M: Yeah, it'll do.
> T: How does it look in there?
> M: Good. (Pause . . .then establishing eye contact) You can peek if you want to.
> T: I'll wait until you tell me. I'll let you tell me how it looks.
> M: (Continuing eye contact and smiling) It looks good.
> T: It looks good?
> M: (Maintaining eye contact and responding quickly) Yeah.

This exchange represents a pivotal and crucial moment in the development of a therapeutic contract. Despite Mickey's ostensible enticement for the therapist to join him in an activity that disregards boundaries of privacy and that has sexual connotations, the therapist responds in nonjudgmental terms that reaffirm his respect for such boundaries. Moreover, by his response the therapist conveys in a metaphorical sense his willingness to wait for the child to look inward and to share with the therapist as he chooses rather than to be examined from an exclusively objective vantage point. Mickey's subsequent expression of pleasure—and almost of gratitude—was made eloquent in his immediate adoption of a relaxed tempo with sustained eye contact.

In other words, Mickey may have been asking, "Are you one of those adult men who is willing to invade privacy when sexual excitement is promised?" When the therapist responded by indicating, in effect, "No, I am not," Mickey's comment, "It looks good," seemed to take on metaphorical meaning in itself, reflecting a sense of relief about the pattern of the therapy process that was beginning to unfold and about the contract that governed it.

> T: Does it? I wonder if it looks sad.
> M: (Pause) Yeah.
> T: Mmm. I wonder if the people inside are crying. (Seeming to be locked in eye contact, both Mickey and therapist shift tempo and tone in a way that nonverbally conveys the impression that both are engaged in the unfolding metaphor and in the feelings that the scene elicits) Are they crying? (Mickey nods affirmatively and the therapist, speaking almost in a whisper, asks) I

> wonder what they're crying about. (*As Mickey shakes his head as if to say he does not know*) It's hard to tell.
>
> M: Mm hmm.
>
> T: (*After a lengthy pause, Mickey leaves the dollhouse area and moves toward the darts, resuming the tempo that characterized his actions before the preceding sequence. The therapist too resumes his earlier tone and volume in a way that clearly acknowledges Mickey's shift*) You know what, Mickey?
>
> M: What?
>
> T: Five more minutes and our time will be up for today. And we'll have to go. (*Pause*) But you know what?
>
> M: What?
>
> T: We'll meet again next week.

Although this sequence has been one that seems to promise access to Mickey's recollections of and feelings about his abuse, he signaled by his shift of tone, tempo, and activity that he was not ready to go further with it. Therapists may at such junctures be tempted to pursue focal issues with persistent inquiry. To do so, however, is likely to precipitate a receding of accessibility in a child whose posture regarding disclosure has been made tentative by consequences she or he experienced earlier when tears were allowed to show. As noted previously, ambivalence regarding disclosure may also stem from the child's anticipation of censure and rejection when details, including the pleasure that may have been experienced, become known. A child's readiness to proceed, in other words, should be hers or his to determine.

The end of a play therapy session should always be preannounced. For young children five minutes usually proves an interval they can comprehend as being short but not immediate.

The importance of preannouncing the end of a play therapy session is well illustrated in this sequence. Children often infer causality from contiguity. Had the session ended at this point, for example, with no previous five-minute preannouncement of its coming to a close, Mickey might easily have concluded that his allusions to having knowledge of sadness— or his unwillingness to engage in further disclosure—led the therapist to call a halt to the process. Instead, the preannouncement essentially carried with it the message that the end point has already been determined. Nothing that Mickey says or does—or fails to say or do—will affect the time when the session ends.

Because this last sequence was particularly powerful and because this is the first meeting, the therapist takes the further step of telling Mickey

that there will indeed be a session next week. By doing so, he further emphasizes the independence of the scheduling process from the events that occur
within each meeting.

> M: Yeah. (*Moving toward the chalkboard*) I need red chalk. Here's the red chalk.
>   To me it looks like paint. Doesn't it to you?
> T: It does to me.
> M: Five more minutes?
> T: Five more minutes and our time is up.
> M: We can't go for a cruise?
> T: We can't go for a what?
> M: (*Making heavy, slashing marks on the chalkboard*) We can't take a ride
>   around?
> T: You'd like to take a ride around. To go for a cruise. Is that what you said,
>   for a cruise?
> M: Yeah.

Although the therapist was puzzled at first by Mickey's suggestion of
a cruise, it led eventually to the speculative hypothesis that Mickey was
seeking to avoid the termination of the session by promising a sexually toned
experience. In other words, he may have been using a term that he had
heard and that he knew had to do in some way with the predatory sexual
behavior of men seeking pleasure. So as not to reinforce Mickey's efforts
to achieve gain by attempting to excite him and to avoid contradicting the
previous message that content and scheduling are independent, the therapist did not pursue this speculative interpretation. Instead he reaffirmed
the previously announced ending of the session while acknowledging the
discontent that presumably led Mickey to attempt a manipulation. Keeping the focus on the affective response that probably motivated him leads
to a productive exchange that strengthens the sense of sharing in the waning minutes of this first meeting.

> T: Five more minutes and our time is up. I think that doesn't make you happy.
>   (*As Mickey looks away from the therapist shaking his head in agreement*)
>   That our time is up does not make you happy. (*Pause*) Maybe it even
>   makes you a little bit sad.
> M: It does.
> T: It does. I know what that's like. I know what sad feelings are like. They're
>   no fun, those sad feelings.
> M: They're not for me.
> T: They're not for you either.

M: Are five minutes up?

T: Five minutes aren't up yet. We have three more minutes.

Like many children in play therapy, Mickey typically increased the speed and tempo of his motor activity during the last few moments of the session. In effect, he seemed intent on accomplishing as much play as possible by compressing more into the rapidly diminishing time available.

It is perhaps useful to recall in this context that children seldom have the experience of being alone with an adult for a full hour during which the agenda is centered solely on the child's needs, interests, and concerns (Landreth and Barkley 1982). Certainly a youngster from dysfunctional circumstances such as Mickey's would find the experience unique. In that sense alone the hour of play therapy, though a tiny percentage of the time constituting the child's week, has a salience that increases its potential impact by an order of magnitude. Recognizing that fact may help to reassure therapists who sometimes feel discouraged by the challenge of making a difference in the relatively brief time available to work with a child.

M: (*As Mickey moves toward the dart board*) Three more?

T: Time to throw some darts.

M: (*Throwing the darts from a point very close to the board*) I want to get some high numbers . . . like fifty, ninety. (*Mickey looks at the therapist and smiles, then looks back at the board and drops a dart*) There's a zero right there. (*Continuing to throw the darts, Mickey succeeds notably with one and looks at the therapist as if seeking approval*) Oh, yeah, that was high, wasn't it?

T: That was pretty high. (*Pause*) And now, Mickey . . .

M: What?

T: Our time is up.

M: (*Referring to a dart*) As soon as I get this one on?

T: You want to get that one on. (*As Mickey succeeds*) And now it's on and our time is up.

M: Six hundred and fifty-five!

T: Six hundred and fifty-five is a good score.

M: And thirty-six!

T: And thirty-six more is even better. (*As the therapist gestures toward the door of the playroom, Mickey goes instead through another door into the observation room and converses with those present*)

In this first session Mickey has learned much about the treatment that is to follow. He has learned, for example, that the playroom is a special place where he can express, directly or through the metaphor of play, his concerns, feelings, fears, and other highly personal issues and that a non-judgmental response will be forthcoming. He has learned that his expressions will be greeted by efforts to help him achieve a more differentiated and integrated perspective, a process he is obviously unlikely to articulate but which he may find experientially to be one that leads to a feeling of being unburdened and to a greater sense of mastery regarding the oppression of the past and the uncertainty of the future. He has learned as well that the mechanics of the therapy that is beginning are independent of its content, that is, that the rules remain intact, that scheduled time remains established, and that he continues to be accorded respect and rights of privacy regardless of what he says or does—or does not say or do.

Mickey has learned also that the therapist respects boundaries and cannot be enticed to abandon that respect, even with the promise of sexually toned experiences. He has learned that, despite the extraordinary freedoms of the playroom, there are rules to be observed, most of which have to do with the safety of persons or the integrity of objects and property.

In effect, a therapeutic contract has been established.

VI

The Development of Metaphor
as a Therapeutic Vehicle

Initial contracting and rapport building having been largely accomplished, the session presented here, one that occurred several weeks later, centered upon several emergent themes that foreshadowed the work to be done by therapist and child.

First alluding to a sense of deprivation and disappointment, Mickey soon speaks of his perception that the vigilance of school authorities recently spared him the fate of further sexual violence. Implicit in his remarks is an admonishment to the therapist that he, the therapist, will also need to be alert to things that may threaten Mickey. In effect, the child is, by metaphorical reference, amending the therapeutic contract with a stipulation that highlights the therapist's responsibility to safeguard him. By further inference it might be said that Mickey's concern is for the therapist to ensure that he will remain unharmed in a literal here-and-now sense as well as with regard to the prospective integrity of his ego functions in anticipation of the daunting task of disclosure ahead.

Although he does not accept the indirect invitation to use anatomically correct dolls to elaborate concerns regarding sexual exploitation, Mickey does launch into a labored but important verbal effort to achieve a more differentiated perspective of sexuality by attempting, with the therapist's help, to define characteristics of sexually expressed "love for a kid" (which he concludes is not love at all) and "love between grown-ups."

In struggling with this early attempt to achieve developmental advance through differentiation and hierarchic integration regarding sexuality, Mickey poses a technical dilemma for the therapist by issuing challenging demands for him to speak of his own sexual behavior. Rather than explicitly respond to the queries, the therapist selectively avoids refuting certain aspects of Mickey's musings. Mickey consequently accepts his own guess about the therapist's exercise of sexuality as a working hypothesis. Apparently feeling thus reassured in terms of safety as he prepares to speak of his sexual victimization, Mickey moves further toward a differentiated and integrated posture with regard to the experience of sexuality by next addressing its affective dimension.

Still later, through visual imagery, Mickey foreshadows the intensity of the disclosure that will occur in later sessions by speaking about frightening representations of that experience having penetrated even his dreams. Also fearful perhaps that having noted his vulnerabilities may have portrayed him as weak, Mickey lapses into counterphobic posturing. For a time he seems more oriented toward that process (i.e., eliciting a desired reaction from the therapist) than toward elaboration of the preceding content.

Though he alludes momentarily but emphatically to a waking experience that seemed to suggest a hallucination, Mickey accepts the therapist's reframing of his remarks into "as if" terms. He thereby affirms that his comments were in fact prompted by the impulse to engage in counterphobic posturing (i.e., to dramatize the strength he wanted to portray) rather than to reveal what might have been construed as a psychotic lapse of reality testing.

M: I want to make another painting today for my sister.
T: Today we have a different kind of paint. We have the other kind, not the messy kind—water paints—but we still have to put a shirt on if we're going to use those paints.
M: (*Referring to the jars of paint he had used in a previous session and throwing his jacket down angrily*) Oh, come on! I think the other ones were better.
T: Well, we can't because we don't have that one to use today.
M: What about . . . you said you'd get me finger paints.
T: We don't have it.
M: Next time will you get me finger paints?

T: (*Helping Mickey on with his smock, a gesture Mickey invites and accepts, approaching with his arms extended*) I don't like to promise things because sometimes I can't do it and I don't want to make you sad. But I'm going to get them as soon as I can. (*Pause*) I wonder if sometimes people promise things and they make you sad because you don't get them. (*Pause*) Does that ever happen?

Several points are noteworthy at this early juncture. First, Mickey's acceptance of the therapist's helping gesture differs dramatically from his earlier avoidance of such offers of physical assistance. The contrast suggests that Mickey was both qualifying and tempering the anger that was implicit in his opening remarks and seeking to further determine the limits of the therapist's benevolence in the face of one or another affective expression. Second, to the extent that Mickey was in fact expressing annoyance and disappointment, the therapist had the option of encouraging further expression of those feelings or of attempting to extend Mickey's awareness of his frustration to parallel experiences outside the playroom. To the extent that the therapy circumstance allows reflection and potential developmental advance in ways that are at best fleeting in the context of metaphorical reference, the therapist chooses the latter.

M: Huh?
T: (*As Mickey assembles the top-access dollhouse on the low table*) Does that ever happen to you?
M: Yeah. My mom doesn't do that though.

In one sense Mickey's response implies a willingness to confront the reality of adversity and deprivation he has known. His quick exempting of his mother from that indictment, however, represents in effect the high ground on the topography of his denial: he is not yet ready to acknowledge within himself that some of the hardship he has known traces to her failings.

T: She promises you things?
M: She said "I might buy you a candy."
T: Uh huh. (*Pause*) I wonder how Mickey feels when people make a promise and then they don't keep it.

It is at this point, once the reality of parallel experiences outside the playroom has been cited and acknowledged, that the therapist seeks to help

Mickey express increasingly differentiated affective dimensions of his self–world relationship. The alternative would have been to restrict consideration of emotional experience to the here and now, a sequence that would have occurred had Mickey's feelings been referenced when he first expressed frustration about the paints. Because this is still a relatively early stage in treatment, however, the therapist does not extend the metaphorical reference to those instances in which adults have left Mickey hurt by their abrogation of trust and their sexual exploitation of him.

> *M:* I don't like it. Sometimes I call them "cheap pants." (Several internal walls of the dollhouse that Mickey has set in place fall and he asks) Can you help me?
> *T:* (*Picking up the walls of the dollhouse*) I wonder how Mickey feels when people make promises and then they don't keep them.
> *M:* I don't like it. Sometimes I call them "cheap pants."
> *T:* Cheap pants? I never heard anybody called that before. I wonder if you made it up.
> *M:* Me, I did.
> *T:* That's your special word.
> *M:* I say it.
> *T:* I wonder if you made that word up.

Proceeding on the speculative inference that Mickey's persistence in focusing on the phrase *cheap pants* may signal his unarticulated impulse to extend earlier references to abrogation of trust and disappointment to the realm of sexual exploitation, the therapist here provides Mickey the opportunity to pursue his associations. Mickey does not do so, however, and the therapist does not reintroduce the remarks once they have submerged.

> *M:* (*Trying again to assemble the dollhouse on the table*) Can you help?
> *T:* You want me to help you. (*As Mickey carries the dollhouse to the corner of the room with the therapist helping him in that effort*) I remember when we first started meeting here, you never wanted me to help you. But now you let me help you. Things are changing, things are a little bit different. (*As Mickey and the therapist carry the doll furniture away as well*) Before you didn't feel all right about me helping you. Now you feel okay about me helping you.

From the point of view of playroom technique, this intervention illustrates the frequently beneficial practice of reinforcing the child's readiness to accept help. To do so by framing comments in ways that reference by implication both the literal (e.g., help with playthings) and the metaphorical (e.g., help in achieving developmental advance) reaffirms the basic premise of the therapeutic contract. Perhaps as a consequence, Mickey moves next toward a more focused reference concerning adult males who sexually assault children.

> M: You know that guy who usually picks me up?
>
> T: The guy who usually picks you up?
>
> M: (*Initiating and maintaining the direct eye contact that previously had not been the case*) Yeah, my principal, the principal of the school, thought he was a stranger here to rape me.
>
> T: A stranger to rape you? Oh, my goodness!
>
> M: She thought. But it wasn't. I knew him.
>
> T: (*As if breathing a sigh of relief*) Oh. (*Pause*) Who said it was a stranger to rape you, I wonder.
>
> M: Huh?
>
> T: I wonder who said it was stranger to rape you.
>
> M: She thought.
>
> T: She said to you, "Mickey, I think there's a stranger here to rape you"?
>
> M: (*As Mickey climbs upon and stands on a chair next to the easel of newsprint and as he adjusts the paper*) She said, "Do you know him?" and I said "yes."
>
> T: (*Helping Mickey to adjust the paper*) Oh. (*Referring to Mickey's moving the paper from the easel to place it on the table*) You don't want it up here, you want it down here.
>
> M: (*Referring to a picture he had painted previously*) Can you tear my picture off, please?
>
> T: Mmm?
>
> M: Can you tear my picture off please? I want to take it with me today.
>
> T: (*As Mickey jumps from the chair, turns his back to the therapist, and busies himself with paintbrushes on the table*) I wonder how you know that the principal thought the stranger was going to rape you. I wonder how you could tell that.

It should be noted that, although Mickey's reference to the issue of rape was said in a rather matter-of-fact manner and seemed almost incidental to his greater investment in the ongoing play, the therapist did not assume it to be inconsequential. Instead he pursued it, even while relating to Mickey in terms of the ostensibly innocuous aspects of his concurrent play activities.

In this instance the dramatic content of Mickey's choice of words renders unlikely that his comments would be shrugged off by the therapist. Circumstances do occur, however, in which children express less dramatic but no less important concerns in an almost off-handed way and embed them in activities that seem much more focal for the child. In those instances it is nevertheless important that the therapist weigh the seemingly secondary focus as perhaps being reflective of the child's ambivalence about addressing a potentially affect-laden concern against the possibility that it is, in fact, of minor consequence to the therapy process. It is particularly incumbent upon the therapist to do so in that children often express denial and avoidance through such matter-of-fact behaviors stripped of problematic affect.

> M: I was warned about that.
> T: (*Tearing Mickey's picture from the pad of newsprint and placing it aside for him*) You know we have some other things to do here too, Mickey.
> M: What?
> T: (*Referring to the anatomically correct dolls that Mickey had previously seen when he was first screened for play therapy but which had not been present in the playroom since then*) We have some dolls here that we didn't have before.

The anatomically correct dolls had been purposely left out of the playroom during the initial several individual therapy sessions. During those meetings it was deemed important to focus on the development of rapport and on the negotiation of a therapeutic contract in an environment that was not overly stimulating or narrow in terms of its recollection of recall of trauma. That Mickey's victimization and its effects would be of focal concern nevertheless became clear almost from the outset through interactions centering upon definition of the therapy process and of the trust that is essential to it.

To include in initial sessions play objects that have a circumscribed and very powerful stimulus value can often rigidify a child's defenses. Such countertherapeutic impact can occur particularly when, as had been the case with Mickey through his recent grand jury appearances, disclosure prompts repeated efforts to encourage the psychologically unprepared child to recall and express the literal and stark aspects of abuse. Instead, therapy should help children address the more broadly defined impact of victimization on her or his emotional life, self concept, and the resulting constructions and exercise of self–world relationships in general.

> *M:* (*Looking across the room at the fully clothed dolls*) That girl is . . . that girl is fine.
>
> *T:* That girl is what?
>
> *M:* That girlie doll.
>
> *T:* And there's a boy doll too. (*Pause*) So we've got girl dolls and we've got boy dolls.
>
> *M:* (*Maintaining his position at the desk while painting and referring to his stroking several of the brushes with another one*) I'm using one to wet them.

Rather than challenge Mickey's resistance to incorporating the anatomically correct dolls in his explanation, the therapist invites him to return verbally to an elaboration of his sense of the danger that was said to confront him at school. At this early juncture to persist in encouraging use of the dolls would risk conveying to Mickey that his introducing certain topics would lead to diminished degrees of freedom for him in discussion of them. Therefore, to have made explicit the potential symbolic meaning of Mickey's having used a phallic-shaped object to stroke other such objects while commenting, "I'm using one to wet them," would probably trigger, for him, an impulse to retreat defensively.

From an orthogenetic perspective, it is also the case that poor timing by the therapist in making threatening issues focal is particularly problematic. Persistence in doing so, despite signals from the child that she or he is not ready to address them, could precipitate regression to a more dedifferentiated experiential posture and render more difficult the achievement of therapeutic goals.

> *T:* So the principal said to you, "There's a stranger here . . . (*Pause*) and I think he's here to rape you." (*Pause*) Is that what the principal said?
>
> *M:* She thought.
>
> *T:* Well, how . . . how can you tell that's what she thought?
>
> *M:* She looked like it. I went back into the school to get a note and she was watching me while I went into the car.

This comment reflects a frequently occurring sequela to a child's victimization, namely, reliance on projection as a defense in a way that erodes the potential for trust, sustains a sense of danger in the interpersonal environment, and at times blurs the perception of reality. In this instance the therapist does not argue with Mickey's comment but responds in a simple, monosyllabic way that gently conveys, through tone and furrowed brow, that he does not affirm the premise from which Mickey reasoned, but at the same time encourages the child to further elaborate his perception. The goal here is to foster movement toward increased differentiation and integration rather than to continue the posture of relative dedifferentiation or differentiation and isolation rather than integration.

T: Mmm.

M: That's how I could tell she thought it was a stranger.

T: You know, Mickey?

M: (Interrupting with a quick response) What?

T: You never did tell me what rape means.

M: I don't know.

T: You told me about rape a few times but you never really told me what it means.

M: (Rising quickly, Mickey looks the therapist in the eye and points the paintbrush he is holding at him in a momentarily defensive gesture. He then moves quickly with arms waving above his shoulders in a kind of controlled flailing. Mickey speaks with a tense and impatiently raised voice) It begins with an S, I said.

In the sequence that follows, several emotionally charged and critical therapeutic issues emerge on the heels of Mickey's apparent struggle with the conflict between his impulse to maintain a guarded posture on the one hand, and on the other to move forward in discussion of troubling concerns. The latter becomes the direction taken, partly as a result of titrated persistence on the part of the therapist in the face of continuing yet gradually yielding resistance.

Mickey begins with a somewhat defensive but assertively stated challenge to the therapist regarding the therapist's presumed exercise of his own sexuality. Reflected in Mickey's persistent inquiry regarding the therapist's sexuality is a degree of fusion between love and sex incorporating, in a vague way, the notion of rape as well. Further, Mickey associates those fused notions with the question of whether the therapist is a father. He adds that men who want children engage in rape. In doing so, he again raises the issue of whether he may be seen by the therapist as a child to be preyed upon. That concern becomes yet more strident as he explicitly asks if the therapist engages in acts that might be the equivalent of rape.

The therapist's tact is to encourage Mickey to share his assumptions before factual answers are provided. As often occurs, Mickey accepts his own increasingly differentiated and integrated musings as premises from which to operate rather than insist upon their confirmation, even after he has met the prerequisite condition imposed by the therapist for responding to such questions.

Although most children, like Mickey, drop the demand for factual data after being helped to elaborate their own speculations, it is always preferable in any case to ask a child for his or her guess before the therapist responds by providing specific information, even when a particular circumstance or treatment plan renders such self-definition advisable. Unless those fantasies are first elicited, they quickly become lost data that evaporate or submerge in the wake of the child's learning the reality-based facts.

Importantly, in the sequence that follows Mickey moves strikingly and explicitly toward increased differentiation and integration of the concepts of love, sex, rape, child, and adult. Further, he does so in a way that allows the trust between therapist and child to continue, and indeed, to grow. One effective result of that process in terms of the sequence is the subsequent emergence of discussion of Mickey's emotional experience with regard to his victimization, an act of sharing and vulnerability that could not have occurred without sufficient trust having been established. In a larger sense Mickey here takes a quantum step forward in terms of developmental advance with regard to his construction of self, the world, and the potential relationship between the two.

> T: Well, you told me it begins with an S . . . and you told me it was called "sex," but you never told me what people do when they rape people.
> M: (*Continuing to face away from the therapist*) You know what!
> T: Mm.
> M: You know what you do to your wife, don't you?!?
> T: People do all kinds of stuff.
> M: (*As Mickey walks back to the table holding the paintbrush steady before him*) Do you got a baby?
> T: You make a guess. What do you think?
> M: (*Seeming to be intently absorbed in his painting*) Yes.
> T: You think that I have a baby. (*Pause*) But I thought you told me that raping and babies are not the same.
> M: (*Mickey rises from his painting, looks at the therapist, gestures in a repeated pointing motion at him with the paintbrush and speaks with a seemingly exasperated sigh*) Do you have a kid?
> T: You make a guess.

M: (Standing facing the therapist and speaking plaintively) No, I want to know!

T: You make a guess first.

M: (Walking toward the desk with an unusual gait) Yes.

T: (Walking to a point several feet to the side of Mickey so as to be within his range of vision should he choose to look up) Yes. So . . . what does that mean. . .if I have a kid.

M: (Ostensibly attending to the painting materials and avoiding eye contact) You do.

T: How does that tell me what rape is?

M: What do you do if you want a kid . . . with your wife?

T: What do you think?

M: Sex!

T: Sex . . . is that the same as rape?

M: It is.

T: (Referring to a comment Mickey had made during an earlier session) I thought . . . there was a certain kind of sex that was love and a certain kind of sex that was rape.

M: They're both the same.

T: They're the same? I thought they were different. I thought rape was nasty and love was nice.

M: There's a love for a kid and there's a mean love . . . for a kid . . . and there's a nice love for a parent.

T: There's a nice love for a parent and a mean love for a kid.

M: (Moving back and forth from the desk where he wets the paintbrush and carries it to the table where he continues to paint a picture of an outdoor scene) And a nice love for a kid.

T: And a nice love for a kid. (Pause) And the mean love for a kid is the kind that has sex with it.

M: Mmhmm.

T: I see. (Pause) So it is different then. Nice love for a kid and mean love for a kid are very different.

M: Them two are different.

T: So love for a grown-up . . .

M: (Interrupting to complete the therapist's sentence) . . . it's like sex.

T: So for grown-ups its okay to have sex but for a kid . . . that makes it mean.

M: Yeah.

Having helped Mickey achieve a more developmentally advanced cognitive construction of sex and love with regard to the relationship between self and the interpersonal environment, the therapist next encourages Mickey to extend the more differentiated and integrated perspective to the affective dimension.

T: Now I understand. I think maybe that's the way it is. (*Pause*) That's not a
  very happy thing to think about. You know all about the mean kind, I
  think.

M: I know more than you.

T: You know all about the mean kind.

M: How come you don't? You're supposed to.

T: Do you think maybe you could help me to understand?

This response exemplifies the way in which a therapist can, rather than
become defensive and rush to assure the child that he is, in fact, knowledgeable, let stand the judgment that he may be lacking in a way that the
child is not. The therapist in effect accepts the premise that he may have a
problem that the child can remedy, that is, his lack of understanding. By
structuring the sequence in this manner, the child is empowered even at
the same time that he is confessing a vulnerability.

M: (*The therapist stands across the table as Mickey continues to walk back and
  forth alternately wetting the brush and adding to the picture he is painting*) I
  just told you. I just helped you understand.

T: Yes, you did. But you didn't help me understand how it makes a kid feel.

M: Sad!

T: It makes a kid feel sad.

M: Now that's all I'm telling you.

T: You don't want to say anymore. Maybe you think I shouldn't know about
  that.

M: (*Referring to the painting*) No, I want to get my work done.

T: I see.

M: I want to concentrate.

T: Stuff like that keeps a guy from concentrating. (*Pause*) All the talk about sex
  and rape and stuff like that makes it very hard for a guy to concentrate.

M: (*Referring to the picture he is continuing to paint*) I've got to get one for my
  sister . . . just like for my mother. (*Stretching across the table, Mickey in
  effect lies on the table and gets paint on his hands*) Oh God! Get me some
  napkins.

T: I think we need some paper towels. (*Indirectly addressing the observers behind
  the one-way mirror*) Maybe someone will bring us some paper towels.
  (*As Mickey slides off the table and heads toward the playroom door*) Maybe
  you'll get some for yourself. (*As Mickey leaves the room, the therapist follows him out*)

To avoid the implication that Mickey's leave-taking constitutes a kind
of violation, the therapist speaks of its purpose, implicitly allowing him to

continue reliance upon the device of temporary absence when material of the dialogue reaches threatening intensity that the child can no longer sustain. Although not all treatment contexts lend themselves to extending this freedom of movement, and indeed not all children would benefit from it, some means should be provided by which a child can clearly demarcate the end of a sequence that has for the time being become overwhelming.

At a speculative level regarding the symbolism of content, it may be noteworthy that Mickey ends the discussion of sex and rape by asking for paper towels to clean the mess left in the wake, ostensibly, of his painting.

> M: (*Returning to the playroom with paper towels after several moments*) Now don't bother me.
> T: (*Standing across the room*) I shouldn't bother you about that stuff, huh?
> M: (*With his back to the therapist as he wets his brush in the jar on the desk*) No, I'm trying . . . (*Mickey's words trail off without his completing the sentence*)
> T: Maybe there's just one thing I would like to ask.
> M: What?
> T: Because I need to understand and you've got to help me figure it out.
> M: (*Walking toward the therapist, glancing quickly at him, and then sprawling on the table next to the painting that he continues to dab*) What?
> T: If it makes a kid feel bad, how can a kid get over feeling bad? How can he get all better?

To encourage Mickey to look beyond the pain he has acknowledged and to consider ways in which resolution might be sought, the therapist invites him to focus on available instrumentalities, various means by which he may transact with his world and the options available to him for bringing about change in his relationship with that world. These too on first emergence are likely to reflect developmental primitivity that will require movement toward further differentiation and integration if therapeutic gains are to be made. Alternatively, to encourage only emotional expression by the child simply for the sake of catharsis is insufficient.

In addition, the therapist's fostering consideration of actions that can be taken provides a substrate within the therapy process for the metaphorical retribution that needs to occur later. By moving from consideration of relatively global and undifferentiated options for action toward those more developmentally advanced, the child will progressively gain a frame of reference by which to experience and express his trauma-induced rage more effectively. In the metaphor of play the emotions that are the partial legacy of his abuse will find enhanced expression rather than the truncated externalization that would probably eventuate had Mickey's first expression of his pain been taken as an end point in the preceding sequence. In keeping with the overarching goals of treatment, this process will enable the child to move beyond the enveloping impact of trauma to more developmentally advanced constructions and transactional patterns.

M: When he's arrested!
T: When the guy who did it is arrested.
M: Yes.
T: That makes the kid all better.
M: Do you get it?
T: I think I understand. (*Pause*) That means that you're all better now? You don't feel sad any more?
M: I still feel a little sad. (*Pause*) Because I want to live with my mother.
T: You still feel a little sad.
M: (*In an indignant tone*) They took me away from my mother!
T: Uh huh!
M: (*Having stood up from his sprawled position on the table and speaking in an angry tone as he makes a kicking motion*) I'll kick them and they'll go flying right to the sky.

Having addressed the issue of victimization in terms of sexual violation but having stopped short of externalizing the rage left in its wake when he was violated, Mickey is prepared to access his feelings of anger. He does so, however, in a different realm, one that is both less central to the reality of his being vulnerable to others for use as an object of sexual gratification and at the same time more poignant with regard to his needs for protection and nurturance, that is, his longing for his mother.

T: I wonder who did that.
M: Charlene!
T: You're very angry at Charlene.
M: I'm going to tell her . . . I'm never ever going back to my—whatever her name is—my foster mother.
T: There's one thing a guy would like after going through all that business . . . to be able to go back to his mother and live with her.
M: And I'm going to tell them why I'm not going back there. And I'm also going to tell my new one.
T: Your new one?
M: My new social worker. I've got a new social worker.
T: I wonder what her name is.

M: I don't know.

T: You don't know yet.

M: Charlene didn't tell me. I hope it's a white one too.

T: I see. That's important to you.

M: I'm not having no black one.

This racially pejorative comment exemplifies the frequently occurring tendency for children to reflect values and perspectives that they have acquired within troubled familial or subcultural contexts. Such comments often collide with the values of the therapist. Although such views can be associated with psychopathological processes, they may at any given juncture serve as a distraction from the current focus of the session and indeed might be introduced by the child for that unarticulated purpose.

With success in the effort to foster developmental advance eventually there will be a re-examination and revision of beliefs and perspectives rooted in distortion; eventually, therefore, issues such as racial prejudice may become focal. At this point, however, Mickey is still struggling to define self as having worth. For the therapist to dialogue with him about social attitudes toward others whom he has been told are inferior would be ill timed. The therapist thus must put aside his own adverse reactions to such comments and continue on a path that may eventually return to correct such distorted perceptions.

T: Mmm. (*Pause*) That's something else you worry about. (*Pause*) It sounds to me like you have a lot of worries. Goodness, how does a guy go to school and stuff when he has all those worries? (*Pause*) Or even sleep at night; I wonder if you sleep at night okay.

M: No.

T: You don't sleep so good.

M: (*In a tone bordering on disgust*) I have to dream about it!

T: Mmm. I wonder what part you have to dream about.

M: (*Continuing, as he has been, to work on the picture and continuing as well to avoid eye contact*) The meanest part of all.

T: The meanest part of all?

M: The one I had to explain to you.

T: The one that begins with *S*? (*Pause*) I see. And you dream about it every night?

M: Yeah.

T: Oh, that doesn't sound like a very good dream. (*Pause*) But maybe in some ways it is a good dream.

M: Nope.

T: It's not a good dream, no way!

M: How would you feel dreaming about it?

T: I don't think I would like it.

M: Then how do you think I would feel?

T: I think you probably don't like it. (*Pause*) I think maybe I might even wake up crying sometimes if I had dreams like that.

In this sequence Mickey has relied on indirect references to share with the therapist the pervasiveness and intensity of the distress left by his abuse. He has learned from the therapist's response that his code is understood such that he does not need to label or describe in literal, behavioral terms the acts of his victimization in ways that might frighten and/or embarrass him. Still, the abuse can remain focal in interactions with the therapist. Should Mickey have difficulty sharing what might reasonably be inferred to be his response of crying, the therapist legitimizes that option. Simultaneously, he seeks to erase any fear that Mickey might harbor that he would be seen as lacking by the therapist who admits that under similar circumstances he too would likely cry.

M: And you might even wake up seeing a ghost at night.

T: Might even see a ghost at night.

M: Like I do!

T: You see a ghost at night?

M: (*In an apparently counterphobic tone that sounds like bragging*) Yup!

T: Holy smoke! (*As Mickey makes brief eye contact*) What kind of ghost?

M: A skeleton ghost.

T: Oh, my!

M: (*Maintaining extended eye contact and gesturing with his hands on his face, Mickey speaks in a tone that seems intended to impress the therapist with his ability to withstand symbolic onslaught and remain composed rather than becoming fearful*) Dressed like a ghost . . . so you can just see his head, his face, his skeleton, his mouth, blood coming out of his eyes, nose and mouth and skeleton hands with blood coming out.

T: Oh, my goodness! And what does the ghost do to you in your dreams?

M: He walks.

T: He walks.

M: And then he takes a knife and kills me.

T: He kills you with a knife?

M: I scream to the bottom of my lungs.

T: I guess you do! (*Pause*) And then you wake up.

M: Mmhmm.

T: I wonder if there's any stuff that happens when you're awake that's like that.

M: (*Bent over the paints at the desk and intently wetting the brushes*) Yes, same thing.

T: Same thing happens when you're awake?

M: Same ghost, too.

T: Uh-huh.

M: Once I get up that same night, I see him again.

T: Feels like you see a ghost at night. It seems to you like you do.

In his response the therapist affirms through reflection the impact of Mickey's experience but frames his intervention in a way—"feels like," "seems like"—that avoids endorsing the notion that there is concrete reality behind it. In doing so he conveys an empathic sense of the impact on Mickey but avoids compounding the child's stated distress. To affirm in any way, even in jest, the notion that ghosts or other supernatural entities in fact pose a real menace risks profound regression, particularly with a traumatized child who has yet to abandon fully the expectation of punishment born of an egocentric construction of his or her own victimization.

M: (*Abruptly changing the subject*) You got any tape?

T: I don't think I have any tape.

In recalling his dream, Mickey has presented an emotionally laden account of his terror and victimization by violent penetration at the hands of a specter he cannot challenge or resist. Further, he maintains a fear that nightly, and perhaps during waking hours as well, a return of the attacker is possible. Implied is the unrelenting nature of Mickey's sense of helplessness and immobilizing fear. At the same time, both his compelling adherence to symbolic referents and the counterphobic tone of bravado in his statements further suggest that the full disclosure toward which he is moving will likely be filled with yet more power and pathos.

As in previous emotionally charged sequences, Mickey abruptly signals his need to let go of the topic, presumably because his tolerance to remain with it has reached its limit. Because the therapist seeks to foster developmental advance rather than invite the dedifferentiation that could result from requiring Mickey to remain with a threatening topic beyond his tolerance, the signal is respected and unchallenged. The therapist's strategy is based on confidence that this issue, of obvious importance to Mickey, will re-emerge in similarly metaphorical ways or perhaps in more direct references.

M: (*Quickly dropping the brush on the desk and heading toward the door to the observation room*) Then I'm going next door.

T: To try to get some tape. But Diane's not there today.

M: Oh, drats! (*Heading toward the door to the hallway*) Then I'll go this way.

T: (*As Mickey returns quickly from an adjoining office with a roll of tape*) I wonder if that ghost reminds Mickey of anybody.

M: (*Taping a tear in the picture he has been painting on the table*) The bogeyman.

T: The bogeyman.

M: (*Scrutinizing the repair he has accomplished on the painting*) I'm gonna be embarrassed, taping right over it. (*Giving the taping a second glance*) That's gonna look nice.

Mickey's comments here might be seen as metaphorically reflecting his ambivalence about disclosure and about the image he will project in that process; on the one hand he anticipates embarrassment; on the other he hopes for an eventually positive outcome.

T: I can see you're the kind of guy who likes to fix things after they've been hurt . . . to put things back together. (*Pause*) You're the kind of guy who likes to have things fixed. (*Pause*) Maybe that's how you feel about things at home. (*Pause*) And about your own feelings.

M: I hate people who yell at me.

T: That's another thing you don't like. Yelling at you is something you know about.

M: And I'll bust their noses if I get very mad!

T: You think about busting things, but you also think about fixing things. I can tell by the way you put that tape on that you think about fixing things too.

M: And I think about busting people's noses if I have to.

T: Sometimes you think about busting and sometimes you think about fixing.

M: If somebody gets me really, really mad, I bust their nose up.

T: But then after things get busted, you think about fixing things, about putting them back together.

M: Not people who tease me.

T: Oh, not those people. (*Pause*) But maybe your own feelings and stuff.

M: (*Without making eye contact Mickey continues to work on the painting. On it he has begun to add heavy lines, coloring in the outline of the ground he drew as part of an outdoor scene*) Only if I got my own feelings back.

Mickey's persistence reflects the power of the aggressive impulse once located. The therapist's equal persistence in the face of that power is intended to convey to Mickey the premise that coherence can be achieved between the impulse to accomplish retribution and the eventual need for healing in the wake of violation and consequent rage.

> T: Maybe you try to figure out how to put your own feelings back together . . . after they've been all busted up. (*Pause*) That's important to you, I think. (*Pause*) It's not an easy thing to do. (*Pause*) One thing that Mickey knows about is how hard that is to do, how hard it is to get those feelings back together again.
>
> M: It's very hard.
>
> T: (*Maintaining a position across the low table from Mickey as he walks around it*) It's very hard. Mickey knows about that. (*Pause*) But Mickey's the kind of guy who keeps working at it.
>
> M: (*In an almost wistful tone*) I get my feelings back.
>
> T: He gets his feelings back together.
>
> M: But I know somebody right up beside me that will help.
>
> T: There is somebody who will help you do that.
>
> M: (*Making eye contact with the therapist and pointing to the ceiling*) Who's up there that is your only father?
>
> T: I wonder who that is.
>
> M: We're his son. Right up above. Who's Jesus' father?
>
> T: You tell me.
>
> M: You know.
>
> T: You tell me.
>
> M: No.
>
> T: Well I don't know what name you use.
>
> M: (*In an angry tone*) Yes you do, God!

It should be recalled that Mickey's first placement outside his home following the discovery of widespread abuse in the family was with his uncle and aunt who maintained themselves through strong involvement in a fundamentalist church. They often brought Mickey to church and religious classes during his several months' stay. Mickey's recalling those perspectives at this juncture reflects the importance and urgency he attaches to the effort to "get his feelings back" through the intercession and benevolence of a source of power equal to the enormity of the challenge he faces.

> T: Oh, I didn't know what you meant.
>
> M: Who's Jesus' son? (*Pause*) And then you'll find out.
>
> T: Hmm. And that helps you in putting things together. When feelings are all broken up, thinking about that helps you put them back together.
>
> M: I always think about God.

T: I see. (*Pause*) That's an important thing for you.

M: (*In a barely audible, almost timid tone*) For me? Yes.

T: And it sounds like that helps a lot.

M: (*Speaking somewhat abruptly*) I need more tape.

As in other sequences, Mickey is probably introducing this abrupt shift to signal his wish to stem associations that have reached his limit of tolerance. It is possible, however, that in a way that is unarticulated within his own awareness Mickey may also be endorsing the notion that "God helps those who help themselves" and he therefore needs to take an active role in the mending process.

T: Tape is important. (*Mickey jumps up and runs toward the hallway door before the therapist completes his statement*) If you're going to fix . . .

M: (*As he leaves the room*) More.

T: (*Mickey re-enters the room with several pieces of tape and sticks them to the table. He uses one of the pieces to repair the picture he had been working on*) Oop, Mickey's in the business of fixing things again. (*Pause, then speaking slowly*) Fixing things is important business.

M: I don't . . . I don't leave them ripped . . .

T: You don't like to leave things all messed up.

M: (*Almost interrupting the therapist again before he completes his statement and standing across from the therapist making eye contact*) You got any scissors?

T: I don't think I have scissors.

M: Oh, drats!

T: (*Referring to a tear that Mickey is inspecting*) But I think you can probably fold that tape over it, over the end of the paper.

M: (*Standing and intently trying to untangle a piece of tape, Mickey speaks in a low tone as if to himself*) Oh, come on. (*Pause*) Made a mistake, drats. (*Beginning to hum and eventually succeeding in untangling the tape, which he then uses to repair the painting*) Got it!

T: (*As Mickey resumes humming, and then begins to add words to the tune*) When you fix something, you feel so good you feel like singing. (*Pause, while Mickey continues to vocalize as if between humming and singing*) Fixing things gives a guy a good feeling. (*Pause*) Especially when you fix your own hurts. Then it feels even better.

By highlighting Mickey's expressions of positive affect, the therapist seeks to define and reinforce the attitude that resolution of conflict and, in metatheoretical terms, developmental advance can yield moments of relief that offset the intermittent anguish that occurs as the process unfolds.

M: (*Mickey continues to vocalize for a few moments, then begins to paint over the tear he has just repaired with the tape*) I've got to do something. (*Pause, then speaking playfully*) Smarter than the average . . . (*Realizing that the black paint he is applying is not adhering to the tape surface*) You mean black won't help?

T: Sometimes the paint doesn't stick to the tape too good.

M: Yeah, I'm going to do something. I need more tape. (*Leaving the room and returning with more tape, Mickey begins repairing the painting again. He then takes note of noise outside the window as several people pass talking loudly*) Oh, shut up!

T: You don't like the people outside talking.

M: They're disturbing me. (*Pause, as the therapist helps Mickey place the pieces of tape on the edge of the table holding the painting*) See, it won't stick. (*Pause*) I'm going to try it now . . . see if some paint sticks.

T: To see if the paint will stick to the tape.

M: (*A piece of tape sticks to the brush as Mickey attempts to paint it*) Huh?

T: Sometimes things don't work out the way you want them to.

M: (*As Mickey carries the errant piece of tape to the trash bucket*) It won't work.

T: It's not as easy to fix something as it looks at first.

M: (*Bending over the paper and diligently continuing his effort to paint the taped surface*) So I'll just go like this.

T: It looks like you're going to keep at it until you fix even the things that are hard to fix. (*Pause*) It just takes a lot of work.

In this sequence the therapist and Mickey are communicating within a metaphor, speaking ostensibly about the difficulty of mending playthings, but also about the difficulty of mending the effects of the trauma Mickey has suffered.)

M: (*Speaking in a seemingly strained tone of voice*) It takes me time to do it.

T: Mmm. It takes work and it takes time. (*Pause*) I think that's the way it is when you try to help yourself through a hurt time. It takes work and it takes time.

Here the therapist makes explicit the metaphorical referents of the dialogue in which he and Mickey are engaged. Affirming that linkage by his silence, Mickey continues below to exclaim the sense of futility he sometimes feels in the effort.

M: (*Speaking with frustration as he continues to encounter difficulty in painting the taped surface*) Gosh! Everything doesn't work for me. (*Apparently*

> *referring to the painting on which he has been drawing a wide band at the base*) I could break this city to bits and then use the sidewalk.

T: Sometimes, when you're trying to fix things, it makes you angry . . . and you feel like breaking things.

M: (*In a tone of agreement*) Mmhmm. (*Pause . . . then referring to the paints*) Why didn't you get the other ones? They're better.

T: These are the ones we have today. (*Sliding the chair with the paints on it toward the table*) I think if we move it closer it will work better. (*Placing a paper towel under the paint tray to steady it*) If we put this right here, it will work even better.

M: (*Choosing another paint from the one he has been using*) I better use one of these. (*Pause . . . then taking note again of the renewed noise outside the window, Mickey remains near the paints but shouts toward the window*) Shut up! (*Lowering his volume to softly spoken words*) Dumb-dumbs. I'm trying to work.

T: Sometimes people . . . (*Mickey begins to strike a container of paint, ostensibly to loosen the cover, but in the process he produces a loud hammering noise*) . . . just don't let you do what you want to do.

M: (*When the paint container he has been striking falls to the floor, Mickey asks in a soft and almost doleful way*) Will you get it?

Mickey's question, following on the heels of the therapist's noting that others are often not helpful, suggests that Mickey is assessing the possibility that the therapist may be an exception to that frequent pattern and perhaps may be respectful of the posture of vulnerability that disclosure will require.

> T: (*After the therapist picks up the paint and places it back on the chair, and as Mickey resumes painting*) Pretty soon there's a special day coming.
> M: Christmas!
> T: Christmas is coming.

Because the end of the session was drawing closer, the therapist sought here to introduce a potentially lighter and more upbeat topic. Mickey responds for a while but soon returns to emotionally laden issues. His doing so speaks in one sense to the power of his need to uncover noxious concerns in the context of the comfort he has acquired in the session to this point.

Although in this instance Mickey resisted the therapist's efforts along these lines, it is often prudent to bring a sense of affective relief to a child toward the end of the session. Obviously, to send a child home without having assisted in her or his emotional reconstituting after some emotionally trying therapy experience can be problematic. A youngster might otherwise return home preoccupied with concerns and feelings that threaten to overwhelm without a therapist present to help manage them productively. Further, interactions with others prompted by the child's agitation could easily lead to interpersonal conflict. In simpler terms, it is unfair to the child to open up difficult feelings without later closing up.

> M: (*In contrast to his previously exaggerated tone of assertiveness and feigned authority, Mickey begins to speak almost in the manner of a preschooler. He maintains the pattern throughout the following sequence*) Now it's for children.
>
> T: It's a special time for children.
>
> M: The parents had their fun. Now it's for kids.
>
> T: Now it's the kids' time. I wonder when the parents had their fun.
>
> M: Thanksgiving.
>
> T: Thanksgiving was for the parents, Christmas is for the kids.
>
> M: And I'm lucky I'm a kid. I can get all my toys now.
>
> T: You like being a kid. (*Pause*) Maybe there are sometimes you wish you were a grown-up instead of being a kid.
>
> M: (*Continuing to work on the painting*) Yeah, because of what I face.
>
> T: There are those times. (*Pause*) Sometimes Mickey says to himself, "It's fun being a kid but I wish I were grown up right now." (*Pause*) "Because if I were grown up right now . . ."

The therapist's intervention seeks to facilitate dialogue in a productive way by reframing the child's words as an incomplete sentence and letting the tone of the last few words hang as if to beg completion. In effect, the therapist joins the child's cadence and maintains it, thereby creating a need to continue. It should be noted, however, that this approach quickly loses its efficacy and in fact may become counterproductive if it is overdone.

> M: . . . I could do what I want.
>
> T: "I could do what I want." (*Pause*) ". . . And what I would do would be . . ."
>
> M: . . . go to the store.
>
> T: "Go to the store."
>
> M: I'd pick up $500.
>
> T: "Take $500 to the store . . ."
>
> M: No, take out $500.
>
> T: "Take out $500."

M: And I'll have a party.

T: And have a party with $500.

M: With my friends.

T: And at the party everybody would . . .

M: Eat.

T: . . . Would eat.

M: I'd give my . . . (*Mickey begins humming* "The Twelve Days of Christmas" *as he lifts the bottom of the painting and attempts to repair the tear by taping the underside*)

T: It looks to me like you figured out another way to fix that . . . by fixing it from the other side. (*Pause*) Sometimes there's more than one way to fix a thing.

By this intervention the therapist invites Mickey to revisit the metaphor regarding healing.

M: I'm smarter than the average kid.

T: You're smarter than the average kid.

M: Yup.

T: I think that's true. (*Pause*) I think that's a good thing to be, too.

M: I'm smarter than the average . . .

T: (*Attempting to clarify Mickey's last words, which had trailed off into an inaudible mumble*) Smarter than the . . . than what?

M: Whoever that guy is . . . even if he's a pig, I'm smarter than him.

At subsequent points in the play therapy, Mickey referred to the perpetrators of his abuse as "pigs." Retrospectively, it can perhaps be assumed that he was doing so here as well and seeking, prior to explicit disclosure, to move toward a sense of mastery over them and over the threat they represent by asserting his superior intelligence. In a sense his associations at this point might be understood as a kind of preparation for the challenge that is unfolding.

T: Hmm. (*Pause*) That's pretty smart. (*Pause*) Sometimes being smart is not enough.

In metaphorical terms, the therapist is affirming the notion that Mickey is bright but adding that even his intellectual abilities are not a shield against exploitation by those willing to overwhelm him with other forms of power.

M: (*Leaving the picture he has been absorbed in repairing, Mickey walks to the desk*) You got a stapler?

T: I don't think we've got a stapler. (*Groaning in an exasperated way, Mickey walks to the door and exits the room. He quickly returns. The therapist follows, carrying a stapler borrowed from a nearby office*) The rule is that I use the stapler over here, but I'll use it the way you tell me to. Just tell me how to use it. (*As Mickey holds the corner of the paper up*) I see what you want. (*As he staples*) All right, here, I'll do it this way. (*Mickey guides the stapler as the therapist fastens the corner of the paper*) You know what? It's empty.

M: (*Jumping up and attempting to grab the stapler*) I don't think so.

T: Yes, it is.

M: (*As Mickey attempts to take the stapler from the therapist's hand*) Let me see!

T: No, no, it's empty. (*The therapist demonstrates by pressing the empty stapler. Gesturing with his hands and vocalizing, Mickey then expresses exasperation and exits the playroom once again. Returning momentarily after replenishing staples, both Mickey and the therapist resume the effort to secure the corner of the picture*) You know what?

When particularly difficult issues are being addressed, even in metaphorical terms, therapists are often less inclined to enforce limits within the playroom. It is important, however, to recognize that limits are an integral part of the therapy process and may in fact reassure a child who is venturing into threatening areas. A youngster engaged in addressing difficult problems that imply profound vulnerability, despite protests, typically finds reassurance in the strength of a therapist who decisively sets protective limits.

M: What?

T: (*Referring to the painting*) I think if we get a piece of paper behind it . . .

M: Yeah?

T: And put it like this . . .

M: It'll be even better. (*Using the stapler with a paper placed behind the torn painting, the therapist accomplishes the repair. Mickey resumes painting the bottom of the picture depicting the ground in the outdoor scene he is constructing*)

Nonparticipation in the play of a child is the guideline in this play therapy approach, with exceptions made only when a clear rationale can be articulated. In this instance the joint effort of the therapist and child metaphorically represents and reinforces the notion that together they will attempt to repair the damage that has been done to Mickey.

T: *(Referring to the stapler)* Now it's time to take this back.

M: Can you take it back while I paint?

T: I think I'd like you to come with me.

M: Why?

T: Because I'd like to have you come with me.

Leaving a child alone in a playroom is, of course, imprudent, certainly from the point of view of his potential safety. Further, the therapist here seeks to avoid any basis for Mickey's inferring that he might be abandoned should a requirement of greater urgency arise. It is equally important for a child not to feel overly empowered—for example, by sending the therapist out of the room on an errand—in a way that might spring from misguided indulgence on the part of the therapist in an effort to compensate the child for the hardships that have been disclosed.

Taken here in light of the metaphorical implication of the preceding sequence, the therapist's request that Mickey join him is a further statement of his commitment to the notion that they are in this together.

M: Can you wait for one second?

T: Yes, I can wait one second.

M: *(Abruptly jumping up, and reaching for the stapler in the therapist's hand as he heads to the door)* I'll take it back.

T: No, I'll carry it. *(Upon returning from the mission of bringing the stapler back, Mickey leaps into the room and returns to the painting)* Thank you for walking back with me.

M: *(Referring again to the painting)* I think my sister will like it.

T: This is a picture for Carol.

M: *(With a tone of slight challenge)* I already got one for my mother, don't I?

T: I think you already have one to give to whomever you want to give it to.

M: I'll make one some other day for my Nana.

T: You're going to make one for Nana too.

M: Some other day.

T: There's a lot of people you want to give things to. *(Pause)* It sounds like those people are very important to you, Mickey.

By first dismissing the need to present anything further to his mother and then dismissing the worthiness of another maternal figure for his largesse, Mickey, in effect, affirms the importance of his bond with his sister. Indeed, they were co-victims, and in a tragic way laden with pathos there was a kind of nuptial bond between them, forged when they were required to have sexual involvement with each other for the entertainment of the perpetrators.

Though the therapist's comments are initially addressed to Mickey's apparent impulse of generosity, the remarks that follow suggest that Mickey is instead propelled in his associations by what might be termed *the power of the pathology*, that is, his continuing to subordinate himself in a depression-inducing way to the authority of even those family members who treat him in a punishing way. In one sense, however, it might be said that Mickey is incrementalizing his attempt to embolden himself such that he might denounce the malevolence of family members, beginning first with the "mean" grandmother and leading later to the abusing uncles and the atrocities they committed.

> *M:* Well, sometimes my Nana is mean.
> *T:* Nana can be mean sometimes.
> *M:* Yeah.
> *T:* Hmm. I wonder how Nana is mean sometimes.
> *M:* (*Laughing as if to mimic a witch*) Wah hah ha!
> *T:* Wah hah ha! (*Pause*) What does that mean?
> *M:* Huh?
> *T:* What does that mean?
> *M:* She's meaner than a witch!
> *T:* She's meaner than a witch? Oh, that's very mean. That is . . . very mean!
> *M:* I mean REAL mean!
> *T:* Real mean.
> *M:* She can chew people up!
> *T:* Oh my goodness, this is major meanness! (*Pause*) But still, you want to give her a picture.
> *M:* Yeah. Probably she'll be nice to me.

Despite the misgivings he seemed to suggest in his previous statements, Mickey's perspective in this context implies that he continues to endorse the premise that, to establish affiliation with adults who might ordinarily be assumed to seek such a relationship because of inherent family ties, it is nonetheless necessary to give of oneself in ways that meet the needs of those adults before caring can be assumed to define the relationship. In a poignant way his assumption still recalls the typical egocentric construction of the child incest victim who assumes that exploitation is somehow explainable in terms of his or her own failings.

T: Mmmm.

M: I might see her today.

T: You're looking forward to seeing her today.

M: (*With the tempo of his speech slowing as he continues to work intently on the ground portion of the scene he is painting, Mickey still avoids eye contact*) I might . . . and I might not.

T: It's hard to decide what to do.

M: She might have made an appointment. (*Pause, then referring to the painting*) I think my sister will like that.

T: It looks like something Carol would like. (*Pause*) I wonder when you're going to see Carol.

M: Probably today.

T: Today's a special day.

M: I think . . . today I go to see my mother.

T: You know, somebody besides Diane may drive you home today.

M: Who, the bogeyman?

T: No, not the bogeyman.

M: You?

T: I don't think so . . .

M: (*As Mickey shakes his hand on which he has spilled paint*) Yuk.

T: . . . it depends whether Diane is back or not.

M: (*Referring to the painting*) I made a yellow spring flower. Now I'll make my sister. (*Working carefully to construct a figure next to the flower*) Here's the shoes. That's her shoes. Slip, slip . . . here's the slip part. Here's the other part. I'm going to make water. (*Proceeding to paint rapidly in a swirling motion on the surface of the ground he has drawn*) Somebody was sick in school today.

Although it is highly speculative, Mickey's remarks here suggest a recapitulation of sexual involvement with his sister, indicating perhaps that his earlier associations were indeed of the illicit bond he was required by contrivers of the scene to have with her; after announcing that he will "make his sister," he systematically, but gently, recalls first the covering of her extremities, then her "parts," and with a swirling motion speaks eventually of "making water." His subsequent association was of sick feelings that occurred in the context of required learning.

It is unlikely that the inferred referents of these actions and comments were explicit within his awareness, but Mickey's veiled associations nonetheless support the inference that he is moving slowly but inexorably toward the disclosure that he feels compelled to accomplish.

T: Somebody in school was sick. (*Pause*) I wonder who that was.

M: Natitia!

T: The teacher was sick today.

M: Not the teacher.

T: Not the teacher.

M: Natitia!

T: I wonder what Latitia is.

M: Natitia. (*Making eye contact with the therapist*) Say Na . . .

T: Na . . .

M: Tish . . .

T: Tish . . .

M: A . . .

T: A . . .

M: *Natitia!*

T: Natitia.

M: Now, what did I say?

T: Natitia.

M: (*Making eye contact with the therapist*) It's a girl . . . Natitia!

T: Oh, its a girl named Natitia!

M: (*Adding heavy blue strokes to the sky in the picture he has drawn*) Okay, just making a little rain.

T: Maybe the girl named Natitia is a girl Mickey thinks about.

M: No. She's a girl.

T: She's a girl.

M: I've got another one to think about that's my girlfriend.

T: Mmm. Mickey has a girlfriend.

M: Ah huh. (*Pause*) You don't, do you?

T: You make a guess.

M: (*Continuing to add rain to his painting with heavy, broad blue strokes*) No.

T: No, you don't want to guess. Tell me about your girlfriend.

M: No.

T: You don't want to tell me about your girlfriend. That's okay, you don't have to.

M: I don't like people telling her, otherwise I'll bust their noses.

T: You're afraid somebody will say to her, "Mickey likes you" and you don't want anybody to say that to her.

M: (*Winding up and feigning a roundhouse punch in the air*) Or I'll bust their noses and say pshhsshh!

T: Bam! There goes their nose, right in.

M: (*Punching the air again, Mickey makes more sound effects to convey explosive impact, then walks away from the table toward the door*) I'm all done painting.

T: Well, you know, most artists sign their pictures.

M: Huh?

T: Most artists sign their pictures. They put their name on it so that everybody knows who drew the painting. I wonder if you're going to sign your picture.

M: (*Walking back toward the table*) Yeah, different colors. Where should I sign it?

T: Wherever you want to.

M: (*As Mickey spells out his name, saying each letter as he paints it, the phone rings and he dashes to answer it*) Hello? I don't know. (*Handing the phone to the therapist*) Here. (*While the therapist again instructs the switchboard to direct all calls elsewhere, Mickey returns to painting his name on the picture*) A lot of artists like to scribble out their names and make a mess.

Mickey's reluctance to sign the painting in a clear way may well represent his ambivalence about fully owning at this point the metaphorical and symbolic meaning of his preceding remarks and actions.

T: Is that what artists do?

M: (*Painting over his name*) Yes. (*Looking at the paint containers*) Look, this is a bucket—black and purple.

T: Know what it looks like?

M: No.

T: It looks like a cloud in the sky.

M: It might be.

T: It could be a cloud in the sky. (*Pause*) And inside that cloud it says Mickey. (*Pause*) It looks like a rain cloud. (*Pause*) Sometimes artists draw rain clouds in pictures when they want to show how sad something is. (*Pause . . . then, while Mickey remains still and motionless near the paints*) Then they put a sun in the picture when they want to show how happy it is. (*With the last statement of the therapist, Mickey resumes movement*) And sometimes they put both in to show they feel both ways.

M: Huh? (*Glancing quickly at the therapist*)

T: Sometimes an artist puts a sun in and a cloud in when he wants to show that he's happy sometimes and sad sometimes.

M: (*Painting a dark cloud*) That's the cloud.

As though to affirm that the primary emotion stirred by his associations and recollections is one of sadness, Mickey adopts the symbolism suggested as being that typically employed by artists and thereby imbues his own painting with that meaning.

T: That's the cloud.

M: (*Painting his name again on the picture, this time in the ground portion of the picture*) M-I-C-K-E-Y.

T: Mickey.

M: Mickey. (*Referring to his other picture*) I need the other one . . .

T: (*The therapist drapes the other picture over the upright easel and Mickey again spells his name aloud while painting each letter in the ground of that picture*) Very good. (*The therapist suggests that Mickey might wash his hands while the pictures dry. As Mickey returns from doing so*) Mickey, there are just a few more minutes. (*As Mickey tries to unfasten his painting smock—an old, oversized shirt worn backwards—the therapist asks*) Would you like some help with that?

M: (*Ignoring the therapist's offer of help*) It unbuttons like this?

T: It unbuttons like that. (*Pause*) You're not sure you want me to help you take that off. Taking things off is not something you like to have people help you with.

This intervention, following soon after Mickey's apparent references to sexual exploitation, serves again to reassure him that, even when he speaks of his vulnerability, the therapist will respect his rights and take no freedoms with him.

M: (*Succeeding in taking the smock off*) I already got it.

T: (*Inspecting the picture hung over the easel*) You know what?

M: What?

T: This name is dry. I think it's all set for Mickey to take it with him if he wants.

M: (*As the therapist folds the painting and hands it to Mickey*) I'd better be careful.

T: I guess we're all finished.

M: (*Spreading the painting on the floor*) I want to write a card to my mother.

T: We have a couple more minutes. I guess you can write a card.

M: How do you write *I*?

T: I.

M: How do you write *love*?

T: L

M: L

T: O

M: O

T: V

M: V

T: E

M: E. You. How do you spell *Mommy*?
T: *M-o-m-m-y*.
M: How do you write *from*?
T: *F-r-o-m*. (*Pause*) How do you write *Mickey*?

Though it is again highly speculative and probably unarticulated in Mickey's awareness, his impulse to send a card to his mother declaring his love for her seems to have a poignant and compelling sense of importance for him. Specifically, he may be conveying a need to apologize to his mother because of a fused sense of guilt, affection, and neediness that he experiences as a result of the dedifferentiating impact of his co-victimization with his sister.

M: *M-i-c-k-e-y*. (*Pause*) I want to do another card for my sister's picture.
T: That one's not dry yet. You can do that one next week.
M: All right, I'll do that one next week. (*Donning his coat, Mickey makes reference to his trip to his foster home with the social worker*) And she better not take me home or I'll break her stupid neck. I just thought right now. My social worker.

Mickey's closing remarks seemed at the time a counterphobic gesture toward the world by which he sought to reclaim his self-image as capable and not to be trifled with. It was subsequently learned that he was being sexually accosted in his new foster home by an eleven-year-old girl, another foster child who was herself an abuse victim. His ending words and their tone of anger thus may have reflected his reaction to that circumstance as well and foreshadowed his disclosure of it several sessions later.

VII

Setting the Stage
for Recall of Trauma

The session highlighted here, an example of sequences related to the recall of trauma, took place during the fifth month of treatment. The session began sedately enough with the therapist responding to the child's wish to paint by assisting in setting up the necessary materials. The controlled and measured tempo of the process reflected that of most of the previous sessions. The contained quality of the child's activity up to this point seemed to convey what Spotnitz and colleagues (1976a) have referred to as "the need for emotional insulation" required by children who have been brutalized as a prerequisite to eventual reintegration. Mickey's need in that regard was proportionate to the profound brutality he had experienced. Accordingly, the therapist had assumed a measured pace without forcing issues, following Mickey's lead with regard to the symbolic referents of play sequences. This was often accomplished by his assuming a reflective tack through which potential meaning of interactions was ventured but withdrawn with a comment akin to "Oh, I was wrong about that" when Mickey signaled that he was not ready to consider the issue referenced by the therapist's statement.

The session excerpted below also exemplifies the therapist's attempt to convey respect in physical terms for the child's need for emotional insulation. Specifically, the therapist monitors the actual physical distance between himself and the child trying on a moment-to-moment basis to maintain a balance. By so doing, the therapist avoids arousing the child's anxiety while making available the opportunity for the child to engage the therapist.

The ways in which closeness and distance are varied depends upon a therapist's interpretation of a variety of cues. These include variations in the child's eye contact, gaze aversion, demeanor, or bodily postures; changes in the tempo and content of verbal statements or motoric expressions; discontinuation of initiated statements by the child; changes in the manner of onset, frequency, and duration of silences; and shifts along the dimension of self-contained versus open-ended play.

Once Mickey again felt assured that his need for emotional insulation would be respected by the therapist as it had been previously, he ventured further during this session, presumably sustained by his awareness that he could take refuge in distance if he needed to. Given the increased latitude for reflection and interpretively toned probes made possible by Mickey's more animated expressions, the therapist was more able to refer to areas of potential dissonance or conflict.

Mickey seemed to preserve a sense of comfort in his wanderings beyond previously established defensive boundaries. The therapist was thus able to approximate in his reflections issues that, though not related to the abuse by his uncles, were nevertheless associated for Mickey with the potential for strong anger. As such, they represented a midpoint in his effort to reapproach and resolve the effects of his original trauma.

Mickey had previously told the therapist about a foster sister who was in his view causing trouble in the house. In this session he said that he could "kill her" for breaking his toys. Later in the session the therapist attempted indirectly to reference the original trauma by saying, "I'm wondering if you're angry at other folks too." This "wondering" whether the child has a similar sense about other events or people beyond those alluded to in play, or in its initially accepted interpretive import, is a strategy the therapist uses with some frequency. Through it he is able to invite the child to consider the quality of more broadly defined self–world relationships than those represented concretely in the playroom. At the same time it is possible, by establishing such a metaphor, to preserve the child's option to retreat defensively to the concrete referent of play while preserving the option of later returning to the generalized frame of reference.

For Mickey, the abuse by his uncles, as well as its reverberations, were a prominent and fearfully looming potential referent of his play. "Wondering" by the therapist about possible parallels between the data at hand and the trauma Mickey had suffered was always made in a careful and tentative manner. Such caution was exercised to avoid triggering a retreat by Mickey into a more guarded posture of emotional insulation that might leave him unwilling to see the import of his play in anything but concrete terms.

At the outset of the session excerpted below Mickey and the therapist spoke about having missed three previous appointments (because of transportation problems) and then prepared to use finger paints that had been discussed as an option in an earlier session. During that initial sequence, Mickey signaled his apparent willingness to address troublesome issues by approaching the therapist in a friendly way and maintaining physical proximity and eye contact. In response, the therapist gave Mickey an opening to pursue the agenda that seemed to have some urgency for him. That intervention was phrased in a way that avoided infusing a demand quality into the process and preserved for Mickey the option of regulating his degree of disclosure.

T: I bet a lot of things have happened since I saw you last.

Note that this intervention invites a response based on the child's cognitive construction of his interpersonal environment.

M: My [foster] mother and [foster] sister was back.
T: The last time I saw you, you were having a lot of trouble with your sister.

During this interaction, both the therapist and Mickey were opening the jars of paint he was preparing to use. Note that the comment by the therapist is phrased in terms that approximate the as yet undifferentiated quality of Mickey's concern, "trouble with sister."

M: Humm . . . (*Mickey tries to use his teeth to open the jar*)
T: You were having a lot of trouble. (*The therapist finishes opening his paint jar and reaches over to Mickey's in an attempt to assist him. The child does not acknowledge this effort and continues instead to look down at and struggle alone with the jar, finally opening it*)
T: There you go.
M: Got more? (*Mickey and the therapist each open another jar*)

T: Yes, we do.
M: Opened it before you did.
T: Yes, you did.

Note that the therapist often takes such opportunities to satisfy the child's need for ego enhancement, even when it is reflected in mildly positive self attributions or statements that convey some sense of pride.

M: These four.
T: Now these are the ones I promised you a long time ago but we never got them. Now we have them.

Through this comment the therapist seeks to reaffirm the reliability of himself as a constant object in Mickey's often fluid world. It is noteworthy that during this interaction Mickey busies himself with placing the paint jar caps in a neatly aligned row, reflecting perhaps the importance he attaches to the predictability highlighted by the therapist.

M: What, did you buy them?
T: Uh huh.
M: You bought them?!
T: Uh huh.

Mickey's response of incredulousness and pleasure reflected his cognitive construction of an interpersonal environment that frequently ignored or violated his needs. It also marked, perhaps, the beginning of his revising that view into a more differentiated one that included some aspects of the world as potentially positive and valuing of him.

T: (*Therapist gestures, offering the child some paint from one of the jars*)
M: Okay, some. (*Mickey then picks up a stick as the therapist holds flat the paper on which Mickey then dabs some of the finger paint*)
T: You remember all the trouble you were having with your sister?

Again the therapist invites the child to move through recall in the direction of increased differentiation of a cognitive construction of one aspect of the interpersonal environment and of his transactions with it.

M: Yeah.
T: (*As Mickey continues to paint*) I wonder how that turned out?

Note that the therapist poses the question indirectly to minimize any implied demand for a response arising from the child's sense of the built-in power dimension.

> M: (*Without establishing eye contact*) She's not causing any trouble for me but she's causing a lot for my mother.
> T: No trouble for you but some trouble for your mother . . .

This technique of simply repeating the child's words, with inflection and intonation that suggests those words were the beginning of an as yet unfinished series of statements, is one that serves effectively as a "maintainer" of the child's self-reflection. This technique can be especially helpful when the child, in the therapist's estimation, may be moving toward an increasingly differentiated and integrated perspective with regard to his self–world relationships. When used for that reason it is important that the intervention be without any hint of a judgmental or questioning attitude on the part of the therapist.

> M: (*Continuing to paint and addressing his attention to the yellow orb he has produced*) That's supposed to be for the sun, that big spot is for the sun.
> T: Yeah. If you did decide to use your fingers, it washes off pretty good.

By inviting Mickey to become more tactually involved with the play materials, the therapist is in effect encouraging more intimate engagement in the therapy as well as in the self-reflection and disclosure that it may involve.

> M: What, this stuff?!?

From Mickey's remark it could be speculated that the above-characterized invitation to greater disclosure registered with him. If indeed that were the case, his words here might reflect his wariness about the unarticulated prospect of loosening his grip on the defenses by which he contains the reverberating impact of the "stuff" associated with the sexual abuse he suffered.

> T: Uh huh.
> M: (*Starting to manipulate the globs of paint with his fingers*) Do you think I'm stupid, I had it before.

Proceeding along the lines of the speculative interpretation suggested above, it may be that Mickey's words and actions at this juncture signal his readiness to accept the invitation to engage problem issues more directly.

T: You had it before, huh? I thought you never had it before.

Continuing to develop the unspoken metaphor, the therapist in one sense raises a question about Mickey's past efforts to share in an unguarded and vulnerable way. At the same time the therapist demonstrates his willingness to accept expressions of irritation that the child is making. Mickey's irritation may be viewed as a counterphobic emboldening of himself as he launches into the finger painting and into the increased experiential engagement that it may symbolize for him.

M: I told you . . .
T: (*As Mickey, with a mildly distressed facial expression, wipes his hands with the clean stick and attempts to rub remaining smudges from his fingers onto the paint jar*) You're not so sure you like it on your hands. Would you like me to get you paper towels?

By acknowledging Mickey's nonverbal communication with a non-judgmental and nonprobing reflection, the therapist reaffirms Mickey's prerogative to choose the pace at which he moves into difficult areas and his right to change course from previously stated determinations. The therapist's following with the offer to provide paper towels carries with it the message that assistance will be available when concerns arise so that excessive caution, based on an assumption of irreversibility, is not necessary. Note also that the therapist asks Mickey whether he would like this assistance rather than simply extending it in a well-intentioned manner that nevertheless could be experienced by Mickey as intrusive.

M: Yeah.
T: All right. I can tell you have some mixed feelings about that. (*As the therapist leaves the room to get paper towels*) I'll be right back.

This comment by the therapist represents an interpretively toned reflection of a construction by the child of one aspect of his transactions with the physical environment and potentially, by extrapolation of the symbolism involved, with the interpersonal surroundings.

M: (*While the therapist is out of the room for a moment, Mickey wanders about. As the therapist re-enters the room, Mickey approaches him with his arms raised as though trying to prevent staining himself or things around him with the mess on his hands*)

T: (*As Mickey takes a paper towel from the therapist*) Messiness is something you don't like so much, huh?

Note that this interpretive formulation seeks to encourage increased differentiation of a valuative construction regarding the physical environment. Additionally, through symbolic association that advances development of the assumed parallel between play activities and previous experience, it encourages the child to orient toward eventual recollection of the abuse he suffered and the mess that it recalls for him.

M: No.

T: (*As Mickey kneels at the table, addressing his attention to the paint materials*) You're the kind of guy that likes things nice and neat. Except maybe sometimes you like to have things messy? I don't know.

By framing this generalization of an interpretively toned reflection in terms that acknowledge its being a preference shared by others, the therapist communicates his sense that Mickey's response is not an idiosyncratically distorted one, but is a statement of his individuality. Through the intervention the therapist is able to preserve the basis for the rapport that has developed to this point: the sense of respect he has for Mickey despite Mickey's initial assumption, borne of experience, that adults have little regard for the rights of children. Implied also is respect for his defense as well as for him as a person. By adding the qualifier to his comment, the therapist is further able to convey to Mickey his awareness that not all feelings or preferences are constant or maintained without ambivalence. Rather, it is acknowledged, they may wax and wane with time and circumstance.

M: My sister messes everything up on me!

By extending use of the term *mess* beyond its immediate and concrete reference to the play activity, Mickey implicitly but clearly acknowledges the metaphorical import of the process in which he is engaged.

T: Oh, so she's the messy one, huh? (*As Mickey wipes off the table with a paper towel*) I think you mean your foster sister.

In addition to acknowledging Mickey's complaint about his sister, the therapist encourages increased differentiation in the construction of the interpersonal environment that Mickey has offered by noting that he is actually referring to his foster sister.

M: Yeah, I'm going to kill her some day for destroying all my toys on me.

In this response Mickey reveals his sense that transactions with the interpersonal environment that follow angrily toned constructions may need to be of an extreme if not violent nature. That perspective can be seen as another aspect of the legacy of his having been the object of extreme action by adults who construed his role in their worlds in effectively laden self-serving terms that took no account of his rights.

T: Oh boy!
M: All I have now is one toy car!
T: (As Mickey wipes off his paint stick with a paper towel, using quick, firm strokes) Sounds like you're very angry at her, Mickey.

In this intervention the therapist reflects Mickey's anger in a non-judgmental way that legitimizes the experience and any further discourse about it. In developmental terms the therapist's remark can be considered to reflect the child's construction of his interpersonal environment in a way that seeks further differentiation from the previously global expression of anger inherent in his statement, "I'm going to kill her some day." It should be noted that this interaction also marks the beginning of an effort to encourage Mickey toward modulation and gradual externalization of the contained rage that had sustained his depression and its episodically suicidal manifestation.

M: . . . don't even have anything to play with. She broke my "put-together things."

By further dramatizing his plight, Mickey seems to indicate that he values the therapist's reflection and in effect seems to invite similar remarks.

T: (As Mickey begins to paint again, this time using a tongue depressor to spread the paint) Yeah.
M: I would use them to build things with.

At this point the therapist has the option of responding in a way that would invite development of a metaphor regarding Mickey's challenge of rebuilding his self concept and his self–world relationships in the wake of the abuse he suffered. An intervention along those lines might take the form, for example: "Maybe sometimes it seems really hard to put things together when other people don't let you have what you need."

Another option for the therapist is to respond in a way that preserves the dialogue regarding anger and encourages the child to consider analogous experiences. To do so essentially invites Mickey to focus on anger related to his abuse. The therapist chooses the latter option.

> T: I wonder if you're angry at other folks too.
> M: What do you think?
> T: I don't know, I think maybe you are. But it feels safer talking about your sister.

By his response the therapist encourages further differentiation in Mickey's construction of his interpersonal experience and highlights the likely use of substitutes in his transactions with that aspect of his world. In psychodynamic terms the therapist is identifying the defense of substitution as being one means by which Mickey seeks to shield himself from the full and direct awareness of his rage and from explicit recall of the circumstances that gave rise to it.

> M: (*Starting to use his fingers to spread the paint*) I'm not angry at anyone else.

Despite his earlier allusions of rage toward those who would assault children, Mickey at this juncture chooses to deny that his anger toward his foster sister has any parallel in his feelings about others. Particularly in view of his next response, which shifts the focus away from this issue, it is apparent that Mickey is unwilling to tolerate the full emergence of his anger. His reluctance may also have been rooted in this being the first instance of dialogue regarding such feelings that did not take place as part of his initial testing of the therapist. Some of this he did by proclaiming his abuse in a defiant fashion and by issuing warnings to anyone who might seek again to victimize him.

> M: I need some scissors.
> T: I don't have any scissors. Tell you what, why don't we just fold it under like this. How's that? (*As Mickey draws with a black marker and hums*) You know what?

> M: What?
> T: I think you got bigger since I saw you last.
> M: I grow every day. So, what do you think?
> T: I think you're growing a lot.
> M: Very, very, very big!

Here it is clear that Mickey needs to emphasize his size and strength. His comment might be taken to reflect his sense that he is gaining strength from the attention, acceptance, and other aspects of the therapy process, but it may also represent a counterphobic expression of his reaction to the prospect of addressing the dangers that beset his self–world relationship.

> T: Very, very, very big! Not just big. I wonder what you would do if you were really big right now, what would you do differently?

At the level of technique, the simple repetition of the child's words by the therapist typically serves to convey their acceptance without judgment. A child is then likely to further elaborate the theme of the repeated words, particularly when the therapist's presentation of them is done in an affectively accentuated way. In this context the therapist essentially invites Mickey to reconsider his earlier denial of strong feelings that range beyond his foster sister and to do so with the protection of fantasized strength. In a developmental sense the therapist is calling upon the child to formulate a more differentiated cognitive construction of his circumstances and of the transactions in which he might aspire to engage with the world thus defined.

> M: I'd be a policeman!
> T: Make sure people don't do bad stuff?

The therapist here attempts to explore Mickey's feelings about transactions sanctioned and empowered by authority, particularly in view of his having been brutally exploited in a power relationship. In that connection the therapist also invites any expression that Mickey might venture of his associations to his trauma.

> M: And if they do, I'll give them a good beating!

In effect, Mickey accepts the invitation to work toward restoring confidence in his capacity to be an agent of ongoing experience rather than simply a passive recipient of it. By proposing an action he might take if offended, Mickey continues the process of effectively externalizing his anger rather than depressively containing it.

> T: What kind of bad stuff would you keep them from doing?

The therapist persists in his effort to facilitate Mickey's making reference to the abuse sexual abuse he has suffered. In doing so the therapist is inviting the child to move toward greater differentiation in his cognitive construction of his interpersonal experience.

> M: Robbing people.
> T: Robbing, yeah . . .
> M: Trying to kill other people.
> T: Trying to kill other people.
> M: . . . And breaking things.
> T: . . . And breaking things. How about raping kids?

Mickey had first introduced the word "rape" in an early session when he spoke of the difference between sex and love and when he noted what a superhero would do if anyone tried to rape him. Those words, however, were spoken in a context of his testing the new circumstance of play therapy and of implicitly warning the therapist not to intrude upon his boundaries. In this current interchange reference is made to rape for the first time since an implicit therapy contract has been in force and both child and therapist are aware of the likelihood that its discussion will continue rather than be simply sounded as a warning.

> M: Yeah!
> T: Policemen ought to get after people for doing that too. Especially those people. That's something you know about too.

In this comment the therapist offers a valuative construction of the sociocultural dimensions of interpersonal experience for Mickey's consideration. In doing so he acknowledges Mickey's having already formulated a cognitive construction of the potential for people to violate others. The sequence, somewhat in content but more so in tone, conveys an understanding and compassion that strengthens the rapport.

> M: That's something I wouldn't let them do. If they do, I take my gun and say "bang!" (*Mickey "shoots" with his finger and then resumes drawing*)

Having briefly ventured some reference to the relationship between angry feelings and his victimization, Mickey quickly returned to the safety of painting. The beginning differentiation of trauma-related thought and affect that occurred in this sequence, however, remains compelling. That developmental advance makes possible Mickey's dramatic references to the perpetrators later in the session.

> M: (*Again pointing his finger like a gun, and turning toward the therapist, Mickey says loudly*) Stick 'em up! Bang! Bang! Bang!

In one sense Mickey's reaction might suggest that he is at least ambivalent about the therapist's beginning effort toward challenging his defensive resistance to the recall of thoughts and feelings pertinent to the abuse, particularly those that bring a sense of rage closer to direct awareness.

> T: I wonder if you're just a little tiny bit angry at me for not being here the last couple of weeks.

So that Mickey might achieve the differentiation that accompanies verbal formulation of otherwise unarticulated affective experience, the therapist does not allow Mickey's communication to remain only at a non-verbal level. Instead the therapist states the obvious in the form of an indirect question. The content and nonjudgmental tone of the intervention also carries the message that feelings toward the therapist are both understandable and allowable as direct expressions.

> M: Huh?
> T: I wonder if you're a little bit angry at me for not being here the last couple of weeks.
> M: I'm not angry . . . at least I know my two tables and three tables a little. (*Mickey then walks to the corner of the room, out of the therapist's sight, picks up a toy gun, and steps in a box on the floor*)

Mickey not only denies the anger that has been obvious in his play but goes on to commend himself to the therapist. One implication is that Mickey probably assumes that the anger he senses within himself and that is now being summoned to awareness discredits him and may prompt the therapist to punish or abandon him. Another—and not mutually exclusive—possibility is that Mickey seeks not to own the anger to which allusion is being made but instead projects it onto the therapist such that he feels he may have to defend himself against some form of attack. Hence his movement away from the therapist's sight, his seeking the boundaries provided, at least to the level of his knees, by the box, and his arming himself with the toy gun.

> T: You learned your tables?
> M: Two tables. I don't know them by heart.
> T: Oh, maybe you think it was because of not knowing your tables that we didn't have our meeting. But that wasn't the reason, it was just a mix-up.

Two previous therapy sessions had been missed because of problems with the taxi that was supposed to pick Mickey up. This sequence, however, stresses that therapists must be mindful of children's tendency to explain events in egocentric terms and to engage in what Sullivan (1953, pp. 28–29) has called "parataxic" logic, the inference of causality from the contiguity of two events. In this instance, and almost always in play therapy, therapists need to make explicit any such notion a child might have come to through such reasoning. Often the events that the child construes as causal may not even be known to the therapist. It is possible, for example, that Mickey may have failed a test at school and concluded that his missing the play therapy session that afternoon was the consequence of his not knowing his tables.

> M: (*Mickey steps out of the box and walks toward the window while pointing the toy gun into his mouth*) I knew that, I knew that even before you called.

By pointing the gun into his mouth, Mickey may be symbolically attempting to continue the process of containing feelings of rage in a very basic, oral, incorporative way. At the same time his gesture also reflects the self-destructive impulse that had previously led him to suicidal behavior.

> T: (*As Mickey goes to a chair and stands on it to look out the window*) I see, even before I called.
> M: I knew it got mixed up. (*Mickey sits on the corner of the widow sill and the therapist stands near the window's other corner about eight feet away*) My mother gave me two and three tables. I knew them that first day she gave them to me.

Despite Mickey's having previously dismissed the notion that his failure to learn his tables may have been construed as leading to an unwelcome consequence, his musings here again raise the question of whether he considers that to some degree such might be the case. The unwelcome consequence in this context would be the loss of his biological mother.

> T: You are one smart guy! How did you learn them so fast?
> M: How did I learn them so fast? I knew them! I learned them a long time ago.
> T: Oh, I didn't know that. You're a very smart fellow.
> M: Even before I came here I knew them.

Self-aggrandizing remarks were frequently a part of Mickey's presentation. As in this instance both their tone and their timing suggested they were defensive in nature with their assertion perhaps serving as a compensation against the fear that he might be seen as having failed by allowing the abuse to occur. Mickey's assumption of responsibility in this regard reflected his accustomed role as the parentified protector of his siblings.

> T: Sometimes even when a guy's a really smart fellow, even then he still can't figure out the reason why people do certain things to him. Even when you're smart, sometimes you can't figure that out. Because people are very hard to figure out sometimes.

By this intervention the therapist extends to Mickey the recognition sought by the child. The therapist structures his remarks in a way that allows for subsequent discussion of the abuse without calling Mickey's capabilities into question. In effect the therapist here proposes a cognitive construction of the interpersonal environment that, in its increased differentiation, invites refocus toward the abuse experience without diminishing Mickey's self-esteem.

> M: Do you think I could throw this way, way, way over there near the door? (*As Mickey, still sitting on the window sill, asks the question, he motions with a toy gun*)
> T: I don't think that's a good idea because that will break. That's plastic. If you want something to throw, I'll give you something else. (*The therapist walks across the room, picks up a stuffed dog, and returns to the area of the window sill, handing the dog to Mickey*)

From the point of view of technique, this sequence illustrates the principle that holds irreversible play—including the breaking of objects that cannot be restored—to be typically counterproductive. Instead a child needs to be immediately provided an alternative instrumentality by which to accomplish the intended transaction. The interpretive import of Mickey's wish to throw the toy gun may well be a reflection of his ambivalence regarding aggressive impulses elicited by oblique reference to his abuse. Specifically, his stated intent to throw the gun "way, way, way over there" implies a wish to distance himself from the of aggressive action, but the means by which he proposes to accomplish that distancing—vigorous throwing—in itself requires at least assertive if not aggressive action. In effect he attempts to rid himself of anger in an angry way.

Climbing down from the window sill—which actually was a wide benchlike area about four feet from the floor—Mickey stated that he had to go to the rest room. It is of note that his trips to the rest room were often precipitously announced following sequences that were obviously anxiety provoking for him. No challenge was made by the therapist of Mickey's use of this strategy for modulating anxiety.

Upon returning to the playroom Mickey began kicking the stuffed dog and made growling noises.

T: You know what he could stand for? Anybody you want it to stand for.
M: (*Continuing to kick the stuffed dog around the room*) Boogie!
T: It could stand for Uncle Buddy . . . is that what you said?
M: No. Boogies.
T: Oh, Boogies. I thought you said "Buddy."
M: No! I'm going to the bathroom. See you later.

Mickey's quick return to the rest room probably reflects his wish once again to escape anxiety. At this juncture he seems discomforted by recognition of an inner compulsion to follow the path being encouraged by the therapist. In effect Mickey seems wary of, yet drawn toward, developing a metaphor by which feelings related to the abuse and its perpetrators might emerge.

M: (*Returning from the rest room, Mickey picks up the stuffed dog and again perches himself on the window sill. As the therapist walks toward the window sill, Mickey gestures as if he is throwing the dog*) Do you think this will make it all the way over there?
T: I betcha it will.
M: (*Throws the dog across the room*)
T: You're a pretty strong guy. (*Looking at where the dog landed*) Almost . . . pretty close.

M: (*Walking across the room and retrieving the stuffed dog with the therapist following*) That's where I meant for it to go.

Here Mickey again seems to steel himself against the fear of perceived ineptitude that may threaten him as he moves closer to feelings associated with recollection of abuse. By affirming his capabilities, Mickey may also be acting out transference issues having to do with his victimization. Specifically, he may fear that unless he issues a warning that he is not to be underestimated, the therapist, like other adult men he has known, may exploit the vulnerability inherent in the therapeutic process by violating his boundaries.

T: I thought for sure when you were playing with that before you said it could stand for Uncle Buddy.
M: I said *Boogies*.
T: You said "Boogies"; I got mixed up.

Mickey has begun to participate in the metaphor proposed by the therapist as a beginning reference to the perpetrators. To do so, however, he gives himself the safety of distance by renaming them, thus excluding the full symbolic presence of their threatening identities.

M: (*Returning to the window sill*) Okay, you stay there and see if you can catch it.
T: (*Referring to the stuffed animal*) Who does it stand for first? You decide this time who it stands for.
M: Each time it stands for Buddy and Freddy.
T: For Buddy and Freddy. (*Pausing and shifting toward a wondering aloud tone*) What should we do if it stands for Buddy and Freddy?
M: Say *Dookie* if it stands for Bud and *Hi* if it stands for Freddy.
T: Dookie . . . what does that mean?
M: (*Throwing the stuffed animal to the therapist*) I don't know.
T: So if it stands for Buddy I say *Dookie* and if it stands for Freddy I say *Hi*?
M: No, change Freddy. Turn it to *Ku-ku head*.
T: Ku-ku head?

Here Mickey not only renames the perpetrators, but he also uses demeaning terms that denude them of their potential for harming him by implying impotence. Moreover, he chooses words that approximate children's slang for excrement thereby beginning to express his anger toward them.

When appropriate affect is joined to conflict-laden cognitions, developmental advance often occurs. In this instance Mickey gives evidence of that by differentiating one perpetrator from another rather than continuing to make attributions regarding the potential for abuse to all adult men.

> M: (*Therapist and child continue to throw the stuffed animal back and forth, with Mickey becoming more vigorous and punishing toward the displacement object as the process continues*) Okay, come on!
> T: So I have to guess which one it stands for?
> M: (*Winding up to swing at the stuffed animal tossed to him by the therapist*) Dookie!
> T: Stands for Uncle Buddy! (*Tossing the stuffed animal again to Mickey*) Let's see who it stands for this time.

With regard to technique, this sequence is an example of a therapist enabling play that the child could not otherwise accomplish; it is more facilitative than participatory.

> M: You're going to get it, Ku-ku head!
> T: Oop, stands for Uncle Freddy. Was I right that time?
> M: Yeah.
> T: It looks a little like him . . . or maybe it doesn't.

The therapist introduces this light note to remind Mickey that play and playfulness remain available vehicles of expression even as he draws closer to the rage within. This is a kind of preventive effort geared toward offsetting the child's potential to feel frightened and overwhelmed by his own anger.

> M: (*Giggling*) Yeah. (*Again throwing the stuffed animal to the therapist and playfully challenging him to identify it*) Ku-ku head!
> T: It's Uncle Freddy again!
> M: (*Grasping the stuffed animal that the therapist has tossed back to him*) Dookie!
> T: Oop, stands for Uncle Buddy! (*Pause*) I think it was no fun having Uncle Buddy and Uncle Freddy pawing at you like that.

Here the therapist invites the child to step away from the safety of the motorically animated metaphor for a moment of direct recollection of the event and the affect associated with it.

> M: (*Ignoring the therapist's last comment and continuing the activity that preceded it*) Let's throw and play catch.

At this juncture, Mickey's first reaction is one of defensive denial and avoidance as he seeks to remain within the play that refers to his abuse only indirectly.

> T: Oh, okay. You like to play catch. I wonder if Mickey thinks of Uncle Buddy and Uncle Freddy these days?

Having judged the child's capacity to tolerate persistent reference of a literal sort to the perpetrators, the therapist continues to maintain that effort. By the sequence of his remarks the therapist also indicates that Mickey can continue the tension-reducing playful activity while such dialogue unfolds.

> M: No.
> T: You don't think of them. (*Shifting to a "wondering aloud" tone after a brief pause*) I wonder if Mickey dreams about them or about what they did. . . .

In his response the therapist accepts Mickey's denial but follows with a further "wondering" about dreams to expand the scope of inquiry. The sequence in effect reframes Mickey's denial to one having to do only with volitional thought.

With regard to therapeutic technique, the therapist avoids becoming caught in a trap of his own making; therapists often present either/or choices in the form of reflective interventions. When the response defensively denies the premise from which the therapist speaks, little forward progress within that theme is possible. By extending the range of possible experiential dimensions that the client might affirm, therapeutic advance remains possible.

In this instance reference to the possibility of dreams legitimizes consideration of those aspects of experience and, by implication, other dimensions of awareness that may be fragmentary, diffuse, or less than fully articulated.

> M: No. (*Gesturing toward the stuffed animal*) Pass it to me.
> T: (*Again adopting a "thinking aloud" tone*) I wonder if Mickey has dreams about what Uncle Buddy and Uncle Freddy did . . . (*After a pause*) Looks like Mickey doesn't want to tell me. That probably means he has the dreams.

In an earlier session the therapist had laid the foundation for the strategy employed above. In a parallel sequence the therapist had wondered aloud about an aspect of Mickey's construction of his world. Receiving no response, he added that "I must be right about that because I know that Mickey is the kind of guy that would tell someone if they were wrong when they said something about him. Mickey's not saying anything so it must be that I was right."

Several similar sequences followed that initial interpretation of silence as implying affirmation and allowing its inference. In some of them Mickey negated the musing aloud; in others he acknowledged the accuracy of the therapist's inferring affirmation by his silence. That intermittently reinforced precedent enabled the therapist to continue reflective sequences without requiring Mickey to agree at every juncture. The therapist could then introduce alternative constructions without Mickey having to indicate explicitly that he had not thought in those terms previously.

> M: (*Laughing*) I play funny.
> T: I wonder if the dreams happen a lot . . .
> M: (*Again laughing and throwing the stuffed animal*) I try to get it back to you.
> T: I wonder if they happen every day or just sometimes.
> M: I never dream about them.
> T: Oh, you don't? I thought you dreamed about what they did.
> M: No.
> T: Oh, I was wrong about that. I guess because they're in jail now you don't have to worry about them anymore.

In this intervention the therapist accepts Mickey's denial. Again, however, the therapist leaves an opening for Mickey to acknowledge thoughts or dreams about the abuse. In this instance he does so by expanding the temporal scope beyond that implied by the sequence, that is, *now* you don't have to worry—implying that perhaps he did previously or that he may once again in the future.

In developmental terms this intervention by the therapist also invites Mickey to move toward a more differentiated perspective with regard to his own affect in relation to interpersonal and physical aspects of the environment.

> M: Buddy's not in prison.
> T: He's not in prison? I thought he was in prison.
> M: He's living with O'Malley.
> T: Who's O'Malley?
> M: The guy he's staying with.

> *T:* He's staying with another guy? I thought Buddy went to prison too. How come he didn't go to prison?

Note that at this point the therapist in fact was under the impression that both perpetrators were still imprisoned. It was later learned that Buddy had been furloughed to the custody of a friend because, being intellectually limited, he was seen as a somewhat unwitting accomplice of his more capable brother. Mickey's information about Buddy's release was therefore accurate. As the following sequence indicates, however, the expla...ation that Mickey put to this development reflected his continuing sense of Buddy's culpability and perhaps of the danger he might still pose.

> *M:* He's lying.
> *T:* He lied. What did he say?
> *M:* I don't know, but he said a lie.
> *T:* (*Continuing to toss the stuffed animal back and forth to Mickey*) Hmm . . . I wonder who was the worse guy when they were doing that nasty stuff. . . .

By this intervention the therapist seeks to encourage Mickey toward increased differentiation in his recollection of the abuse experience by invoking a kind of valuative dimension that may be tied closely to strong and troublesome constructions. The former, however, allows recourse to a more intellectually oriented perspective should those feelings threaten to overwhelm Mickey as he ventures to recall his abuse.

Note also that these direct references introduced on the heels of a somewhat objective exchange of facts implies by their sequence a kind of safety for Mickey to further share his personal experience of the abuse. Mickey presented facts that he owned, which bestowed on him a sense of mastery that the therapist then sought to extend to reflection upon the new and more subjectively threatening material.

> *M:* Both of them.
> *T:* They were both bad.

VIII

Overcoming Remaining Defenses: Full Disclosure

Although the dialogue that follows is a continuation of the same session recounted in the previous chapter, the sequence assumes a qualitatively different tone. Specifically, Mickey moved toward more explicit disclosure of his abuse and of its emotional sequelae by more energetically and literally enacting a motoric metaphor while engaging in ego-enhancing play.

During the second half of this session, the therapist's persistence finally led to Mickey's fully revealing even painful details of his and his sister's abuse. The story he shares is one of fear, desperation, pathos, and courage. Mickey's sharing of his experience in terms that represent for him a statement of vulnerability occurred only after several months in which the therapist, through persistent questioning that nevertheless respected Mickey's needs and sensitivities, worked to create a safe environment defined by trust.

In developmental terms Mickey's more literal account of his abuse became the means by which he achieved greater differentiation with progression from the more global concern about "people doing bad stuff to other people" to direct commentary upon the abuse and the abusers. This advance was achieved through a motoric metaphor in which thrown play objects represented the abusing uncles whose actions were then described in literal terms.

The sequence that follows was characterized also by an increased effort on the part of the therapist to empower Mickey by providing him with the basis for enhanced self-esteem. As Mickey engaged in play that required some level of skill, for example, the therapist offered a commentary of praise and admiration, both for the effort Mickey made and for the successes he realized. Positive remarks about the intelligence and strength evident in his play seemed to encourage Mickey to venture full disclosure and move toward the developmental advance that it allowed.

Viewed from another perspective this sequence can be considered an example of the healing potential of memories reframed in their meaning by the impact of treatment. Informed by alternative constructions of the here-and-now symbolic referents of larger self-world interactions past and present, such memories take on new dimensions and point toward new perspectives. The play that unfolds, and the reflections upon it, enable Mickey to view himself less as a victim and more as a capable, albeit vanquished, competitor who made valiant attempts to do battle with the perpetrators to protect his sister and himself.

> T: (*Throwing the stuffed animal back and forth with Mickey*) Who does this stand for?
> M: Anyone.
> T: You decide.
> M: No one. We're just playing catch.
> T: Oh, okay.
> M: (*Pointing to the other side of the room*) If I get one out I go back there.
> T: Close! What a shot! You have a good aim. You're a very strong fellow. I wonder what makes you so strong?
> M: That's because I do exercises.
> T: That's it!
> M: Yeah.
> T: I see. (*Pause*) I wonder if you tried to be strong when Uncle Freddy and Uncle Buddy came around?

Here the therapist implicitly invites Mickey to affirm that his strength has remained intact despite the abuse he suffered. The therapist implies that Mickey's recalling his abuse would not detract from the strength inherent in his persona. As is evident in his subsequent remarks, Mickey quickly endorses that perspective by describing his abuse in angry, defiant tones rather than self-consciously or timidly.

M: (*Wrapping his hands and arms around his own neck*) Yeah, they had me like this! Aaaghhh!

T: (*Elevating his tone and tempo to acknowledge the gravity and alarm inherent in the scene that Mickey had dramatized*) They had you like that?! And what did you do?!

M: Tried to punch them but my hands were blocked.

T: Punched them?!

Note that at this point the therapist spoke in an affect-laden tone to convey both outrage at the perpetrators and respect for Mickey as a survivor of atrocity so great that it seems to startle even the adult to whom he has begun to reveal it. The affect experienced by the therapist is dramatized but not contrived. Rather, it reflects the therapist's willingness to engage even the most affectively painful memories of the child with empathy and genuine caring.

From a psychoanalytic perspective Mickey could be said to have elicited an objective countertransference on the part of the therapist, thus conveying his need for intimate emotional understanding of the terror and rage associated with the abuse.

As noted previously, the response of compassion is repeatedly engendered in a treatment context by children who have been abuse victims. Its occurrence reaffirms the importance that the therapist maintain a clear sense of the treatment plan rather than allow the process to deteriorate to one of well-intended, but minimally effective, supportive interventions, dictated in their timing and content more by the therapist's need than by the child's.

M: I tried to bite them and they moved their heads down.

T: They moved their heads down so you couldn't bite them!

M: Yeah.

T: Oh, my goodness! Was that when you were trying to help Carol or when you were trying to help yourself?

In this intervention, and in the sequence that follows, the therapist is quite active in presenting both questions and comments. By them, he seeks to help the child achieve increased differentiation of the affective and valuative aspects of the experience associated with the now explicitly detailed abuse and to move toward their more developmentally advanced integration.

M: When I was trying to help both of us.
T: Help both of you!? I see.
M: They were doing it at the same time! Freddy would. . . . Buddy was on
    me and Freddy was on my sister.
T: At the same time!?
M: Yeah.
T: . . . and you were both crying and yelling . . .
M: I wasn't crying. I was trying to do the best I can. . . . My Uncle Freddy, he
    stuck it right in my sister. She was crying.

By his response Mickey reminds the therapist of the importance to
him that the abuse not be construed as any indication of weakness, but
rather as a reflection of his strong and valiant effort. In doing so Mickey
reaffirms the importance to him of that construction, which had been suggested previously by the therapist.

T: He stuck it right into your sister and you tried to help her!

Here the therapist takes his cue from Mickey and reaffirms his awareness of the child's strong effort in the face of overwhelming physical
strength. Note also that the therapist respects Mickey's need to stay focused
for the moment on his sister's abuse rather than on his own.

M: Yeah, my sister was crying. I tried to pull him. Then I got loose and I pulled
    him off me. I had to put my head over like I was getting ready to duck.
    He let go of me and I bit him. He went to put water on his hand and
    then I bit my Uncle Freddy.
T: Oh, that was Buddy you bit first, then you bit Freddy.

Because Mickey here presents a very dramatically detailed account,
the therapist does not continue his tack—evident in the immediately preceding sequence—of escalating the intensity of tone through his remarks.
Instead he turns to a cognitive construction geared toward clarifying factual dimensions of the scene depicted. This downshift of intensity seeks to
keep Mickey's anxiety level within bounds that allow forward movement
to continue rather than engendering overwhelming feelings that could trigger retreat into a more defensive posture.

M: Yeah, to get him off my sister.
T: Did he get off?

M: Yeah.
T: Then he got mad at you.
M: Yeah.

In this response Mickey appears to signal his readiness to focus on his own sexual violation.

T: Then he did some bad stuff to you.
M: Yeah. I almost karate-kicked him in the face!
T: Oh, my goodness! Oh, my goodness! That must have felt awfully scary! What a scary time that was!

In this response the therapist obviously seeks to convey his awareness of the enormity of the trauma Mickey has suffered. Perhaps this expression could also be considered an effort to put into words the cry of panic that Mickey may have felt at the moment he realized in horror that his innocence, his "goodness," was about to be assaulted.

T: I wonder if you and your sister talk about that when you see her.
M: Nah ah.
T: You don't talk about that . . . that's too scary to talk about.

By this comment the therapist seeks to acknowledge the fear that has blocked the child's communication with others close to him regarding his abuse. Implied also is a recognition of the sense of isolation and loneliness Mickey has likely felt in his victimization and the therapist's willingness to address that dimension of experience. Acceptance and legitimization of this most important affect, fear, further fosters trust and understanding in the therapeutic relationship.

M: (*While tossing the stuffed animal about, Mickey nearly knocks a pile of papers off the top of a file cabinet in the corner of the playroom and speaks about this unanticipated event in a surprised tone*) Wow! I almost knocked that down!
T: Yeah, we have to be careful. You don't want to do that.
M: I won't do it again.

In a concrete sense Mickey here seems concerned that he came close to doing damage to the playroom and may suffer some consequence. In a metaphorical sense, however, Mickey's words may be taken as referring to the avoidance noted moments before. He may be presenting an unarticulated recognition that he almost knocked down connections with others because of his fear that discussion of the abuse might prompt overwhelming consequences. The therapist's response addresses the metaphorical implication while remaining consistent with the sequence of literal meaning. The therapist acknowledges and affirms Mickey's call for caution at the behavioral level, but also conveys an admonition to avoid self-imposed isolation born of fear.

> *T:* (*Returning to the interrupted discussion of Mickey's abuse*) Did that happen a lot or just one time?
> *M:* (*Continuing to toss the stuffed animal*) A lot of times.
> *T:* A lot of times! Even when you were little, little babies . . . ?
> *M:* Not babies . . . around 5 or 4.

The following sequence includes a number of questions that maintain structure for Mickey as he continues the process of disclosure. Introducing event-defining questions at this point serves to reassure him in the midst of that threatening process by casting him as an expert who remains in control and worthy of respect by virtue of his being knowledgeable about the facts of the situation. In the process Mickey is also moving toward increased differentiation and integration of the experience, diminishing its global threat and achieving the increased mastery that allows substantive disclosure to continue.

> *T:* Five or 4?
> *M:* . . . and 6.
> *T:* How come no one else also knew about it?
> *M:* (*Tying his shoes*) I told them. (*Responding to the therapist's gesture to toss the ball to Mickey*) Not yet, when I'm done tying my shoe we'll start.
> *T:* I wonder how come your father and mother didn't know about it when it was happening?
> *M:* I told them . . . I told them!
> *T:* When it was happening did you tell them?

Here the therapist invites Mickey to formulate a cognitive construction of a sociocultural experience by defining his interaction with the family in temporal terms.

> *M:* Nope, I told them a couple of days after.
> *T:* I see. (*Pause*) I wonder what they said?

M: They said if they done it again, tell them.
T: I see.

It may be that the therapist's use of a visual reference ("I see") to convey understanding of the picture Mickey has drawn verbally implies a sense of being there with him in an empathic way that preserves, despite the immediacy of the abuse, a nonjudgmental but respectful regard for Mickey. In any case this was the goal of the therapist at this juncture.

M: (*Referring ostensibly to the ongoing back-and-forth tossing of the ball*) I have only one chance . . . you have four chances.
T: I wonder if Mark and Phil [Mickey's cousins who were also abused] were there with you at the same time?
M: Yeah, it happened to them too.
T: Same time or different time?
M: Same time as doing it to us.
T: Same room and everything?

By inviting Mickey to re-create the moment in potentially painful detail, the therapist seeks to enhance the immediacy of the experience such that its affective impact might emerge as well. An effort is made to proceed, however, without violating Mickey's sense of mastery or the respect he feels he is receiving from the therapist.

M: (*Again referring to the tossing of the ball*) I'll go over there. Give me the ball. (*Pause*) We'll call it a ball now.
T: I thought we were going to call it Uncle Buddy and Uncle Freddy, but I guess we're not.

Here the therapist phrases his intervention as an instance of thinking out loud such that the demand component with regard to Mickey's responding is minimized—he can comment or not, as he chooses, without feeling he has violated an expectation. In effect the therapist acknowledges that Mickey may need a respite after a flurry of disclosure statements. The therapist's comment legitimizes engaging in motoric interaction qua play while reminding Mickey that he can return to the immediacy of the metaphorical dimension when he chooses to do so.

M: (*Dropping the ball*) First time didn't catch it! Oh boy, we're starting up a game losing!
T: Looks that way. (*Pause*) Did you hear that noise?

M: Yeah. Me kicking. Me. I was kicking.

T: I don't think it was you.

M: If someone gets two outs, we take a rest for a while.

T: (*As the tossing of the ball continues*) I wonder what else Uncle Buddy and Uncle Freddy made you do?

Having participated with Mickey in a time-out from direct reference to the abuse, the therapist here invites a return to it.

M: They made me touch my sister.

T: They did?

M: Yeah.

T: The same day or a different day?

Again the therapist seeks to encourage the emergence of Mickey's recollection of a painful self–world transaction in differentiated terms that allow feelings of mastery.

M: Same day. Came in and . . . (*Suddenly jumping and catching the ball*) Oh, oh . . . all right!

T: That sounds like an awful, awful time. (*Pause*) But maybe it wasn't so awful sometimes. I don't know.

Recall that often for a child the most difficult part of disclosing abuse is acknowledging that some pleasurable feelings may have occurred. Here the therapist legitimizes that aspect of the experiential dimension of abuse and implicitly invites Mickey to speak about it or simply to affirm the notion by silence. Whether or not a child decides to focus explicitly on that issue, it is important for the therapist to convey a nonjudgmental awareness that some pleasure may have occurred in order to offset the potential for the development in the child of an insidious and unspoken guilt.

M: Do you think I touched my sister!?

Mickey clearly took from the therapist's comment the implication that pleasure may have been part of the experience. His affect-laden response in turn foreshadowed a short-lived return to denial regarding the sexual involvement with his sister that he had disclosed moments earlier.

T: I don't know.
M: (*Spelling out his response*) N-O! I never . . .
T: I thought you told me you did.

It should be noted that the therapist's tone here was not one that conveyed "gotcha," but instead was spoken in a matter-of-fact way to convey to Mickey that he could retreat for a time from the intensity that his disclosure had invited if wanted to.

M: (*Referring to the ball tossing*) Over there.
T: They said if you didn't they were going to hit you? Is that what they said?
M: Yeah.
T: Oh. ·
M: When they were walking out the door and said they were going to hit me, I said "tough luck!" and I kicked them in the behind. They go, "What the heck was that?"
T: Is that what they said?
M: Then I bit them a second time. See how they like it!
T: Then they came back and did it again.

Knowing that there had been ongoing abuse, the therapist here encourages Mickey to continue his disclosure.

M: Oh God! (*Ostensibly referring to the tossing of the ball*) I go back over there. (*Mickey switches to the other side of the room where he resumes throwing the ball*)

Mickey's words here have concrete reference to the ball tossing, but might also reflect his recognition that, by recalling with poignancy the events of his abuse, he is, in a sense, re-living it. Another implication of his remark might be one of self blame; i.e., lamenting his failure to avoid the place and circumstance where his victimization could, and did, recur.

T: I wonder if they came back and did it again?
M: What do you think? (*Spelling his response*) Y-E-S!
T: (*Spelling*) Y-E-S!
M: What does that stand for?
T: It stands for *yes*. (*Pause*) We only have about five minutes left. What do you think, should we keep doing this or should we do something else in our last five minutes?

Mickey emphasizes the point by asking that it be defined by the therapist. By doing so in an assertive way, he affirms his strength while continuing his disclosure. At the same time he affords himself a margin of distance as he recounts his repeated humiliation. Because the effective result is facilitative, the therapist cooperates in this process.

This intervention also illustrates the practice of announcing the end of the session five minutes before it occurs. As noted previously, children seldom keep track of the hour as well as adults. This preannouncement often triggers a flurry of communication, in words or in play, by which the child may parallel the frequently evident pattern of adults who abruptly share pivotal concerns that they have been saving until the end. Further, the announcement precludes parataxic distortion that might subsequently rigidify defenses; the child is discouraged from assuming that, because of the contiguity of events, something he or she said or did led to the session's end. By preannouncing the conclusion the therapist helps the child recognize, through experience, that the session ends at a predetermined time independent of what transpires in the process.

For children who have been the object of violence, this practice has further relevance. Specifically, the child who has suffered trauma may find that sudden shifts in transactional contexts recall the onset of their traumatic ordeal. Accordingly, it is helpful to introduce change gradually.

A further implication of the exchange here involves providing Mickey with the option of respite from the difficult process of disclosure before the end of the session. Thus the therapist acknowledges that Mickey may want to wind down before the session ends and legitimizes that option should Mickey choose it.

> M: Let's play ball.
> T: You want to throw this back and forth?
> M: (*Referring to the toy closet in the playroom*) Find something else in there.
> T: You must have felt that there was nobody around that could help you. I guess that was an awful feeling. (*Pause*) Was that an awful feeling? (*Pause*) Or was it not so bad?
> M: It was an awful feeling.
> T: It was an awful feeling.

Unless overdone, repeating the child's words with affect that mirrors and/or sharpens the accompanying feeling has powerful impact. The synchronous understanding conveyed typically leads to a strengthening of the therapist–client alliance and often to further elaboration of the child's experience.

In developmental terms the response affirms that Mickey offered further differentiation of experience through construction of what was a painful interpersonal transaction. That trauma may otherwise have continued to be so global and diffuse in its impact as to sustain regression in all spheres.

In fact, pathological regression had previously led Mickey to suicidal behavior that continued to be in evidence until developmental advance allowed him to consider alternate constructions of the experience. He eventually came to impose meaning upon the abuse that relieved him of feelings of culpability and diminished worth.

> M: (*Referring to the continuing process of throwing the Nerf ball back and forth*) See how I catch it good!
> T: I guess you sure do! (*Pause*) You know, it's good that we're here now because we can make sure that nothing ever happens to you again. (*Pause*) And that's a pretty good feeling.

Mickey here seems to make an effort to ground himself in conflict-free aspects of the present, enthusiastically taking pride in his prowess and seeking acknowledgment of his accomplishments. In doing so he moves from a focus on painful recollections to the reassurance of the here-and-now relationship with the therapist.

The therapist takes Mickey's shift of temporal focus as an indication of the importance that recourse to the alliance, and the refuge it provides, be fully available to the child as he attempts to differentiate the fearsome components of his abuse. In his response the therapist first provides Mickey with the adulation he seeks, then reminds him that the therapeutic alliance is indeed a safe place.

By reaffirming that it feels good to have available the safety of the here-and-now relationship, the therapist also encourages Mickey's developmental advance. With this differentiated focus the expression of trust and sharing becomes once again an available instrumentality for transacting with the interpersonal environment.

> M: (*Changing position in the playroom to improve his performance*) Give me a break, let me get over here. (*Throwing the ball*) Catch! Score! (*Again changing position*) I go over here.

As occurred frequently throughout treatment, Mickey's pace and tempo quickens markedly as the end of the hour approaches. At those times he seemed to be trying to get in as much activity as possible before the session ended.

That tendency, frequent among children, can sometimes represent a kind of denial: the child who has one more activity to look forward to, no matter how brief it may be, has momentarily obviated the need to accept the end of his or her special time. For the abused child in particular there is reluctance to give up the insulation that the hour provides from a world that has been very hurtful. Hence a frantic, almost desperate rapidity may emerge, followed, when the end can no longer be forestalled, by an equally sudden shift toward a ponderously slow pace and reticent manner.

> T: (*Preparing to toss the ball*) Ready?
> M: I'm ready anytime. (*Hitting the ball*) Okay, score one! (*Pause*) I only get five chances.
> T: You know what? We're running out of time.
> M: Okay.
> T: Pretty soon . . . a little bit more. (*Pause*) I would like it if you came here next week.

Here the therapist seeks to dispel any possible doubt Mickey might harbor about having gone too far in his disclosures and potentially having fallen into the therapist's disfavor. The therapist's comment also addresses the fact that Mickey's life experiences since the discovery of his abuse have been highly unpredictable. Specifically, he was first taken from his parents and then abruptly moved from one foster home placement to the next. Consequently, a continuing effort is made throughout treatment to help Mickey experience the sessions as a predictable anchor point in his self–world transactions rather than as a reiteration of the disruption and loss he experienced when he first disclosed the abuse.

> M: Huh?
> T: Will you come see me next week?
> M: Yeah.
> T: (*As Mickey tosses the ball*) Oh, that's a great throw.
> M: (*Swatting the ball successfully*) Wow!
> T: I think we're setting up the world championship of throwing this back and forth. I think we probably have the championship of the whole world of throwing this back and forth. What do you think?

M: Yeah!

T: You could be the champion!

M: If I get another one out I won't be the champion!

At a metaphorical level Mickey's words might be taken to indicate that he does indeed harbor misgivings about the wisdom of further disclosure, particularly with regard to the jeopardy it may invite in terms of his being seen as a champion worthy of respect and admiration.

> T: Sure you will be! Because nobody else does this. So you're the champion of the whole world when it comes to throwing this back and forth.

This emphatically expressed intervention seeks to accomplish several objectives. For one, it strongly reaffirms the therapist's high regard for Mickey. Second, it carries the message that the tossing back and forth and, more to the point, the disclosure and trust that it symbolizes should represent a source of pride and accomplishment for Mickey rather than shame and failure. The comment serves a kind of ego-binding purpose, encouraging Mickey to reconstitute in the wake of anxiety-provoking recollections by coalescing around positive self-attributions as he prepares to leave the safety of the therapeutic context.

> M: (*Throwing the ball up and catching it himself*) I have one of these things at home.

Here Mickey invokes his own transitional object reference. It should be noted, however, that children often ask to take an object home with them after a play therapy session. Typically, the effort to take comfort in a transitional object, and to gain the reassurance that a return to the playroom will happen, becomes very obvious by the child's promise to bring it back next time.

In the play therapy approach outlined here, the practice of lending is discouraged because children often lose or break objects and as a result may feel guilty and fearful of rejection. Moreover, it is not realistic to allow a playroom to be depleted of supplies by providing each child seen with a transitional object. Should another child subsequently search in vain for a favorite toy that has been loaned to some other youngster, problematic transference and countertransference reactions are likely to occur in the treatment of both children.

A better choice for providing assistance in managing transition or gaining reassurance that sessions will continue is for the therapist to entrust the child with some responsibility to be carried out during the next session. A therapist might, for example, ask a child to "please be sure to remind me next week," mentioning perhaps where some toy or supply is stored. The reminder should be incidental to the treatment rather than, for example, an admonition to "remind me to ask you about. . .".

T: You do?
M: (*Walking toward his coat and starting to put it on*) Time to go home.
T: Pretty soon.
M: How come pretty soon?
T: Well, actually two more minutes.
M: (*Walking to the phone and making reference to the foster mother with whom he was staying during the bereavement of his current foster mother*) I want to call my aunt.
T: (*Referring to having made arrangements for Mickey's transportation*) I already called them.
M: When did you call?
T: When you were in the bathroom.
M: (*Playing at the chalkboard*) Why did you call them while I was in the bathroom? (*Pause*) I wanted to tell her to leave me here forever.
T: Forever. You want to stay here forever, huh?
M: Never leave.
T: Sounds like you like this place.
M: I can play all I want.
T: It's nice for us to be here together.

In this session Mickey was helped to recall, disclose, and represent in play and in language progressively differentiated aspects of his trauma and of the self–world relationship that it implied. By developing new perspectives and constructions regarding that self–world relationship, Mickey was encouraged to increase integration and the direction was set for further developmental advance in a way that has been highlighted by Landreth (1991). The resulting sense of relief and empowerment that Mickey experienced seemed evident in his wish to remain forever in the relationship that helped him achieve this.

IX

Accessing the Rage

In a session that took place three weeks after the one outlined in the preceding chapter, Mickey spoke with counterphobic bravado about his vulnerability in a world of danger. He referred to one incident in which he thought himself close to being stabbed or cut by another child who had brought a knife to school. He detailed another occasion in which he was nearly hit by an automobile as he retrieved mail for his foster mother from the mailbox.

Parental failure had left Mickey's dependency needs unmet. For him to achieve developmental advance in self–world relationships, it was necessary that he acknowledge hardships rather than attempt to shield himself from their reality through denial. Accordingly, the therapist's response represented an effort to lessen Mickey's inordinate reliance on counterphobic defenses and help him acknowledge the legitimacy of his dependency needs. Initially the therapist noted that "sometimes when a kid feels like things are dangerous, he feels better if he knows his parents are there to help him stay safe. Sometimes a kid needs his parents."

Although Mickey agreed on the surface with the therapist, his acknowledgment of the notion was perfunctory at best and gave way quickly to a litany of ways in which he had helped others with schoolwork and assignments. The quality of omnipotence that colored his remarks represented a return to the counterphobic denial that he might at times need the help of others, such as his parents.

For the moment the therapist adopted the premise inherent in Mickey's proudly stated bravado that he was extremely capable and, by implication, able to manage without parental support. In doing so, however, the therapist took Mickey's premise a step further, suggesting that, given his ability, his parents "must be very proud."

Mickey could not sustain the denial upon which his counterphobic defenses rested; to do so would require that he affirm the presence of parental involvement in his life, which in fact was disastrously absent. Mickey's subsequent reaction could be interpreted to have two levels of meaning. Specifically, he began through the metaphor of play to punish the therapist by shooting him with a toy gun. His actions in one sense seemed to express his anger toward the therapist for forcing the issue and making clear the untenability of his defensive posture. In another sense, however, Mickey, having approached within himself the previously denied anger toward his parents, turned through transference to the therapist as a parent figure and symbolically vented his rage. Apparently unable to tolerate that externalization of aggression, Mickey shot himself with the toy gun and fell to the ground. The symbolic murder-suicide captures both Mickey's fury toward the failure of his parents and the lingering egocentric thinking by which he may have considered himself unworthy of their investment and deserving of death for his own failure. From that point, however, the therapist was able to help Mickey access his rage about his vulnerability, born of parental failure and having been so horribly exploited by the perpetrators of his abuse. As in this instance aggressive play in therapy often represents the storm before the calm (Madonna and Chandler 1986).

> T: You don't want me to say that your mother's proud of you. That made
> you feel like you wanted to shoot me. That's not something Mickey wants
> me to say.
> M: (*Lying on the floor*) I'm dead.
> T: He feels like he's dead. I see that.

Note that the therapist, in repeating Mickey's words to encourage him to elaborate them, inserts the phrase "feels like." From a technical point of view it is generally good practice to recall explicitly that metaphor and not literal reality is being portrayed, particularly when symbolic reference is made to a child's expression of injury or death.

In this context in particular Mickey has just ventured close, albeit reluctantly, to feelings he had previously encapsulated in counterproductive defenses. To qualify his statement that "I'm dead" by framing it as a simile avoids agreeing with any potential fear that his anger is lethal or that suicide is a viable option.

> M: You're going to die! (*Mickey gestures toward the therapist with the toy gun*)
> T: You'll pay me back for saying that. I shouldn't be saying things about your parents.
> M: (*Again gesturing toward the therapist with the toy gun as he gets up from the floor*) No! Die! Please die!

When he externalized his fury through the transference, this time without symbolically punishing himself for doing so, Mickey seemed poised to confront the perpetrators of his abuse within the metaphor of play. Later in the session he did so.

After a short time Mickey took the microphone used for recording the session and, feigning the gestures of a frenzied rock star, began to scream wildly. The therapist supported Mickey's departure from his previous demeanor by remarking in an approving way, "It feels good to yell, doesn't it?" Seeking to encourage further differentiation of those feelings, the therapist then suggested that Mickey sing a song about the uncles who had abused him. Mickey accepted that suggestion and redirected his frenzy toward the perpetrators, repeatedly wailing his protest into the microphone: "I'll bop them in the head! I'll bop them in the head!"

As he sang, Mickey's lament quickly became a sexualized one: "I've got a hard-on! Is that what you say? But all I can do is shake my behind!" His tempo and rhythm were intended to mimic those of rock tunes. Mickey's words, however, exemplified the frequently evident pathological phenomenon in play therapy of erupting sexualization of the self concept as a reflection of the malignant persistence of the effects of abusive experiences.

In this instance Mickey seemed unable to tolerate his sexualization of his self concept; he pointed the toy gun first at his mouth and then at his head.

Parenthetically, it should be noted that too often the suddenness and intensity of expressions such as Mickey's "song" prompt little more than benign neglect on the part of a startled therapist. In remaining silent the therapist may rely on the rationalization that the episode has provided the child an emotionally corrective measure of catharsis. That perspective, however, is at best an oversimplified one parallel, in the primitivity of its assumptions, to the four humors theory of bodily functions extant in archaic practice: to emote some sadness, some anger, some love, or some fear is the means by which balance is restored.

From a developmental vantage point, however, the individual's potential to advance, despite the dedifferentiating impact of trauma, requires more than simple emotional expression alone; it requires, in self–world relationships, the achievement of alternative perspectives, constructions, instrumentalities, and transactional patterns. It is therefore the therapist's task to lead the child not simply *to* but *beyond* expressions of emotion while welcoming, yet not resting upon, the cathartic value they provide.

From a psychodynamic view of the transference process, Mickey's song lyrics may be considered to convey a subconscious conflict between a wish for intimacy with the therapist and a fear that his vulnerability will invite that intimacy to assume the intrusively abusive form his experience has defined as likely. In this instance the therapist took care not to lend support to either pole of the conflict. Instead he continued to encourage further differentiation in Mickey's construction of his memories and of the feelings they engendered as well as in his expression of them.

This tactic does not address conflict directly, but instead seeks resolution by helping the child move beyond the fusion of disparate emotions. In that way the child achieves the first step in conflict resolution—the freedom to consider, accept, reject, and express various impulses without their seeming each necessarily contingent upon the other. In this context the effort is to help Mickey accept the sense of closeness he has begun to experience with the therapist without feeling that inappropriate sexualization is a necessary contingency. Conflict resolution, including that reflected in this transference process, thus rests on increasing differentiation of experience and proceeds through developmental advance in self–world relationships.

In the unfolding playroom sequence that followed Mickey's song, the therapist continued to encourage activities that would foster increased differentiation of feelings regarding the abuse. Specifically, the therapist suggested that Mickey might use the microphone to make a speech. Mickey's frenzied energy, however, continued to find expression in more diffuse form until gradually he moved from chaotic tossing of a Nerf ball to a more goal-directed version of that play in which he announced that the ball stood for the perpetrators of his abuse.

T: (*Tapping the ball into the air as Mickey shoots at it with his toy gun*) I think you've got it! You shot it right out of my hand. . . . (*Pause*) . . . Who does it stand for?

M: (*Throwing a stuffed toy animal to the therapist*) Uncle Fred. Get him! Wait. (*Seemingly addressing the toy*) Turn around, Uncle Fred! (*Addressing the therapist*) Turn his head around! (*Addressing the toy again*) I'll get your behind!

M: (*As Mickey continues to shoot at the stuffed animal he has identified as Uncle Fred*) I'm having great fun.

T: I guess.

M: Give me darts.

T: Did he ever get your behind?

M: He stuck his private up it!

T: He stuck his private up your behind? (*Pause*) I understand the way you feel about that. You really feel like shooting him.

M: (*Continuing to target the stuffed animal*) Okay, Uncle Freddy . . . watch this up your behind!

T: (*Pretending to address the stuffed animal*) It's going right up your behind.

M: (*Motioning to the therapist*) Come a little bit closer so I can get him.

T: (*Having moved closer as Mickey shoots the toy gun*) You got him!

M: (*Sliding off the window sill*) I got him, but he made me fall off.

T: That must have felt just awful when he put his private up your behind.

Note that the therapist has allowed the animated and emotionally charged sequence to play itself out before inviting Mickey to reflect on it. He then offers a supportive construction of the pain ingredient in the recollections Mickey is expressing. This strategy, and particularly its timing, allows a kind of microgenetic consolidation subsequent to a child's pushing the envelope in terms of what he allows himself to articulate. As such, it facilitates the hierarchic integration (i.e., organization of the parts in subordination to the whole of experience) of the newly achieved level of differentiated recall.

M: He put his private up my sister!

T: He put his private up your sister too?!

M: (*With toy gun in hand and shooting vigorously into the air, Mickey moves closer to the therapist*) She was crying and I kicked him in the behind! (*Yelling loudly and gesturing with the toy gun toward the stuffed animal*) Hold it right there! I'm going to kill him!

T: (*Mickey shoots at the stuffed animal, which the therapist has been holding at his request. The therapist then releases it amid Mickey's fusillade of imagined bullets*) You hit it!

M: Wait, hold him!

T: (*The therapist picks up the toy stuffed animal and Mickey then hits it out of his hands*) Good shot, Mickey, good shot! (*As Mickey begins screaming wildly and thrashing about on the floor while throwing the stuffed animal in a punishing way*) You are mad at that sucker, boy oh boy! That's how you really feel about that!

M: (*As the therapist hands the stuffed animal back to Mickey, who continues to yell loudly as he hits it*) Let go of my hands! Gimme! Watch me whip you, boy! Whip it! (*Frantically looking about, Mickey addresses the therapist*) Give me something! I'll really whip him! (*Mickey then takes the microphone from its stand and begins to sing while using its cord to whip the stuffed animal violently*) Come on, fight! Fight!

Mickey's reference to his hands being restrained when that was clearly not the case in his play strongly indicates that this intense sequence had an abreactive quality for him. He was reliving the desperation as well as the terror and rage that fused in his initial experience of the abuse. The retributive fury portrayed in this play sequence reframes the atrocities he experienced by adding to them a dimension denied expression by the terror and threat that accompanied the actual abuse. By bringing this new dimension of punishing fury to abreactive recall, Mickey achieved therapeutic gain. In developmental terms this process made possible movement beyond the paralysis of fear to more advanced constructions of self and of self–world relationships.

T: He's not going to stick his private up anybody's behind anymore! (*Mickey puts the stuffed animal on the table and hits it. He then lies on the table as well. As Mickey screams wildly*) You'll teach him!

M: (*Addressing the stuffed animal*) I'll teach you!

T: That'll fix him!

M: (*Tearing at the stuffed animal with his hands*) Hey, watch it! Watch me, Buddy!

T: You're so angry at that guy, you could tear him up. I know how you feel, Mickey.

M: Where's his mouth? I'll tear it off him!

T: (*As Mickey kicks the toy animal in the behind*) You just feel like kicking his behind. There it goes!

M: (*Now holding the stuffed animal with one hand and hitting it with the other*) Sit!

T: (*Referring to the stuffed animal*) That guy! Meaner than mean! That guy Freddy is meaner than mean, doing that stuff with his private!

M: (*Lying on the floor, Mickey hits the stuffed animal with his fists. He then gets up and kicks it around the room screaming*) How do you like that?

T: Crazy, no good, mean guy!

M: I'll kick you against this door!

T: Get him good! Give him a drop kick! There, you've got it.

M: (*Kicking the stuffed animal violently*) Wait, I'll really get this guy!

T: (*As Mickey successfully kicks the stuffed animal across the room*) There he goes!

M: (*With a tone and gesture indicating a wish to inflict yet more punishment on the metaphorically represented perpetrator*) Wait, just wait!

T: You'll get him this time . . . like no one ever got him. He'll be sorry he ever stuck his private up anybody's behind.

M: (*Addressing the stuffed animal*) Be sorry!

T: (*As Mickey forcefully throws the stuffed animal*) There it goes!

M: (*Running to where the stuffed animal has landed*) Watch me, Buddy!

T: You'll show him how you feel, Mickey. . . . I know just how you feel.

M: (*As he first screams, then bites the stuffed animal and tears its leg off*) Just let me tear off this leg!

Although it might be speculated with some confidence that in symbolic terms Mickey's wish to tear off the stuffed animal's leg reflects his rageful impulse to excise the penis of the perpetrator, the therapist chooses not to raise that allusion to literal interpretation. Instead he leaves it embedded in the unfolding metaphor. The therapist thus avoids activating defenses that might truncate the play sequence.

T: Maybe if you leave one leg on there it will remind him how he lost the other one. Then he'll really be sorry because then he'll remember how he used to have more legs.

With reference to the symbolic import of this sequence, the therapist here empathetically legitimizes the retributive fury that Mickey feels about having been penetrated by the perpetrator's penis. By responding within the metaphor that Mickey has constructed, the therapist allows the growing awareness of affect to continue without distraction that might otherwise emanate from the potential sensationalism of literal reference to sexual organs.

M: (*Kicking the stuffed animal*) Here. See how you like that!

T: (*Addressing Mickey as he lay on the small table rubbing his eye after accidentally hitting himself*) Did Uncle Freddy hit you back?

M: It happened before.

> T: (*Kneeling close to the child*) What happened before?
>
> M: When I was going through the woods a thing got stuck in my eye and turned it around.
>
> T: (*After Mickey resumes kicking the stuffed animal about the room*) Your eye is the way it's supposed to be. It's just fine.
>
> M: (*Kicking the stuffed animal and yelling*) Wait until I get you, dummy!
>
> T: (*As Mickey kicks the stuffed animal with increased force*) There he goes!
>
> M: (*Racing to where the toy has landed*) Oh, I really want to get him!
>
> T: I think you've taken away his private.

With the affect engendered by Mickey's immersion in the metaphor having reached fever pitch, the therapist here recalls the child's earlier references to assault by the perpetrator's "private," linking it to the play sequence that has developed in the wake of those allusions. In this manner an effort is made to help Mickey integrate the affect that has reached expression through the metaphor with the impact of his abuse, previously articulated in primarily factual, intellectualized terms.

The momentum established by the intensity of affect in Mickey's play may carry this sequence further despite the therapist's linking it to explicit memory. The therapist, however, accepts the risk that this metaphor may for now be abandoned should the child's defenses require that no further linkage be allowed. In either case benefit has accrued to the process of developmental advance and, if a period of consolidation is to occur, the likelihood is that the metaphor will be resumed later.

> M: (*Continuing to kick the stuffed animal with much energy*) Kick him in his behind!
>
> T: Kick him in his behind!
>
> M: (*Throwing the stuffed animal in the wastepaper basket*) Kick him in the trash!
>
> T: That's where he belongs.
>
> M: (*Retrieving the stuffed animal, screaming and striking it fiercely*) That dumb, dumb, dumb!
>
> T: (*Addressing Mickey who has again thrown the stuffed animal into the wastepaper basket*) Good work!
>
> M: (*After walking toward the therapist and shaking hands with him as if to accept the congratulations just offered*) Now look at that. I threw it away!
>
> T: I think he deserved it. What do you think? . . . Sticking his private up people's behinds like that! That's about the meanest thing anybody can do!

Clearly, the therapist's linking Mickey's rage with his memory of abuse in an explicit way did not short-circuit the unfolding metaphor in this instance. Instead Mickey's subsequent play suggests that the process of his working through the trauma of abuse—achieving developmental advance in its wake—in fact gathered force from the increased explicitness of the referents.

> *M:* Take him out of the trash can, okay? I'm not finished.
> *T:* (*Retrieving the stuffed animal from the wastepaper basket and walking toward Mickey with it*) You're going to finish him off!
> *M:* Yeah! Put him right down!
> *T:* Where should we put him?
> *M:* (*Gesturing toward the floor near his feet*) Right down here!
> *T:* All right Mickey, get ready!
> *M:* (*Taking the microphone from its stand and hitting the stuffed animal with such energy that he tears it*) I put a hole in him!
> *T:* And he deserves it! You know what I think? It's okay because when he stands for Freddy, he deserves it. What do you think?
> *M:* He does. But I'm going to get in trouble.
> *T:* (*Shaking hands with Mickey*) You know what? No trouble. You know why? Because you are so angry at Uncle Freddy—and I know how you feel— that it's okay.
> *M:* (*As therapist and child sit close to each other, Mickey is playing with the microphone stand but obviously thinking about something else*) So you're not going to tell?

It becomes apparent here that Mickey is preoccupied with the consequences of his having torn the stuffed animal in his rage. In addition, Mickey has abruptly become riveted to the literal dimension of his play, abandoning for the moment its metaphorical implications. Viewed from the perspective of the relationship between therapist and child, it may be speculated that Mickey fears he has gone too far in this play sequence and has invited the censure of the therapist. In a repeated effort to affirm the relationship as one in which Mickey can freely engage in emotional as well as informational disclosure, the therapist emphasizes his acceptance and approval of open expression by Mickey and seeks to assure him that no punishment will follow.

> *T:* No.
> *M:* (*Referring to the stuffed animal*) Where are you going to put it?
> *T:* I'm going to fix it. It's all right to get that angry. (*Pause*) You know what?
> *M:* What?
> *T:* All those angry feelings? . . . It's okay to have those. (*Pause*) Because Uncle Freddy did some terrible stuff. (*Pause*) Right?
> *M:* But how are we going to put the legs and the arms back on?

Several points are worthy of note in this context. For one, the technical principle that in play therapy irreversible acts such as the destruction of a toy are typically counterproductive, despite short-term cathartic release, is here well illustrated by Mickey's continuing worry. The destruction in this instance was accidental yet required attention in the course of ensuing therapeutic dialogue. To invite these complications deliberately by encouraging irreversible acts of destruction, however, is almost always ill-advised. Also, children often fear their potential to cause irreversible damage should they express conflicted feelings openly; to demonstrate to a child that such potential is real and salient is likely, in the long run, to rigidify defenses. Guilt that springs from the irreversibility of angry acts may further complicate the therapeutic process.

Finally, as this vignette also demonstrates, irreversible acts upon playthings can distract a child from the developing play metaphor. When dramatic gestures of anger with visible consequences on playthings are necessary in a child's treatment, the use of Play-doh, clay, or some other material that can later be restored to the wholeness of its original configuration is preferable to a ceramic doll or a plastic one. If, for example, a child decapitates a doll and later decides that there may be conditions under which that object might be reintegrated in a world defined differently by virtue of therapeutic gain and developmental advance, representation of its newly assigned role can be accomplished in play only if the object can be restored.

T: I'll take care of it.

M: Would it be ready for next time?

T: Would you like it to be here?

M: If you want to . . . but I don't want to get in trouble!

T: No trouble. (*Pause*) It's okay to be angry like that.

M: (*After a period of quiet, low-energy play during which Mickey has busied himself without speaking*) I want to stay here. I want to stay with you. I want to play with you. (*Finding a piece of chalk, Mickey writes* I love you *on the blackboard and then quickly erases it*)

T: Is that for me?

M: (*Appearing reticent and avoiding eye contact*) I don't know.

T: Thank you for writing that. (*Pause*) Because that's how I feel about you too.

For Mickey to express love for an adult man after repeated and unspeakable atrocities at the hands of men is a resounding statement of his willingness to again risk trust. Through the developing positive transference toward a man he perceives as loving in the right way, Mickey has again come to see the world as peopled, at least in part, by men who can be trusted.

In that sense Mickey's communication may well reflect recovery from the dedifferentiating impact of his abuse with regard to the critical dimension of vulnerability, that is, recognition that the trust basic to the expression of caring and affection does not always lead to physical contact, much less to unwelcome intrusion. In this context he has come to recognize that he can express caring without touching or expecting to be touched by the therapist; in the world at large he may tentatively venture similar trust toward others who care for him.

Mickey's written message—"I love you"—may also be taken to indicate that the abreactive expression of cognitive, affective, and valuative constructions of his abuse relieved him in ways that led to the expression of gratitude. To that extent he will be in subsequent sessions empowered to address the challenge of developing new perspectives and constructions of self, the world he inhabits, and the relationship between the two.

X

Retribution through
the Metaphor of Play

For several weeks after the session last described, the anger Mickey felt at the perpetrators of his abuse continued to surface and Mickey, tentatively, in short-lived ways, continued to express it. Increasingly, however, his feelings had a more differentiated focus. His rage grew more intense as he cited the perpetrators more often by name.

Mickey seemed to remain apprehensive about whether he might risk losing the therapist's positive regard by going too far with his anger; he continued with a watchful eye and presented tentative requests for approval in nonverbal ways. After an angry expression, for example, he would pause and glance for a moment at the therapist with wide-eyed uncertainty, waiting for a smile or some similar response before resuming the theme.

It could be argued, in learning theory terms, that the therapist was reinforcing if not shaping Mickey's behavior pattern. Indeed it was the therapist's intention to provide reinforcement, not necessarily of the content but of the process by which Mickey expressed himself. From the videotape records of the sessions it was clear that the direction of Mickey's focus and the energy that propelled him were not dependent on or shaped by the therapist's actions. The vigor and freedom of his expressions, however, were encouraged.

Perhaps in part because of his need for assurance that nurturance and approval would continue as he unleashed his anger in play, Mickey sought and obtained permission to solicit orders from clinic staff for a cookie sale being conducted by his school. At the outset of this session Mickey inventoried the cookies he had brought to fill the orders taken previously. At Mickey's urging, he and the therapist began the session by eating some of the cookies.

Parenthetically, several issues should be considered with regard to the role of eating in the context of play therapy. Because of the symbolism of persons being united by breaking bread together and partaking of the same food that then becomes part of each individual, eating can be a powerful and meaningful intervention. By that means relationships can be acknowledged, strengthened, and almost made solemn by a ritual that has been described as having archetypal characteristics.

As noted earlier, that symbolic dimension of meaning regarding the sharing of food can in fact provide part of the process by which termination is eventually accomplished and honored within the therapeutic alliance. Therapist and child can agree that remembering their time together will provide them a kind of continuing solidarity in the memories they share and in the act of recall in which they will both engage. The unity thus achieved can be paralleled in its symbolism by the act of sharing food. Unlike gift giving, sharing food brings a sense of enduring closeness.

Yet another possible advantage of food sharing in play therapy is to provide a means by which to establish a sense of normalcy through an ordinary act of caring. Relaxed eating as a gesture of that sort can be particularly important after a period of psychologically strenuous work such as the abreaction of abuse. Symbolically, and perhaps literally as well, the child can restore the strength lost through the depletion that results from such work. In a sense, partaking of some food can provide a kind of respite preparatory to moving further toward the challenge of developmental advance.

Paradoxically, the therapeutically productive potential of eating as part of the treatment process can shift quickly and completely when it is overdone. It then becomes an activity that triggers dedifferentiation and increased diffusion of therapeutic purpose. Further, it can actually debase the treatment relationship. Excessive feeding, for example, can infantilize the child in the very context intended to empower her or him. Further, it can over-emphasize a sensate focus at the expense of the psychological processes by which the child might accomplish developmental advance. Feeding as a central theme can dramatize both the child's neediness and the limits of the therapist's capacity to meet those needs rather than empowering the child to engage his or her world differently.

When feeding becomes a routine part of the therapy, the child's expectation leads any lapse in the routine, however well explained, to be interpreted in ways the therapist does not intend. At best, the child may construe the shift in terms that are tangential to therapeutic goals; at worst, contradictory to them. Moreover, the therapist caught in such a routine may busy herself or himself before each session with the effort to make food supplies available rather than spend time anticipating the session in terms of the treatment plan. Obviously, countertransference problems can accrue in the form of resentment the therapist may begin to feel about having to provide supplies and wondering whether the food is the aspect of therapy the child most values.

At the outset of this session Mickey and the therapist are standing beside a table piled high with tins of cookies:

> M: (*Addressing the therapist*) Find out which ones are chocolate chips.
> T: (*Handing a tin to Mickey*) These are the chocolate chips. (*Pointing to another tin*) And that's chocolate chip.
> M: How many are there?
> T: Six or seven, I think.
> M: (*Counting the tins of cookies*) One, two, three. . . .
> T: Have you tasted them yet?
> M: One, two, three. . . .
> T: (*Picking up one of the tins*) This isn't the same . . . this is a different one.
> M: I even got paper to see which cookies go to who.
> T: You're a very efficient salesman, Mickey.

At this point casual dialogue ensues, with Mickey comfortably reviewing his list of customers and their orders. In a way similar to that described by Winnicott (1952), a nurturant and safe holding environment has been reestablished, enabling Mickey to engage in a sustained and progressive communication regarding his rage and its precipitants. In the following sequence this takes the form of a spontaneous request for the play object that has come to stand for the abusing uncles. Using highly charged motoric play, Mickey discloses still more about the abuse he sustained and, in the metaphor, enacts retribution.

> M: I want to see if there's anything in here. (*Lifting boxing gloves from a carton of toys and asking the therapist for help in putting them on*) Can you put these on? . . . Now, what else can I do?

> *T:* Most of the toys you like to use I've taken down for you already.
> *M:* What about Uncle Buddy and Uncle Freddy?
> *T:* The lady who takes care of the toys isn't here today. . . . (*Picking up a large Nerf ball*) So I got this instead.

Although the therapist was caught unawares by the absence of the requested toy, he quickly introduced a substitute so as to remain within the thematic metaphor the child uses in his play. As in this instance, and always with children of this age, therapeutic technique should be guided by the importance of facilitating metaphorical communication; rather than expressing regret about the unavailability of some requested plaything, for example, it is often incumbent on a therapist to respond quickly with alternative objects. Substitute objects should, of course, be chosen with an appreciation of the child's frame of reference.

> *T:* This can stand for Uncle Buddy and Uncle Freddy.
> *M:* (*Facing the therapist*) Okay, throw it up.
> *T:* (*Throwing the Nerf ball to Mickey, who punches it back to the therapist as he speaks*) Good shot!
> *M:* (*Addressing the Nerf ball*) Come on, mess around with me and I'll box your head off! (*Addressing the therapist*) Throw him up!
> *T:* (*Throwing the ball to Mickey, who proceeds to punch it vigorously around the playroom*) Wow! Who does it stand for today, Mickey?
> *M:* Uncle Buddy . . . who else? The big fat pig! (*Looking under the chair, Mickey retrieves the ball and continues punching it*) Where the heck are you? (*Addressing the ball, which has landed near the cookies*) Don't eat my cookie! You must be crazy!

Although explicit reference to the perpetrators has been frequent in Mickey's play, the more insidious impact of his abuse experience has not been fully elaborated. The symbolic but potentially graphic reference to sexual abuse—"Don't eat my cookie!"—presents the therapist with a choice of whether to use this emotionally charged fissure on the surface of the metaphor in a way that would tack the whole of it again to reality. The alternative would be to wait in order to use a more emotionally innocuous, and perhaps safer, point on the topography of the metaphor to reaffirm its unfolding reality referents.

In this instance the therapist chooses to attempt the connection and Mickey accepts it. Had Mickey avoided it, the therapist would not have pushed the issue but would have respected the child's response as an indication he was not ready to manage that degree of differentiation and integration of self–world experience.

T: Is that what Uncle Buddy tried to do?
M: Yup.

Having accepted the therapist's translation of his remarks as literal reference to his sexual abuse, Mickey rapidly retreats by utilizing a distracting interlude. "Accidentally," Mickey punches the Nerf ball with such force that it knocks a vase from the window sill, breaking it. The plant it held and pieces of glass scatter about the floor.

M: (*Wide-eyed and startled*) Uh oh! Did I do that on purpose?

Mickey's reaction might be understood in two ways: first, and most obviously, he raises the possibility that ambivalence may have led him to purposely seek a distraction by which to avoid further discussion of the literal events of his sexual abuse. His question, "Did I do that on purpose?" may also reflect the continuing influence of some egocentric construction by which he still harbors fear that he was, in some way, responsible for his own abuse.

T: What do you think?
M: (*Referring to the question of whether his action was purposeful*) No.
T: I don't think so either.

In another context a therapist might, in an effort to challenge defenses, encourage recognition that a purposeful action often masquerades as an accidental event. Here, however, the tack followed is dictated by the impression that Mickey's remarks represent, at least in part, egocentric thinking about his abuse. The therapist therefore encourages Mickey to reframe the idea in a way that negates that construction and enables him instead to recognize the external causality of his victimization.

M: (*Picking up pieces of broken glass and gesturing with a wave of the hand to the debris on the floor*) How'd that happen?
T: It happened by accident.
M: What about the plant?
T: We can put it in the sink.

M: *(Beginning again to punch the ball)* What?

T: We could put it in the sink. How about in that teapot? *(At this point Mickey walks toward the desk, taking off his boxing gloves and placing them on the now vacant window sill. The therapist continues to pick up debris, placing the glass in the wastebasket and the plant in the teapot)* I think you got a little bit scared when that happened.

M: Yeah.

T: I think you—all of a sudden—got surprised. *(Presenting the newly repotted plant for Mickey's inspection)* How's that?

M: Okay.

T: It's as good as new! What do you think?

M: Yeah!

T: Sometimes broken toys can get better . . . it works that way with people too, Mickey.

M: *(Picking up some remaining pieces of glass and putting them in the wastebasket)* I found pieces of glass.

T: I'll get them.

"I found pieces of glass," Mickey's response to the therapist's "broken can get better," might be taken metaphorically to imply awareness that, when healing is attempted, jagged edges have the potential of inflicting further pain. In terms of that implication, the therapist offers his willingness to intercede.

M: I'll get them.

Coming together, both therapist and child place the remaining pieces of glass in the wastebasket. Mickey is perhaps signaling his readiness to continue to work with the therapist to remove hazards from his experience. Extending cooperative interaction, Mickey picks up a plastic ring and tosses it gently to the therapist.

T: Did you ever feel like things were all broken for you?

M: *(Tossing the ring back and forth to the therapist)* Sometimes.

T: It works that way with people . . . in a lot of different ways.

Subsequent interactions take the form of a relatively casual respite from tensions, presumably those triggered by preceding references to abuse. After recalling his victimization, Mickey focuses briefly on one of its sequelae, his placement in foster care. In that vein he momentarily reflects on the differences between being a foster child in someone else's family and being a regular kid. Although it is poignantly clear that he is pained by his removal from his family, Mickey does seem to achieve some increasingly differentiated and integrated perspectives that equip him to formulate plans for his return home. Unable to escape his sense of futility fully, however, Mickey acknowledges that those prospects are uncertain at best.

In response to Mickey's recalling his abuse and considering some of its effects, the therapist seeks to foster ego enhancement in the child's experience of self by initiating an activity that allows him to take pride in his prowess. Specifically, the therapist proposes that Mickey eat cookies while wearing boxing gloves, suggesting that probably no one has ever attempted such a feat and that the success Mickey achieves can therefore be memorialized as a world's record.

> T: You know what would be very difficult? It would be very difficult to eat a cookie with boxing gloves on.
> M: (*Responding almost immediately*) Let me try!
> T: That would be very difficult. (*As Mickey extends his hands so the therapist can put the gloves on him*) Need some help? Here you go. How's that? Now you're going to eat a cookie like that! My goodness! (*As Mickey bangs his gloved hand on the desk*) Want me to get one out for you? (*Mickey eats a cookie with much drama of gesture while the therapist looks on with feigned astonishment*) You can do it! I think you're the only guy I know who can eat a cookie—who can eat a chocolate chip cookie—with boxing gloves on! I think that's really something! You do a lot of things really well, you know that? Like eating cookies with boxing gloves on.

Mickey's smiling demeanor made it clear that he was greatly pleased by his feat and, more important, the adulation offered him. Emboldened by the pride he felt, Mickey began again his use of play as a metaphor for retribution.

> T: (*As Mickey walks to the Nerf ball, picks it up and punches it*) It's Uncle Buddy time again.
> M: (*As he walks around the table*) I have to walk around the circle and get ready.

Although the reference remained obscure, Mickey's comment, "I have to walk around the circle," may carry significant implications. It recalls the archaic behaviors of persons preparing to engage in the primordial expression of aggression. In that sense it can be, like a war dance, a kind of liturgy that calls forth, lends form to, and defines the dimensions of rage before it is unleashed.

In addition, the circling may suggest that during the many months of victimization, Mickey, like many abused children, might have relied on compulsive rituals to brace himself against the terror of not knowing when the abuse would resume.

Clinicians seeking to respond to the problems of sexually abused children understandably tend to focus on the specifics of the trauma itself. Because those events are so abhorrent, they can obscure the subtler but devastating impact during a period of abuse when the child waited in dread for it to happen again. Perhaps to lighten the burden of having to bear witness to atrocity as it is recalled in treatment, therapists might misinterpret the days or nights spent free of abuse as having been a kind of respite for the child. To lie in bed, however, unsure of whether the door will open again this night as it had before, can be a cruel and relentless ordeal. The ritual behavior used as a way to bind the anxiety, that had its roots in previous uncertainty, often emerges in play therapy.

M: (*Referring to the Nerf ball*) Throw him . . . I want to beat him!

T: (*As Mickey punches the ball back and forth*) I think you've got him. Do you think so?

M: Throw him high enough!

T: (*Tossing the ball*) Here it comes.

M: (*Hitting it fiercely*) Aaagh!

T: What a shot!

M: (*Alertly poised to strike*) Throw it!

T: Here it comes . . . ready?

M: (*Smashing the ball with full force*) Yup!

T: What a shot!

M: (*Jubilantly*) Right out! It went right over to the other side!

T: You sure did! Ready?

M: (*Again poised like a spring's coil*) Yup!

T: Here it comes!

M: (*Pounding the ball to the table*) One down!

T: (*Recalling the earlier reference to Uncle Buddy's eating the cookie as the ball lands near the boxes of cookies*) He's after the cookies again.

M: (*Addressing the ball*) Hey, I'm going to get you in the face!

T: He's going to pay!

M: (*Flailing wildly at the ball*) Got him!

T: Wow!

M: (*As the ball bounces, first hitting Mickey in the face and then ricocheting to the cookies*) Hey, you're not supposed to come to me! How dumb! It hit me in the face! Hey, you're after the cookies again!

T: After the cookies again!

M: He'll really know what it feels like!

T: This time he's going to find out for sure! (*As Mickey smashes the ball*) Wow, look at that!

M: I didn't get him.

T: I think you got him pretty good.

M: I didn't. He said, "Oh, you didn't get me!"

T: Is that what he said?

M: Yeah. (*As Mickey smashes the ball across the room again*) Aagh!

T: You got him that time! No question about that now. (*Tossing the ball back to Mickey*) Here he comes. I bet there were lots of times you wished you could hit him like that when he was doing that nasty stuff.

M: I wish I had boxing gloves when he did what he did so I could have punched him out. (*Pantomiming punching*) And punch him out and say "Get out! Knock you out! Knock you out!"

T: When he did all the sex stuff . . . I bet you wanted boxing gloves then.

M: (*Continuing to swing as if punching*) Then I'd say "Uncle Buddy, come here! I have to tell you something. Stop!!!"

Matching and thereby sustaining Mickey's energetic tempo, the therapist has tried to facilitate the child's effort to punish the perpetrators within the metaphor. In the process he has also sought to help Mickey regain a sense of agency or internal locus of control by which he might feel himself able to affect, if not determine, his ongoing experience. In developmental terms this sequence reflects an advance in the differentiation and integration of self–world relationships and the recognition that effective instrumentalities for change are available to him.

From the perspective of technique it is important in animated and emotionally charged sequences such as this for the therapist to remain alert to signals from the child that she or he has had enough for now and needs respite from the intrapsychic pressures involved in the process. In this instance Mickey consistently indicated that he was eager to continue on the track of metaphorical retribution. Had he signaled the opposite, the therapist would have honored his wish; at critical junctures such as this it is considered important in the Synergistic Play Therapy approach to follow the child's lead rather than push him toward further involvement in what could become a psychologically depleting direction.

In the sequence that follows the pathos of the drama intensifies as Mickey shifts to puppet play and enlists the therapist to enact, on a play telephone, a protective role in the metaphor, that of policeman. The benefit of including a play telephone in treatment to facilitate communication by children in conflict has been discussed previously by Spero (1980). The role of policeman is clearly defined: to know what happened and, in the context of the metaphor, what is happening; to offer protection; to assist in punishing the perpetrators; and to secure a future free of abuse sexual abuse.

T: I think we taught him a good lesson.

M: (*As he walks to the desk, picks up a play phone and tosses a puppet to the therapist*) Yeah. Where's the other phone? You're the police, okay?

T: Okay.

M: Okay, now, here's the telephone.

T: (*Putting the police officer puppet on his hand and gesturing toward it with his other hand*) No, I'll hold him . . . you can talk on the phone.

M: (*As he dials*) You be the voice of the policeman too. (*Speaking into the phone*) 911, ring-a-ling-a-ling.

T: (*Holding the puppet in front of him*) Hello, this is the police department.

M: (*With a tone of urgency in his voice as he speaks into the play phone*) Can you come over? This guy named Buddy . . .

T: (*As Mickey's words strain to a halting whisper, the therapist speaks through the police puppet in a way that maintains the dialogue without explicitly highlighting Mickey's apprehension*) Buddy?

M: (*Resuming full voice and speaking in an urgently plaintive way*) He raped me! I'm a child! I'm eight years old! Can you come over?!?

T: (*Continuing to gesture with the police hand as he speaks*) Yeah, I will! Are you okay? How come he's doing that stuff to you?

M: I don't know.

T: We'll put him in jail right away!

M: Yup!

T: (*Still using the authoritative voice of a police officer and gesturing with the puppet*) He shouldn't do that to kids at all! That's awful!

M: (*Speaking loudly and urgently*) Right! Come on! Can you come over?

T: Absolutely! (*As he hangs up the phone*)

M: (*In a loud voice*) Right away!

T: (*Feigning the sound of a police siren as he gestures rapidly toward Mickey with the puppet, the therapist seizes the Nerf ball that has been representing the perpetrator*) Is this the guy here?!?

M: (*Breathlessly*) Yeah!!! (*Issues a cry of delight as the police puppet slams the Nerf ball into the box*)

T: We got him and we put him in jail! We put him in jail, okay?

M: (*The previous tension in his voice relieved*) Yup.

T: (*Placing the puppet down for a moment, dropping the tone of police authority, and speaking in his accustomed voice*) Boy oh boy! You were 8 years old when he did all that stuff to you.

M: Yup.

At this point in the interaction the therapist has stepped out of the metaphor and begun to reflect on the process that has unfolded. Mickey, however, signals his wish to return to the drama so as to dispense with the second perpetrator. The therapist abides by the principle that the child should be allowed to set her or his own time for enacting troublesome issues through play.

Reflecting on intense sequences soon after their emergence is often a fruitful strategy, but the youngster may indicate that the sequence has yet to be fully played out. At other times, though the sequence may indeed be complete, the child may wave off the therapist's efforts to reflect on the process because of what seems like a phenomenon analogous to the negative refractory period in neurophysiological functioning: the rapid and accumulating stimulation resulting from emotionally laden sequences may lead to a period of depletion that requires rest for recovery of function. At other times the reverse may take place: a child may welcome a time-out to obtain emotional distance while preserving the newly acquired sense of mastery. Often, in fact, the child may initiate that process. It therefore remains potentially productive to invite reflection on memories recovered and/or re-enacted through play while remaining alert to signs that the timing may need to be adjusted.

> M: Okay, now get Uncle Freddy! (*Again picking up the play phone*) 911, ring-a-ling-a-ling.
>
> T: (*Quickly stepping back into the role of the police officer by placing the puppet on his hand and speaking again with authority*) Hello! This is the police station!
>
> M: (*In a tone of desperation*) Same person calling! This guy named Freddy is raping me!
>
> T: (*Gesturing forcefully with the puppet*) Another guy is raping you?!?
>
> M: (*With urgency*) Yup!
>
> T: (*In a tone of outrage*) What's going on there?!? How come all these people are bothering this kid?!? Let's go over there! Hurry! (*Feigning the noise of a speeding police car as he gestures with the police puppet toward Mickey's area*) Here I am! (*Addressing the Nerf ball*) Are you the one bothering this kid?!? We'll get you! (*Grabbing the Nerf ball and slamming it as before into the box on the desk while Mickey laughs again in delight*) You'll go right in the jail with the rest of them! (*Addressing Mickey*) How's that? Is that better?
>
> M: (*In a quiet tone of appreciation*) Thank you.
>
> T: (*Pausing, then speaking with a slow tempo and a caring tone*) How do you feel, son? Do you feel okay?

At this point the therapist was concerned about the potentially over-whelming impact of this sequence for Mickey. He was also touched by Mickey's simple "Thank you," which seemed addressed to him outside the metaphor. To emphasize to this child that protection and nonex-ploitative caring remain available to him in this context of recovery and re-enactment, the therapist stepped out of the metaphor and invoked a profound dimension of their relationship, one that approximates a protective father–son bond.

It could certainly be argued that addressing a child as "son" intrudes upon the developing transference in potentially problematic ways. At this point, however, Mickey seemed to be truly a child, needy and receptive rather than guarded and cynical. A term such as *son*, which connotes ulti-mate esteem when spoken at a key moment, can reinforce the restoration of innocence and the development of a self concept rooted in feelings of worth rather than exploitability.

Although this is not presented as an apologia, the reference "son" was clearly outside the metaphor that has been the vehicle for treatment throughout the process for Mickey. As was often stressed by Sandor Feld-man (1968), a participant in Freud's Budapest group, people need to experience the therapist in transferential terms within the treatment pro-cess, but also in human terms outside it. One example he gave was his willingness to kiss a patient's baby in the park. In the office, however, Feldman assumed a tabula rasa posture, allowing the patient to see him as the transferential need of the moment dictated. In this instance with Mickey, stepping outside the metaphor is not the equivalent of happening upon a patient in the park, but it is a kind of deliberately constructed time aside identified as such by the shift of tone and content of the therapist's communication.

As it happens, Mickey again signaled his wish to return to the meta-phor after acknowledging the therapist's expression of caring with a glance.

M: Hmmm . . . yeah
T: Yeah? Are you sure?
M: (*Leaning forward and reaching to strike the Nerf ball in the box*) Kill him!!!
T: We can't do that but we can lock him up so he doesn't hurt anyone else.
M: (*Again shouting*) Shoot him!!!
T: (*Placing the puppet's head against its chest with its arms held over the head as if to portray abject sadness*) Oh, boy. The policeman feels bad about what happened to you. Look at that. He feels so bad he just can't think about how bad it was. He doesn't like guys who do that to kids at all.

M: He doesn't?
T: Nah.

Speaking the thoughts, feelings, questions, or other private experiences of play objects that have a role in a metaphorical drama is often a useful device. In this instance, by speaking for the policeman, the therapist is able to extend a measure of empathic support to Mickey. Since it is the pretend policeman who expresses that compassion, the process here also fosters differentiation in Mickey's perception of the world of adult men. Consequently, even in the midst of his rage, he may avoid dedifferentiation to a global perspective that could leave him feeling fearful of and/or revengeful toward all men. The goal of avoiding future antisocial behavior thus emerges secondary to residual rage toward the more immediate perpetrators of his abuse.

In addition, because of the differentiated response encouraged by the therapist, Mickey may be helped to break the cycle of abused children becoming abusive adults; by identifying alternative forms of expression he is better equipped as an adult man to adopt nonabusive behavior patterns rather than feeling that only one course is open to him. In that connection it is perhaps noteworthy that Mickey returns to his expression of rage by crying again "Kill him," speaking about each perpetrator in turn rather than lapsing into a global reference to "them."

> M: (*Erupting again into near frenzy as he abruptly turns back toward the Nerf ball in the box*) Kill him! Kill him! Kill him!!!
> T: How about we just lock him up?
> M: And don't let him out! Never, ever, ever!!!
> T: Even if he gets better some day?
> M: (*Beginning slowly and in an apparently absentminded way to wrap the cord from the play phone around his neck*) Yup, because they might do it again.

Several possible explanations might account for the emergence of intrapunitive expression at this point. For one, Mickey may have been reacting to his own spoken concern—"they might do it again"—by considering death a preferred alternative to repeat victimization. Perhaps in his fantasy that possibility evoked yet more terror because of a notion that the next round of abuse would be intensified in its brutality as a result of his having dared to identify and denounce the perpetrators.

Another possible explanation is that the intensity of Mickey's rage was such that he felt a measure of guilt about it and, without direct awareness, expressed it impulsively in a gesture that recalled the suicidal behavior he had engaged in before treatment began.

Still another explanation would, retrospectively, suggest that the therapist's question ("Even if he gets better some day?"), intended to help Mickey mediate his rage and cast it in more manageable dimensions, may have been ill-advised. Specifically, Mickey may have interpreted it to imply that his need for revenge was excessive and blameworthy, thus requiring negation through self-punishment.

> T: I wonder if you know any other kids that happened to, Mickey?
> M: My sister.
> T: Besides family, I mean . . . any kids at school or something like that.

Concerned that Mickey had taken from the previous sequence a sense of rebuke for his anger, the therapist began to introduce reference to others. He did so to halt the self-attack symbolized in Mickey's looping the phone cord around his neck. The intention was to move the youngster toward consideration of retributive recourse in circumstances other than those he had known directly. A more general and less personal reference was sought because Mickey had been painfully present for his sister's repeated abuse. Indeed, he held himself responsible for not having stopped it.

The therapist's goal in this instance was to again legitimatize the rage that Mickey felt by quickly reframing it to include outrage on behalf of others. That effort, however, was not completed because of the therapist's determination that a more direct response was necessary in the face of Mickey's accelerating symbolization of suicidal impulses.

As this episode illustrates, an abrupt shift of tactic may be required in play therapy because a previous intervention veered off in unanticipated directions. In one sense there is an analogy here to scientific method in that a willingness to modify hypotheses with the emergence of new data is necessary if rigidity of perspective is not to stifle forward movement. Seat of the pants flying, however, masquerading as empathic intuition, typically leads to diffusion of treatment to the point that it becomes "making nice" rather than psychotherapy. Changes guided by consistently maintained goals and a coherent theoretical perspective are far more likely to contribute to developmental advance.

> M: (As he continues to loop the cord around his neck, Mickey mumbles unintelligibly)

T: I wonder how come you're putting that around your neck.

M: I feel like it. What time is it?

T: Two things, Mickey. I think it's not good to put things around your neck. Also, I think you thought about doing that because . . . maybe . . . you're mad at yourself on account of what happened with Uncle Freddy and Uncle Buddy. (*Pause*) You're mad at yourself. . . . (*Pause*) or just mad at them?

M: (*Biting the cord still looped around his neck in a way that conveyed dramatic expression*) Just mad at them!

M: I wonder how come you put that around your neck. Makes me wonder if you're mad at yourself a little bit too.

In offering an interpretive comment regarding Mickey's intrapunitive impulse, the therapist frames it indirectly—"I wonder" and "Makes me wonder"—and adds the qualifier "a little bit," permitting Mickey to consider the notion without feeling he has endorsed a sweeping characterization that allows no escape from its implications.

M: (*Speaking in a sentence fragment as if distracted by an association from which he abruptly re-emerges*) What?!? . . . Could I ever kill myself?!?

T: Do you want to kill yourself?

M: No.

T: Maybe you used to want to.

M: (*Standing up*) All I want to do is kill Uncle Freddy.

T: (*Repeating Mickey's words in a tone intended to convey mirroring*) Kill Uncle Freddy.

M: (*Making a machine gun noise and gesturing as if "mowing down" the imagined images of the perpetrators*) Kill every one of them!!!

T: (*In a tone intended not to mirror Mickey's excitation but to convey calmly an understanding of the underlying meaning of his behavior*) You just want to put an end to all that stuff.

M: Yup.

In this sequence an important step was successfully taken. Specifically, the therapist was able to help Mickey redirect his rage from its intrapunitive focus onto differentiated aspects of the world around him, that is, his uncles. In one sense this involved encouraging more developmentally advanced affective and cognitive constructions of his experience of himself and of the world of places, people, and customs. To an extent the differentiation might be characterized as Mickey's separating self from surroundings. As a result of that developmental advance, self-punishment no longer promised indirect gratification for Mickey as a substitute for the expression of rage toward the perpetrators.

In psychodynamic terms Mickey might be said to have attempted in part to manage his feelings regarding the abuse through defensive introjection by which he took on aspects of the abusive uncles so that he could "fix things" internally. His rage, however, was such that "fixing" may have required annihilation of the introjected perpetrators and, tragically, of himself. By moving forward developmentally, Mickey no longer felt drawn to that option.

XI

The Closing Stages of Play Therapy

The ramifications of the abuse experience became increasingly differentiated and integrated for Mickey as the course of Synergistic Play Therapy
moved toward its end phase. In effect, the impact of Mickey's victimization had been "detoxified" with regard to his self concept and his self–
world relationships. Accordingly, Mickey began to focus more upon real-
life problems, primarily those regarding his current and prospective living
circumstances.

Mickey's feelings about his shattered family and his desire for its recon-
stitution often found expression in play during this period. As he matured,
explicit dialogue became a more frequent vehicle of such expression. He
spoke thoughtfully, for example, about his hopes, fears, and needs regarding the future.

The following excerpts were drawn from a session eighteen months
after treatment began.

> M: (*Entering the room with the therapist and referring to his new clothes*) I'm
> dressed like a wrestler guy.
> T: You're looking sharp.
> M: (*Momentarily flopping on the couch and rising as he sees a basketball hoop*)
> Oh! Where did you get the net?

T: I brought that up because I thought you might want to use it. (*Pause . . . then referring to a comment Mickey had made in the hallway on the way to the playroom*) It must have been a very special reason that you went shopping that late at night.

M: I couldn't go any other night. (*Walking about the room tossing the ball casually up and down, Mickey notices a present on the chair*) Whose present?

T: Was it a special night?

M: Was it a special night? (*Pause*) No.

T: It wasn't? (*Pause*) Is today a special day?

M: Aaah . . . yeah.

T: That's what I thought. I heard something about that.

M: I had a surprise party.

T: You had a surprise party?

M: Yeah.

T: And the party was because . . .

M: (*In a soft, almost forlorn tone*) I'm leaving.

T: You're going to your new house?

M: (*Continuing to avoid eye contact*) Yeah.

T: When is that happening, Mickey?

M: Five o'clock.

T: First you go home to Aunt Sally's?

M: (*Becoming more animated as he runs and bounces the ball*) Yup!

T: And then . . .

M: (*Interrupting the therapist and energetically feigning a basketball shot*) Larry Bird in the lead!

T: Looks like you don't want to talk about that stuff.

M: (*Mickey races around the therapist as he takes another shot at the basket with the Nerf ball*) It misses! Oh no!

T: (*As Mickey bounces the ball and again circles the therapist*) You know, you look a little like Larry Bird. (*While the therapist sits down, Mickey prepares for and launches another shot*) There's that Celtics form again.

Joining the resistance in a way that seeks therapeutic benefit, that is, continued ego enhancement, paradoxically often leads to a lessening of the defensive component rather than to the rigidification that typically develops when a therapist attempts to challenge or ignore that resistance.

M: I wanted to watch the Celtics last night.

T: (*Referring again to the move to the new foster home slated to occur shortly after this session*) So, Mickey, tell me about this change. What is this all about?

M: (*Continuing to run and shoot at the basket and speaking in a tone that conveys irritation if not disgust*) I don't know what it's all about!

T: And it's happening today. (*Pause*) It's a big change. (*Pause . . . then, as Mickey stands beneath the basket taking quick, repetitive shots as if to intensify the focus of his thoughts*) I wonder if it's a change that makes you happy or makes you sad.

Having joined the resistance for a few moments, the therapist is able to persist in the effort to encourage Mickey to share a differentiated sense of the impact of the impending foster home move. Indeed, Mickey does so.

M: (*Responding instantaneously*) Sad!

T: You know, I talked to your Aunt Sally.

M: (*Moving next to the therapist and standing on the chair*) About what? About lying?

T: She told me about that but she also told me about . . .

M: (*Mickey jumps from the chair and races to the present lying on another chair*) Whose present?

T: Well, let's talk about this first . . . she told me a lot of times you didn't tell the truth.

In this interchange the therapist reframes Mickey's caustic view of himself as a liar. Instead he offers a less damning description based on Mickey's failure to speak the truth, rather than one that implies a willful decision to speak falsehoods. Although the difference may seem more apparent than real, subtle shifts of connotation in reframing, such as in this instance, often foster therapeutic progress. In this example it may be that Mickey's guilt was softened sufficiently to allow open dialogue to continue, to still feel valued and respected by the therapist.

The reframing here implies that Mickey has a goal to achieve rather than a past deed to somehow undo. The issue has particular relevance for Mickey in that he had, before his referral for treatment, felt unmotivated and/or did not deserve to live and had engaged in actual self-attack.

M: (*Slowly moving toward the basketball net*) Yeah.

T: Is that true?

M: Uh huh.

T: How come?

M: I don't know. I just don't.

T: She also told me that you said something in school.

M: What?

T: You got in trouble . . . you yelled something real loud. (*Pause*) What did you yell?

M: I wish I was dead.

T: I wish I was dead.

M: (*Referring to the basketball hoop*) Do we have to have this piece on?

T: Yes.

M: If the ball won't go through . . .

T: The ball will go through.

T: Mickey?

M: What?

T: Do you wish you were dead?

M: (*In a gesture of resignation, Mickey squeezes the Nerf ball and leans into the wall as he speaks softly*) That's what I said because I was mad.

T: Oh, you were mad. (*Pause . . . and as Mickey walks closer to the therapist and gently bounces the ball against the wall*) You weren't sad, you were mad when you said that. (*Pause*) Because sometimes people say that when they're sad. But you say it when you're mad.

Having become aware of a painfully defined affect, Mickey formulates that experience verbally, differentiating the feeling of sadness from anger. In doing so he relieves himself of the tension that characterized the first few minutes of the hour when he seemed unsure about the extent of the therapist's knowledge of what had, and would, occur outside the playroom, that is, the foster home move and the report of Mickey's recent behavior and pronouncements. In effect, the other shoe had dropped.

When a therapist is made aware of recent events in a child's life, it is most often productive to share that knowledge early in the session. To withhold or delay, particularly when a child suspects that the therapist knows some or all of what has occurred, introduces a tension into the process that precludes development of therapeutic metaphor. For the child the nonliteral levels of communication upon which metaphor rests are instead geared toward scanning interactions for clues of what is known and of what reaction it may have stirred in the therapist.

M: (*Resuming an energetic pace as he throws the ball into the hoop above the door and refers to its placement*) Can I just put this in a low spot?

T: That's about the only place that will hold it up.

Having resolved whatever tension may have been inhibiting to the process, the therapist and Mickey develop a metaphor clearly related to his foster home move and his ongoing search for stable moorings.

> M: (*Climbing onto the table near the door*) Uh uh, I can think of another one. (*The table falls and Mickey strikes his leg*) Ow! (*Mickey angrily throws the ball at the hoop, deliberately knocking it off its mooring on the door*)
> T: (*Stands up and walks toward Mickey*) I think it's better up there. I'll hang it up.
> M: (*Quickly snatching the hoop from the floor and running toward the chalkboard*) Over here!
> T: I don't think that will hold it up.
> M: Try it!

From this point the discussion regarding stable moorings continues for a time, punctuated by expressions of hopefulness and frustration on Mickey's part. Although reference is seemingly to the placement and stability of the basketball hoop, it became increasingly apparent that it had to do with Mickey's feelings about the uncertainty of his living circumstances.

Eventually the therapist brings the metaphor to an explicit level. Mickey conveys verbally, and with striking nonverbal communication, his caring for the therapist and his reliance on the therapy process as an enduring source of stability. In a gesture consistent with those feelings he asks the therapist to hold the hoop and, as he stands very near him, gently tosses the ball through it.

> T: Mickey, I didn't get a chance to see you last week because the cab got messed up.
> M: I know.
> T: So you didn't get a chance to tell me what it was like . . . the visit to your new foster home.
> M: (*To contain the results of his efforts from careening about the room, Mickey had previously slipped a small wicker basket beneath the hoop. As he responds, he flips the basket away in a gesture that seems to contradict his words*) It was good.
> T: Well, Sally told me some things.
> M: (*Avoiding the eye contact he had comfortably maintained during the discussion of the therapist holding the hoop and turning his back to the therapist*) What?

T: She told me about the boy who lives over there. He's going to be your new foster brother. He's 15 years old.

M: (*Shuffling across the room with his head down in a way that conveys a sense of dejection*) Uhhh . . . hmmn. . . . His name is Neil.

T: His name is Neil.

M: (*Abruptly changing the topic and focusing on the package he had noticed and discussed earlier*) Whose present?

T: Well, I heard about a party for Mickey. (*Pause*) And everybody who has a party ought to have a present.

M: (*Approaching within inches of the therapist and looking directly at him*) Yeah?

T: So what do you think I did?

M: Uh . . . bought a present for me?

T: Sure I bought a present for you. But not just from me, from everybody.

Gift giving is often overdone and carries potential hazards with regard to therapeutic progress: inhibition of negative transference, engendering of guilt when the child feels angry within the same time frame as the giving of the gift, development of expectations such that the child construes the failure of the therapist to give gifts on the next occasion that might justify doing so as being related to the child's failures or to his having done or said something that invited the therapist's disapproval, and so on. In this instance, however, gift giving was used as a therapeutic tool. Specifically, Mickey has clearly indicated that he had come to feel comfortable in the foster home he was about to leave, that he looked with great uncertainty upon the prospect of the next one, and that he considered the therapy session to be an important source of stability for him.

The gift given to Mickey therefore served as a kind of transitional object, generalizing the comfort and safety he felt in one location to another he was yet to define in terms of its having any positive emotional meaning for him. The strategy is not unlike the frequent recommendation of therapists to parents whose children have difficulty managing transitions, such as from home to school, for example, to allow a favored or stuffed animal to spend the day with the family and to join the child in his or her trip to school.

In this instance the particular toy presented to Mickey, "Connect Four," was chosen to emphasize that symbolic process by its very name. It was intended to link the previous foster home, the playroom, the anticipated foster home, and Mickey's eventual return to his mother's home.

M: (*Conveying mild disappointment as he leans his head against the wall near the therapist but momentarily turning his face away*) From everybody? . . . Oh.

T: Because you know what?

M: (*Resuming direct eye contact*) What?

T: Because when you go to the new foster home, we want you to know that this is still your place.

M: Uh huh.

T: (*With a gesture of emphasis*) And we wanted you to take something with you so that you could know that this is still your place.

M: Oh.

T: You can still feel connected with it. (*Pause*) You know about being connected?

M: (*Rocking back in his chair as if to test his balance*) No.

T: Being connected means feeling like you belong.

M: Uh . . . with the . . .

T: (*As Mickey looks intently at the therapist*) It just means you feel like it's a place where you belong.

M: Can I open it up now?

T: Yes, you can.

M: (*Taking the wrapping from the present*) Ohhh! . . . Now I know!

T: Ohh!

M: (*Reading the name of the game on its box*) Connect Four!

T: Connect Four! (*Pause*) That's a good name for someone to stay connected with! (*Pause*) I wonder if you know about Connect Four?

M: I know how to play it. Do you want to play?

T: Sure! . . . Let's clean up here first. (*As Mickey and the therapist clear the area*) It's tough, this business of moving from one foster home to the next, isn't it?

M: Mm hmm.

T: It's really tough business for a kid.

M: (*Misunderstood by the therapist, Mickey refers to the camera behind the one-way mirror*) How come you have that on there? What if someone's undressing? And you're laying down and you don't know it and you have it on there?

With the move to a new foster home imminent, Mickey was probably experiencing some dedifferentiation in terms of self–world relationships. As a result, his recollection of molestation in the last foster home most likely became salient. He may well have anticipated that those who lived in the new foster home would be fully aware of his history and in a sense would be in a position to judge him.

More immediately, Mickey may have been experiencing intensification of positive transference in response to the kindness of the therapist and the staff for attempting to make his transition less painful. Neverthe-

less, his statement reflects momentary regression to a dedifferentiated confusion between a sense of being regarded in terms of respectful caring and
sexualized exploitation. Such fleeting regressions are commonplace in
psychotherapy and are analogous to the reflexive withdrawal response on
the part of a person who has been traumatized but who, after some period
of hesitation, ventures to approach what initially led to pain.

> T: (*Mickey and the therapist continue to pick up game parts and toys from the
> floor, relating without eye contact and in almost parallel postures*) I don't
> know what you mean . . . have what on there?
> M: Why do you have those cameras? Because what if someone's undressing
> and there's something wrong with them and they're watching . . . ?

Mickey here seems to indicate awareness that those who would be
voyeuristic with children are somehow troubled. In addition, he implies a
fear that they may be free to act out their problems. Alternatively, Mickey's
comment about "maybe something's wrong with them" may refer to the
child whose exposed body would reveal a deformity or mark of some kind
that might elicit a damning judgment. In a less literal interpretation Mickey
may also be expressing concern that the openness to which he is now drawn
in his relationship with the therapist may be misconstrued by others who
are privy to it as a sign of weakness and vulnerability.

> T: I don't think this is a room where people undress. Do you think about
> undressing here in this room?
> M: (*Emphatically*) No!

Mickey's response supports the notion that his previous remarks were
more metaphorical than literal.

> T: I didn't think so. (*Pause*) Undressing is something you know about,
> though. (*Pause*) There were times when you had to undress when you
> didn't want to, weren't there? . . . And people did watch. Do you still
> think about those times, Mickey?
> M: (*Barely audible*) No.
> T: Maybe a little bit.
> M: (*Grasping the Connect Four game and preparing to open it*) I just thought of
> it though.
> T: Just thought of it now. (*Pause*) But sometimes when a guy is going through
> some scary business like changing foster homes, it makes him think of

what other scary stuff is like. (*Pause*) Like the times he had to undress. (*Pause*) Remember the time with Uncle Buddy and Uncle Freddy? . . . that you had to undress?

M: (*In a muffled tone*) Yup.

T: You remember that time, don't you?

M: Mm hmm.

T: There's something about going through tough times that makes a guy remember other tough times.

In this instance Mickey remains only fleetingly in a literal frame of reference as he reflects on his remarks. The interchange nevertheless is an example of the therapeutic strategy of inviting a bridging of the metaphorical and the literal to allow the child in subsequent dialogue to differentiate those dimensions of experience.

For a while the therapist and child played several games of Connect Four. The accompanying exchange had a relaxed quality, a seeming respite from the preceding intensity of affect and recall. Later, reference to those issues resumed.

As the time for Mickey to leave for his new foster home drew closer, he became more animated and aggressive in his play. Reference was made to his not having seen his father the previous weekend as had been planned. The therapist then wondered aloud with the child about his feelings regarding his parents. Mickey's play became yet more animated and aggressive, leading the therapist to comment, "There's something about talking about your feelings about your parents that makes you want to throw things." Mickey asserted that his anger was about having to go to live somewhere else, but he cut short the exchange saying that he did not want to talk about it.

Mickey's attention then returned to the ongoing interaction with the therapist during which he played a game of ringtoss. In a similarly playful way, the Nerf ball was used first as a basketball and then as a baseball that Mickey hit with a plastic tube. When the therapist recalled that the ball previously had been used to represent the perpetrators, Mickey at first declined to pursue the issue, and reaffirmed that "now its just a baseball." His anger erupted, however, and he began a series of karate poses and gestures. The therapist picked up a stuffed animal that Mickey then targeted, saying that it "stands for Uncle Buddy and Uncle Freddy."

The retributive play Mickey engaged in through the pantomime of karate differed in several ways from what had transpired in previous sessions. It was circumscribed and of relatively shorter duration. His intensity in the process was more focused, and both the play and his accompanying comments lacked the sexual connotation of his earlier venting of rage at the perpetrators.

As he lamented the dissolution of his family, the end of the session and the time of Mickey's departure to a new foster home drew closer. Concurrently, Mickey's anger became more manifest, seemingly propelled by his painful awareness that the perpetrators who assaulted him and the parents who failed to protect him had shaken his world loose from its anchors and left him adrift.

In the last few minutes of the session Mickey asked to use the painting materials and produced, with the therapist's help, a series of designs by folding sheets of paper containing globs of paint. Dialogue centered on "making designs out of messes" and Mickey agreed that the results of that effort had been successful. Mickey then presented a design to the therapist as a gift, seemingly affirming that success.

Leaving the gift of a design may also have been an effort by Mickey to remind the therapist of the importance of the differentiating and integrating process of therapy for him. Symbolically, Mickey may also have sought to sustain his sense of ownership and "belongingness" with regard to the therapy, assurance that had particular urgency because of the imminent move to the new foster home. Accordingly, the therapist asked:

T: Mickey, do you know what will happen next week?
M: What?
T: You'll come back here and we'll be together, no matter what.

The session ended with Mickey smiling and seeming to be reassured.

During the ensuing months of treatment, Mickey related to the therapist in a way that could be characterized for the most part as "casual," using the sessions as a kind of anchor point in his uncertain world. In the new foster home—an affluent, middle-class suburban setting—he soon became the scapegoat for the anger of an older child of that family, specifically, a 20-year-old son who was increasingly but secretly involved in drug abuse and targeted Mickey for physical punishment.

Mickey's abuse by the son came to light during a session observed through a one-way mirror by Mickey's Department of Social Services case worker. When she notified his foster parents of her concern, they withdrew, fearing they would be placed on a list of child abusers. Despite repeated reassurances that the intent was to work with them rather than hold them culpable for their son's actions, they refused to communicate directly with either clinic or DSS staff. Instead they referred all communication to their attorney. From that time on Mickey was treated matter-of-factly by the family and was given the clear message that he could remain only until an alternative placement was found.

Concurrently, Mickey's mother showed that she might well succeed in her attempt at rehabilitation and might after all be able to re-establish a home for him. With this recognition, Mickey seemed to construe his therapy sessions as a prerequisite to that eventuality, assuming he could not rejoin his mother until treatment ended. As a result, conflict developed that led him to relate to the therapist at times with hostility and at times with affection. When the conflict was identified and the misunderstanding discussed, Mickey again used the sessions as a source of stability in a world that had finally begun to change in directions that seemed hopeful. In doing so, he resumed a posture with the therapist that often resembled typical father–son interaction in tone and manner.

During the final months of therapy, at Mickey's request, several sessions were conducted in which he and the therapist viewed videotapes of earlier sessions. Watching the very first meeting, Mickey was intent and subdued. He commented several times on how small he had been, an observation that the therapist, through dialogue, developed into a metaphor for the growth that had taken place during treatment.

Mickey paid particularly rapt attention to scenarios in which the differentiation of sex and love had been elaborated, to those in which his concern about peeking had become focal, and then to those in which he vented rage on a doll he had identified as representing the uncles. He seemed almost shaken as he observed the intensity of his own fury, especially when he heard himself yell "faggot! faggot! faggot!" at the representations of the perpetrators.

As if to balance those bracing recollections with events that had helped move him beyond the acute pain of the abuse experience, Mickey also highlighted and asked questions about vignettes in which he had painted increasingly cheery pictures. In addition, he warmly recalled the names of various professionals who had been involved with him early in that process.

Mickey's originally stated intent had been to identify videotape segments he might show his mother, who, with a staff member of the clinic, had begun attending family therapy sessions with Mickey and his sister Carol preparatory to re-establishing a home for the two. After reviewing early tapes in the first session, Mickey stated that he might not want his mother to see them. He gave no reason for his reconsideration, but his manner strongly suggested that he feared that his mother, witnessing the intensity of his anger, might feel frightened or guilty.

During the next session several weeks later, Mickey asked to play a board game while watching videotapes, and in fact selected for viewing a recent session in which the same game had been played. The mirroring that occurred seemed a kind of recapitulation, intended perhaps to hold and extend the experience in anticipation of the impending termination of therapy four sessions later. In a parallel fashion Mickey mirrored the postures and gestures of the therapist as they watched the video together. His behavior seemed to reflect his incorporation of the therapist just as his request to watch previous sessions spoke to his wish to internalize the treatment process.

Toward the second half of the session an earlier tape was selected for viewing and instances of his previously intense rage were again dramatically evident. Mickey's response this time was one of detached amusement, a reaction that seemed to reflect his sense that he was now separate from and beyond those overwhelming emotions. Moreover, he was again prepared to share the experience by viewing the tapes with his mother.

Mickey also began frequently to "slap five" with the therapist, a gesture seemingly calculated to convey that he was now able to be "cool" and was moving toward adolescence with some confidence. He conveyed readiness to address oncoming developmental challenges with fewer emotional encumbrances from his abusive past. Perhaps most important, he had regained some trust in others.

As the agreed-upon time for termination approached, several sessions took on a quality of consolidation of gains, with Mickey's growing trust and confidence identified and reinforced. Mickey had matured to the point that play therapy as an exclusive modality was no longer necessary. Accordingly, he and the therapist increasingly used board games as a vehicle for interaction.

In that context several issues were discussed in anticipation of Mickey's rapidly approaching adolescence. In particular, an effort was made to help Mickey differentiate his own sexual feelings and impulses from those of the uncles who had victimized him and to integrate those feelings into a self concept that allowed an appropriate self–world relationship. As the following dialogue illustrates, interactions between the therapist and Mickey continued in these instances to have a kind of father–son quality.

T: (*As the checkerboard is being set up*) You know, we ought to talk about stuff too. (*Pause*) What should we talk about?

M: I don't know.

T: I suppose we could talk about all the reasons we had been meeting in the first place. (*Pause*) Do you remember why we were meeting in the first place?

M: No.

T: You don't remember?

M: Oh, yeah.

T: What was the reason?

M: Huh?

T: How come we started meeting in the first place?

M: Because of Uncle Buddy and Freddy.

T: Because of Uncle Buddy and Freddy . . . all that abuse stuff, huh? (*Pause*) You know what I was thinking, Mickey?

M: What?

T: I was thinking about that and how, after a guy has been through that kind of experience—and then when he gets older—sometimes, when you get older, when your body starts to change, you start having some sexual feelings yourself. But if you've had a time like you had with Uncle Freddy and Uncle Buddy, sometimes it can get very confusing all over again. (*Pause*) You're getting older now and you're going to have some of those feelings about sexual stuff. (*Pause*) Which is normal . . . everybody gets those kind of feelings. What Uncle Freddy and Uncle Buddy did was not normal. It was a very bad thing. (*Pause . . . as Mickey stares downward at the checkerboard between him and the therapist and listens intently*) But the feelings that guys get when they get older—the feelings that you're going to get—are very normal. (*Pause . . . then, speaking gently*) Do you understand?

M: Mm-hmm.

T: In fact sometimes you're going to feel like you want to touch yourself and it feels good. (*Beginning to play checkers*) Maybe that already happens to you. (*Pause*) But if you've been through an experience like you went through, it can get confusing. Know what I mean?

M: Mm-hmm.

T: (*Focusing on the checkers game*) What are the rules? Do you have to jump?

M: Uh-huh.

T: (*After moving the checkers, each jumping the other*) I wonder if you found some of that stuff kind of confusing already? I wonder if it started happening already. (*As Mickey shrugs*) Maybe sometimes, huh?

M: (*Referring to the game*) Go.

T: It's a little hard to talk about. I understand. (*Pause . . . and as each contin-ues to look at the game board*) But you need to know Mickey, that when those feelings happen it's very, very different from what happened with Uncle Freddy and Uncle Buddy. What they did was wrong. But feelings are not wrong. Do you understand?

M: (*Mickey nods affirmatively*)

With preadolescent children who have been sexually abused, it is important to encourage the differentiation of developmentally appropriate, emergent sexual feelings and impulses from those that fueled the abusive behavior of the perpetrators. Particularly helpful techniques in that process include the use of indirect questions ("Maybe you know about that"); the use of global referents that allow the child to assent to a possibility without endorsing an embarrassingly specific statement (". . . the stuff they did"); the inclusion of interpersonal buffers (games that legitimatize the avoidance of direct eye contact during discussion of sexual experience); the use of a casual manner with references to the here-and-now play activity being sandwiched between references to sexual issues; ongoing, moment-to-moment monitoring of a child's tolerance for remaining focused on sexuality; and a readiness on the part of the therapist to suspend the intervention when necessary until the child regains and signals the availability of sufficient ego strength for the effort to be resumed.

For the remainder of this session the focus was first on the game of checkers and later on Mickey's energetic efforts with the Nerf basketball. Light conversation occurred throughout, with Mickey's manner seeming to reflect a renewed sense of closeness to the therapist.

The next session, which took place a month later, was the third before termination. It was also Mickey's birthday.

T: (*As Mickey enters the room, the therapist hands him a gift*) Happy Birthday.

M: Thank you.

T: (*Sitting down*) And we also have some talking to do . . . about what we're going to do in our last meeting.

M: Yup. (*Opening the gift*) Oh! A watch!

T: When a guy gets older, he needs a watch, Mickey.

M: (*Taking the watch from its case and examining it carefully*) It's a nice watch!

T: It's got a stopwatch on it and everything. (*Reaching for the papers from the case*) Here are the instructions. It has an alarm. Here are all the different things it has listed.

M: Wowie!

T: (*After reading the instructions together, the therapist sets the time on Mickey's watch according to his own*) Here, let's see if we can set it.

In addition to serving as a transitional object, the watch was chosen as a gift because of its multiple metaphorical implications. In one sense it represents a means by which to differentiate past time—the time of abuse—and future time. Moreover, the temporal integration of past, present, and future symbolically parallels the integration that has, in an overarching sense, been the goal of the treatment. At a yet more speculative level, Mickey's setting the watch in synchrony with the therapist's may carry the further symbolic meaning that the cadence of developmental advance begun in treatment will continue to pace his efforts after therapy has ended.

For a while, Mickey and the therapist experimented with the various functions of the watch. Conversation later returned to the anticipated termination. Whether to invite Mickey's mother and sister, along with the family therapist (who had been Carol's individual therapist), to review tapes of Mickey's earlier sessions was discussed.

T: Do you think we should treat them to some food?
M: Okay.
T: It's kind of neat to have food because that way . . .
M: (*Interrupting to complete the therapist's statement*) . . . it will be like a small dinner.
T: Yeah, a dinner, and also it would be like you and I kind of sharing something together. It would always be with us together.
M: Mm-hmm.
T: Because it's something that becomes a part of both of us. (*Pause*) You know what else I was thinking, Mickey?

The act of eating together can have a powerful impact, particularly in anticipation of termination, because the symbolism promises an ongoing connection across time and place. That sense of continuing connection can help the child draw on his experiences in therapy when he faces crises or decisions. To include food routinely in the therapy process dramatically diminishes that potential impact, however. It may even have a negative meaning for the child if an event as seemingly momentous as termination is treated with a sameness that fails to distinguish it from what went on before.

In the exchange that follows the therapist makes another effort to foster a sense of ongoing connection and mutual availability through recall.

> *M:* Mmm?
>
> *T:* I was thinking that a lot of times I'm going to remember back to the time we spent together and I'm going to feel real good about the time you and I spent together.
>
> *M:* Mmm.
>
> *T:* I hope maybe you're going to think back to those times we spent together too. (*Pause*) Do you think you will?
>
> *M:* Yeah.
>
> *T:* You know what might happen?
>
> *M:* What?
>
> *T:* Sometime in the future you and I might be thinking back to the time we spent together at the very same time. Like one day you and I might sit back, each of us, and think about the time we spent together. And we could be doing that at the same time. And that will be really neat because that will almost be like being together again. Know what I mean?

Like the choice of a watch as a gift, this intervention seeks to provide the child with a means by which to access recollections of the therapist as well as the perspectives developed in the context of treatment. The child is thereby empowered to call upon those resources when he encounters troubling situations that require him to make judgments. Not insignificantly, it also helps the therapist manage his own inevitable sense of loss that accompanies termination with a child toward whom a strong attachment has developed.

> *M:* (*Looking up at the therapist*) Mm-hmm. (*Pause . . . then speaking with wide-eyed excitement*) Do you know what happened to one of my friends?
>
> *T:* What happened to one of your friends?
>
> *M:* Well, him and his friend, right? They were just sitting back, right? Then one time, all of a sudden, one time, all of a sudden, together, they would think of the same thing. Then they each had a picture, right? Like his friend had a picture of him and he had a picture of his friend.
>
> *T:* That's kind of the same idea. Would you like us to have a picture of each other?
>
> *M:* Mm-hmm.
>
> *T:* Maybe I could try to get hold of a camera and we could take a picture. Should we do that?
>
> *M:* (*Shrugging his shoulders*) I don't know.

Mickey, by his response, in effect rejects the therapist's shifting dialogue into a literal frame. His doing so supports the notion that the metaphorical meaning related to ongoing connections was more important for him.

T: (*Referring again to the notion of simultaneous recall of times together*) But at least it will be like the same thing, just like your friend and the other guy. (*Pause*) We'll be thinking about the times we spent together and sometimes it will be at the same moment that we're both thinking about those times. (*Pause . . . and as Mickey and the therapist adjust the checkerboard*) It's been a long time, huh?

M: Uh-huh.

For the remainder of this final individual session Mickey and the therapist examined the wristwatch and played a lengthy game of checkers. As they did so they spoke in a low-key, casual way consistent in manner and tone with that of companions about to part. Mickey then "slapped five" with the therapist and asked to shoot baskets. As he did so, he narrated his efforts like a sports announcer. With each shot, Mickey referred to himself as another famous and successful NBA player. He seemed in the process to be asserting a sense of his own strength and of the gains he had made. That presentation stood in dramatic contrast to that of the suicidal youngster who at the outset of therapy had been resigned to hopelessness.

At the very end the plan to invite Mickey's family for a viewing of earlier taped sessions was repeated. Upon leaving the room, the therapist commented again that it had been a long time and that this was the final time just the two of them would meet. Mickey acknowledged the parting as the therapist briefly rested his hand on Mickey's head.

Mickey continued participation in the family therapy that had begun several months earlier with the therapist who had previously seen Carol individually. During that time he sent messages through the family therapist to his play therapist to indicate that all was well.

Mickey and his therapist were not to see each other again until the planned meeting in which videotapes of his playroom sessions would be presented to the family. In the interim Mickey and Carol returned to the home established by their mother. Because several scheduled times were canceled by Mickey's mother, the planned video review meeting took place five months later. When all participants did converge, the session was brief because of the family's late arrival.

Included were Mickey, his individual therapist, his mother and sister, and the family therapist. Brief segments of tapes from each of the three and one half years were presented while Mickey and his mother watched with serious attentiveness. Carol quickly became fidgety, probably attributable to her short attention span as well as to her chagrin at not being as close to the center of attention as her brother was. After the shortened viewing of the tapes, the play therapist asked about the family's current status.

Mickey's mother responded by citing the complexity of the children's adjustment to a new home and a new school.

The family therapist suggested that another session be scheduled in order not to rush the process of tape review. The play therapist asked Mickey which tapes he would like to present to the others. After some thought, he brightened and exclaimed that he wanted to show those in which he had been singing. Carol asked whether they had been rap songs. On learning that indeed they were, she stated with a hint of sarcasm, perhaps rooted in jealousy: "I thought so! That's all he ever listens to."

Two months later this same group met to continue the viewing and discussion of play therapy tapes. The occasion also marked the final separation of Mickey and his play therapist.

The meeting began with Mickey's opening a new tin of cookies and acting the gracious host, walking about the room and offering some to each person present. He then asked that the tapes be presented chronologically by year. Each segment was viewed with the same previously evident attentiveness, but family members offered more comments and reflections during the viewing process. Carol also paid attention after her tendency to distract the process elicited limit-setting responses from her mother.

Both children became quiet and serious when the play therapist recalled various themes that had been enacted in the playroom and captured on tape. Mickey's mother also seemed pained as the play therapist recalled "the time Mickey spoke of being molested by an older foster daughter at one of his placements"; "the time Mickey beat up and kicked around a doll that he said 'stood for Uncle Freddy and Uncle Buddy'"; "the time Mickey talked about the difference between 'good love and bad love' and between sex and love"; "the times Mickey wanted to telephone Sally, the foster mother who had meant the most to him and whom he later began to address as 'aunt'"; "the times Mickey spoke of how hard it was to move from one home to the next"; and other similar references.

From his glances, comments, facial expressions, and gestures, Mickey gave the impression that it was important to him that his mother suffer the burden of that litany. Soon after, however, he seemed equally invested in absolving her of guilt by exclaiming his agreement and breaking into a bright smile when the therapist recalled fun times and Mickey's achievements at various feats of skill. Several times he rose to offer the tin of cookies to his mother, and she accepted those offerings. While it may seem inferential, the eye contact between mother and son gave the impression that healing was occurring.

After showing the segment in which the therapist had spoken about recalling times together, "perhaps even at the same moment," the therapist reiterated that comment in the family gathering. At that point Mickey presented a dream he had had about "a house and everything in it, and the next day I went into that same house." His recollection of the dream at that moment seemed to indicate that Mickey had indeed internalized the notion that experience apart from the routine of everyday life (i.e., dreams or play therapy) might well have an impact that could be carried into ongoing transactions with the world. The shared viewing of the tapes may have become a metaphor reflecting the integration of past, present, and future experiences in a way that defines developmental advance in self–world relationships.

A further meaning of Mickey's recalled dream may have to do with the notion of a "full house," that is, family life that he is now able to anticipate as intact and whole in contrast to the fractured and fragmented family circumstances of the recent past. At a yet more inferential level, the concept of full house may have intrapsychic meaning as well, referring to a sense of his own restoration. In some projective assessment schemas *house* represents the maternal figure; in that sense Mickey may have been acknowledging his feelings of reassurance about his mother's restored capacities without necessarily articulating them within his own awareness.

M: (*Sitting next to his mother and across from the play therapist*) This is the last meeting, right?

T: For me and for you.

C: (*Sitting on the other side of her mother from her brother and next to the family therapist, Janet*) And for me and Janet.

T: I think you're still going to meet as a family, aren't you?

C: Nope.

M: Ha ha, Carol.

T: I'll miss you, Mickey.

C: (*In a mildly oppositional tone*) Because I can quit whenever I want to.

M: (*Addressing the family therapist, Janet*) So can she quit whenever she wants?

C: (*Addressing Janet*) Didn't you say that to me?

J: I told you that we were not going to stop meeting unless it was something we both agreed on. (*Pause*) That I wasn't going to come in some day and say "Well, Carol, I guess this is it. Good-bye." It wouldn't happen like that.

M: Like what me and Bob did, like spreading out the visits?

T: We had more time between our meetings. (*Pause*) I'm still going to miss you a whole lot, you know that? (*As Mickey nods approvingly and throws his head back with a glowing, broad grin*) Think you'll miss me a little bit too?

M: (*Smiling warmly*) Yeah.

T: (*With mother smiling as she listens quietly*) You know what's good, Mickey? You and I can think back to the times that we spent together any time we want to. And we can feel good about it. And we might even think back at the very same time. That will be sort of neat. It will be like being together.

M: (*In a tone consistent with the dialogue to this point*) What does *psychopathic* mean?

T: I think you mean *telepathic*.

M: What does that mean?

T: *Telepathic* means that you can kind of tell what people are thinking.

M: There's . . . something that, it's something . . . people can tell that they're going to do something. (*As Carol imitates noises of flatulence and then laughs, Mickey continues without changing his serious tone as he addresses the play therapist*) Because I had dreams. I had a dream once, right? Of this house and everything in it. And the next day I went into that house. (*As Carol again makes random noises, Mickey turns and addresses his mother*) Remember when I went over to Mitch's house?

Mother: Oh, the manager.

M: I dreamed of that same house, that same one. I went "whoa!" (*Pause*) Okay, now it's time to leave, right?

T: It's close. You've got about five minutes.

M: Five minutes. Why don't we get ready to leave?

Mother: (*As Mickey jingles his mother's keyring, she reaches for them*) Give me the keys, you're really getting me mad.

T: (*As Mickey and his mother engage in a playful tug of war with the ring that holds her car keys*) I think Mickey's telling us that leaving isn't so easy.

Mother: I know.

M: Huh?

T: Leaving isn't so easy. (*Pause*) Leaving's not so easy.

M: Yup.

T: Yeah.

M: (*As if brushing something aside, Mickey waves his hand across his body in the direction of his mother*) Do it and bye.

T: Do it and get it over with. (*Pause*) It's okay to feel funny about it. You know I'm going to miss you and you're going to miss me . . . that's okay, because we'll still remember each other over time.

M: (*In a subdued tone and seeming on the verge of tears*) Mmmm.

C: (*Making a dismissive gesture in response to Mickey's obvious sadness and turning to the play therapist*) Don't let him fool you. (*Looking toward Mickey and*

speaking mockingly as if to echo his words before the session) "'Can I go over
to Kim's house? Can I go over to Kerry's house?"

M: Kerry's house? Kerry's house? Kerry's house? I said Kevin's.

C: I said Kevin. (*Turning toward the family therapist*) He was just about to go
off to Kevin's house and you guys called. (*Pointing toward Mickey*) I said
"ha! ha! ha! ha!"

M: (*Scrunching up his face and attempting an oriental accent*) Weeee have to go
to the meeeeeting.

T: (*Turning to the family therapist and speaking in a joking way*) Did you talk
that way on the phone?

J: (*As mother laughs*) I guess so. At least that's the way Mickey heard it anyway.

M: (*Accentuating the affected accent and speaking in a way seemingly intended to
entertain rather than register distress*) You can't go to Kevin's house because weeee have to go to the meeeeeting.

J: (*Referring to the meeting*) This has been getting put off for a long time.

Mother: Oh, I know.

M: (*Mickey interrupts his mother with the same dismissive gesture he used earlier*) Do it and bye.

Mother: It's Christmas time and we started this way back in the summer time.

M: Two different seasons, two different kids.

In this seemingly delphic musing Mickey paralleled the reflective mood
used by adults regarding the passage of time and its impact on lives. Here
Mickey refers to the seasons of a child's life, which may also have been a
private communication to the therapist he was about to say good-bye to.
In effect, he acknowledged that he would continue his journey at his
mother's side and that the part of the path he and the therapist had walked
together had come to an end. In that context Mickey's dismissive hand
gestures might be interpreted as waving good-bye.

Mother: (*Addressing the family therapist*) The kids went away . . .

T: And the kids were sick, weren't they?

Mother: Yeah, and the last time it was my car and I was "I don't believe this."
(*Turning toward the family therapist*) And when you called me I said,
"Yeah, I know. I can't believe I did this again."

J: You got here, though. That's what counts.

M: It doesn't count.

J: It doesn't count?

M: (*Shakes his head No*)

If the mother's preceding comments are taken to acknowledge her
difficulty in mobilizing herself despite the children's sickness, then Mickey's

response may reflect some unresolved ambivalence toward her in the wake of her failings. The importance of continuing family therapy thereby became explicit.

> T: (Reaching for Christmas candle replicas of the movie character E.T., the lovable lost alien famous for his persistent effort to phone and return home) Hey, will you kids do me a favor?
> M: What?
> T: Will you take care of E.T. for me?
> M: Huh?
> T: Will you take care of one of the E.T.'s for me?
> C: Can I take it home?
> T: Sure.
> M: (As both children jump from their seats, Mickey exclaims excitedly) Yeah! Yeah!

The children leapt to their feet and raced to the video monitor where the candles had been placed. A short, competitive squabble ensued, with Carol and her brother claiming, alternately, one or the other of the two figures.

> T: Each of you takes one home.
> M: Ohhhhh.
> Mother: I think you've done a lot for Mickey, Bob. You know when we were visiting and stuff like that . . .
> M: (Interrupting her with his recollection of the time the therapist observed his birthday when the mother had not remembered it) And on my birthday . . .
> Mother: You know, like sometimes Mickey would talk about the stuff you talked about afterwards . . . you know, I don't think if he didn't have this to come to, you know, to let anything out or anything . . . he had a lot of hard times in the foster homes, along with our home when he was living with me. And you know, the last four years have been really difficult for both of them, for all of us.
> T: I appreciate what you just said. (Pause) I think Mickey's a super kid and I'm very proud of him.
> M: (Standing and pointing toward the therapist) And he's a super guy!
> T: I'm very proud of him. He did a lot of good work. (As Mickey stands facing his mother and sister with a beaming smile) And I think he's going to be just fine. (Pause . . . then glancing toward the family therapist and making reference to that continuing treatment process) You've got to keep working though, of course.

M: Yup. (*Standing and playing with the E.T. candle, gesturing as if to simulate its flight home*) See, there's the spaceship.

T: (*Mickey simulates the sound of ascent and flight*) Hey, Mickey.

M: Yah?

T: Don't forget, you and I each promised to think back to the times we spent together, okay?

M: Yup.

T: (*Mother, who has been looking intently at the therapist, turns and smiles at Mickey, who responds with an equally warm smile*) And that's the way we will sort of keep it.

J: (*Speaking to the play therapist*) Is it okay if I let you know if I have to see Mickey sometime?

T: I think that would be fine.

J: (*Addressing Mickey*) Is it okay if I tell him if I see you?

M: (*With an expression conveying apparent delight at being in the center of and in control over the proposed sharing*) Mmm hmm. (*With playful affectation, as his mother laughs in amusement at his manner*) You have my permission.

J: And if we were to do some more tapes or something and talk about the family, is it okay if I let Bob see them?

M: (*With an even more exaggerated facial expression and affected tone, so extreme as to convey its opposite in a playful way*) You don't have my permission. (*As others laugh, watching Mickey play with power*) You can have my permission now.

J: I can have your permission now. (*Addressing the play therapist*) You may even get to keep seeing him grow up even if you don't see him face to face.

T: Okay, that will be great.

M: (*Continuing his exaggerated facial expression*) Yes.

C: (*Speaking to the family therapist in an obviously irritated tone and scowling*) But you don't have the tapes, Bob has the tapes.

J: Oh, but I have the tapes from when we met together.

M: So, is five minutes up?

T: Well, we've got about . . .

M: Two seconds!

T: We can do a countdown here—we've got about two minutes and counting. (*Handing his watch to Mickey*) Here, I'll let you count down, Mickey.

M: (*Rising from his chair to take the watch, then returning to his seat*) Is that the seconds?

T: (*Leaning toward Mickey and speaking in a paternally instructive way*) Yeah. See here, four thirteen-O-five, four-O-six, four-O-seven . . .

M: Mmm. (*Pause*) I'll count down from a minute.

Mother: (*Referring to the videotape of an earlier session that has been playing silently and taking note of the therapist's weight loss*) I was just going to say, Mickey looks like he got bigger and you got smaller during the tapes.

T: (*Referring to the watch and beginning the final countdown*) Okay, I'm ready to turn this back, okay?

M: (*In a playful, affected tone and saluting*) Yep! Yes, sir! Roger! (*Pause . . . then looking at the watch, Mickey begins to whisper the countdown*) Thirty-four, thirty-five, thirty-six . . .

C: (*Whispering in synch with her brother*) . . . . thirty-seven, thirty-eight, thirty-nine.

Mother: (*Addressing the family therapist as the children continue to count in the background*) Oh, I passed my test.

J: (*As Carol applauds and Mickey continues the whispered count*) Oh, you passed your G.E.D.!

M: (*Shouting and pointing at the family therapist*) One minute!

Mother: I passed four of them. The last test I feel good about. I know I passed.

Having discussed at some length both the tests that she had taken and her plans to enter nursing school, the mother took obvious pleasure in the praise she elicited from the therapists. She was interrupted by Mickey, however, who extended his hand in a motion that conveyed a command to halt.

M: Okay, everybody! (*As Carol becomes increasingly agitated in apparent response to her mother's plans to pursue a nursing career, which Carol associates with needles, Mickey resumes the countdown*) Shut up! Forty-one, forty-two, forty-three . . . (*Carol joins him in the countdown*) fifty-four, fifty-five, fifty-six . . . (*Carol uses her finger to keep the rhythm of the count but falls silent as Mickey's voice grows in volume*) . . . fifty-eight, fifty-nine . . . (*Then, loudly*) Aarhhh!!! Meeting's all ended!

T: (*Rising and giving Mickey a bearhug*) You take care of yourself.

M: Yup.

T: (*With one hand on Mickey's shoulder both walk to the door*) Good man.

M: (*Cradling the candle in his arm as he leaves*) E.T., E.T., E.T. . . . (*Then, as he drops the candle and quickly retrieves it*) E.T., stop falling!

XII

Implications of Synergistic Play Therapy: Retrospect and Prospect

As a frame of reference with roots in developmental metatheory and the clinical tradition promulgated by Ginott, the Synergistic approach has application beyond work with latency-aged children. In a diagnostic context with adolescents and adults, an assessment can also include determination of developmental placement on a continuum of relative primitivity or sophistication of experience and expression. The diagnostician can ask about the extent to which the individual has a relatively differentiated and integrated awareness of the sources of internal discomfort, distress, and/or agitation, or whether only a relatively global and diffuse sense of source issues has been achieved. Does the individual's expression approximate the developmental level of awareness that has been attained, or has mistrust, interpersonal anxiety, and/or the absence of a therapeutic rapport reduced expression to a lesser, more primitive level? To what extent, in other words, are the concerns of the person reflected in simple motoric discharge, heavily veiled reference, revealing metaphor, or direct and focused verbal statements? According to such determinations, the principles of the Synergistic approach will provide guidelines to advance the diagnostic process.

It will be recalled that one guideline of the Synergistic approach is the notion that *with good rapport and a trusting relationship, issues of conflict and concern will emerge, at times tentatively and at times with longstanding intensity.* With adults and adolescents, as with children, a diagnostician or therapist need not force issues, but can allow the individual to determine when concerns are addressed and the extent to which they remain focal each time they appear. With older adolescents and adults the guideline itself can be discussed explicitly. Indeed, improved rapport and therapeutic gain often result when there is explicit acknowledgment, for example, that some issues are difficult to address, that discomfort will be respected, that "it's okay to hold off for a while . . . we can talk about it when you feel ready," and that some issues can be set aside for a while and revisited later.

A second principle of the Synergistic approach refers to the *therapist maintaining rather than blurring the child–adult distinction, yet in a way that reassures rather than threatens the child with the unavoidable power dimension.* Obviously, with adults and older adolescents the terms of this principle would be reframed, but its import remains relevant. The clinician is in fact in a position of authority in the diagnostic or treatment context, but in no way can that be allowed to diminish the rights or dignity of the individual receiving services.

At times, motivated by an eagerness to avoid the arrogance that can characterize service providers, clinicians adopt an extreme but misguided demeanor of exaggerated friendliness or deference that typically fails to improve effectiveness. What it can provide is the basis for defensive resistance rooted in the notion that familiarity breeds contempt; at worst it blurs distinctions that can lead to abrogation of clinical propriety and ethical violation.

With regard to work with children, a third principle of the Synergistic approach holds that *the therapist must remain mindful of the power dimension when reflecting the inferred meaning of a play sequence.* When this principle is translated into terms that have reference to adults and adolescents, the clinician must be aware that she or he is involved in a hypothetical deductive process such that inferences and interpretations need always to retain a flexibility that is responsive to the emergence of new data. Moreover, casting interventions in tentative terms ("Maybe X or maybe Y") and inviting the individual to reflect on the possibilities ("What do you think?") typically has the added benefit of relaxing defenses and encouraging candor in therapeutic discourse. Thinking aloud in a musing fashion and the use of third-person allusions (e.g., "Sometimes people feel that . . ."), mentioned as being useful with children, are devices likely to prove helpful as well in introducing alternative constructions and/or in legitimizing reactions with adults and adolescents.

Another pivotal notion in the Synergistic approach is that *it is neces-sary for the therapist to monitor the degree of intimacy that is required, encour-aged, or allowed*. With children these issues often arise around questions of close physical contact (e.g., "Can I sit on your lap?"), gift giving, or feed-ing. Although these specific behaviors may arise with adults and adoles-cents, related issues are more likely to emerge in subtle fashion, such as in an excessive search for, or extension of, statements and gestures of a highly nurturant, emotionally intimate sort that are incongruent with the person's developmental progress in addressing and resolving presenting concerns.

The 3 x 3 schema, discussed as a way to dimensionalize and address experience with children, likewise has relevance with adults and adoles-cents. For the clinician as well as for the person receiving services, a more differentiated and integrated understanding can result when inquiry and intervention have reference to knowing, having feelings about, and valu-ing aspects of the physical, interpersonal, and sociocultural surroundings. Moreover, treatment goals can often be achieved through shared consid-eration of alternative instrumentalities by which to bring about change in some aspect of self–world relationships thus defined.

In a way even more thoroughgoing with adults and adolescents than with children, the clinical process of psychotherapy is itself a metaphor. In effect, the treatment process metaphorically parallels the person's rela-tionship with the world of his or her past, of the present world, and the world sought for the future. Psychotherapy, as metaphor, is therefore the means by which self–world relationships are restored to effectiveness and developed to their full potential. That process may involve varying degrees of emphasis on self, surroundings, and/or the transactions between the two.

Like the E.T. character, Mickey was eventually able to go home. He did so without being mired in the global, diffuse burdens that sexual abuse imposes upon a child. The developmental progression reflected in the gains that allowed him to do so was fostered by an approach the authors have termed *Synergistic Play Therapy*. The frame of reference thus designated, and the procedures derived therefrom, are an integration and application of the play therapy approach of Ginott and the organismic developmental metatheoretical perspective first articulated by Werner.

The former is itself an integration of several clinical traditions; Ginott drew from psychodynamic theory, learning theory, Rogerian self theory and Piagetian notions of cognitive development. The authors therefore consider the principles and applications of Synergistic Play Therapy to be an integration arising from orthogenetically orderable development in the treatment of children.

A presenting circumstance such as Mickey's obviously has many complex dimensions. The sessions chosen for review here were intended to illustrate two of them: the process by which disclosure unfolds, and the emergence of attendant feelings of rage and retributive impulse. These sessions were also intended to illustrate how a child might be helped to move beyond the enormously burdensome sequelae of sexual abuse and resume the development of a healthy self concept, a realistic sense of the surroundings, and an effective relationship between the two.

In Mickey's case treatment oriented toward those goals was dramatically illustrated by the creativity he brought to the process. Yet it was at the same time slowed by the secondary problem of the uncertain fluidity in his living circumstances. The latter had been set into motion by the initial discovery that abuse had occurred and was sustained by the limitations of the parent figures in his life. Both his biological parents and the foster parents were unable to manage the crises that emerged; the father had little, if any, ability to match his words of promise with appropriate action; the mother for a long time remained addictively tied to substances in a way that undercut her efforts to re-establish a home; one foster mother was immobilized by grief when her husband died; another could not continue the commitments she had made before her husband left her; and the last foster parents assumed a cold, guarded posture when it became known that their biological son had been beating Mickey.

Although treatment goals regarding the psychic impact of the abuse that Mickey had suffered had essentially been achieved after approximately eighteen months, play therapy continued, primarily to provide some constancy and predictability in his otherwise chaotic family living experiences. In addressing that remaining problem, Synergistic Play Therapy proved an effective modality. It provided not only stability in a drastically shifting family situation, but also a means by which to maintain and consolidate the gains Mickey made with regard to self concept and self–world relationships.

Even with successful treatment, gains achieved are often threatened and eroded by the potentially disruptive realignment that can occur in the psychological vectors impinging upon a child. Examples might include a rapidly substituted, tenuously reconstituted or redefined, but still shaky family system; positive changes in school behavior that result in a child's moving beyond the need for the special education services that previously insulated him from academic and social pressures; or increasing expectations on the part of peers or adults who recognize and react to a youngster's developmental advance. To terminate treatment prior to a consolidation phase hazards dedifferentiation and regression as such pressures increase.

Moreover, the emergence of secondary sexual characteristics and the accompanying psychosexual turmoil may require that the treatment serve as an effective psychological inoculation: an implicit goal of developmentally oriented treatment is to equip a child to move forward in the face of such pressures without previous problems resurfacing in ways that lead to dedifferentiation and regression, differentiation and isolation, or differentiation and conflict with regard to self–world transactional patterns.

Circumstances familiar to a child, such as those that define the family experience, include many cues that can trigger regression and re-enactment of past problematic behavior patterns. In Mickey's case there was a literal separation from the home and a later return to it. The resumption of previously familiar cue patterns was therefore an actual event. In most instances, however, children remain in familiar settings while treatment proceeds; encounters with familiar stimulus arrays, and their potential regressive pull, are an ongoing experience. In either case such cues can be intangible (e.g., the tone and demeanor of others in the context) and/or very basic and concrete (e.g., the sights, sounds, smells, and textures that define the surroundings in sensory terms). For a given child cue properties may also accrue to the discrete content of accustomed but emotionally charged interactional pattern; to phrases, sequences, or configuration of interactions that take on the quality of buzz words; to familiar routines in which the child is required to participate; and so on.

Such cues may place the child in continuing jeopardy with regard to her or his potential for regression to previously habituated problematic behavior patterns, particularly when developmental advance has been achieved only recently. The end phase of treatment is thus of paramount importance in psychologically arming a child against such potential triggers of regression.

In Mickey's treatment the consolidation phase was also used by the therapist to establish specific internal markers, including the therapist's musing that, with the passage of time, they might think of each other at the very same moment so that "it would be like being together again."

Reviewing videotapes of earlier key sessions with Mickey as a way of visually patterning in the gains made during those sessions was also significant in this regard (Haworth and Menolascino 1967). Reviewing those same videos with family members helped demarcate, for all concerned, the past from the present and from the future with regard to the meaning that previously familiar cues would now have and the new responses they would now elicit.

With sexually abused children whose victimization was made possible, at least in part, by the negligence or self-absorption of family members charged with their protection, reviewing play therapy session in which the child's rage is dramatically portrayed has the added benefit of bringing to a head feelings of guilt that might otherwise continue, in subtle ways, to affect relationships between the child and family members. In Mickey's case the review of play therapy sessions by the family provided an opportunity for the child to feel acknowledged in his suffering and vindicated by the distress of family members who witnessed his pain. It is also a time in which the child might grant absolution.

Such interventions remain within the contract of confidentiality; the child is given the right to choose which aspects of play therapy will be shared and which will not. When such transactions between the child and family take place as a discrete event, it becomes possible for all concerned to move beyond the otherwise burdensome sequelae that can linger for years without being articulated. In addition, cues associated with parent–child transactions can more readily take on a function different from that previously associated with regression.

These interventions are frequently employed as part of the Synergistic Play Therapy approach. Moreover, when family therapy and/or parent counseling is proceeding concurrently, such strategies can serve as a link between the two treatment efforts, synergistically enhancing the potential benefit of each.

The judicious giving of gifts toward the end of treatment ("Connect Four" and a wristwatch) was another means by which the therapist sought to arm Mickey against the possibility of future regression and differentiation. In one sense those particular gifts served as transitional objects enabling the child to exit treatment more confidently. More important, however, they conveyed the message, as termination approached, that child and therapist could remain symbolically connected over time.

The power of metaphor is a pivotal element in Synergistic Play Therapy and was graphically reflected throughout Mickey's treatment. Largely by that vehicle, discussed with its implications by Burke (1954, 1972) and Cirillo and Kaplan (1983), and by the safe, gradual, and compelling externalization of conflict that it allows, Mickey progressed from suicidality to an excitement about life and a desire to make the most of it. Even the objective sought toward the end of treatment—equipping Mickey to endure the regressive pull of cue patterns previously linked with problematic behavior—was advanced through the use of metaphor. Specifically, breaking bread together as a device to represent the bond between therapist and child and the ability of Mickey to access the perspectives and determinations achieved during treatment were embodied in the sharing of food that became part of each. Therapist and child thus might be linked together over time yet to unfold. As noted previously, and as is the case with metaphor in general as a therapeutic vehicle, it is important to recall that excessive or even routine reliance on a given metaphor strips it of its potential power.

The metaphor of E.T. was introduced at the very end of treatment not only to reflect in a personal way Mickey's yearning to rejoin his mother, but also to embody an almost archetypal need of children, and adults as well, to "return home." In addition to capturing the universal search for a place of safety, acceptance, nurturance, and understanding, the E.T. symbol affirmed at a deeper level Mickey's compelling need to move from a diffuse, unanchored experience of self-in-the-world to one that has differentiated direction and a hierarchically integrated sense of self–world relationships.

Although the character E.T. was popular in a certain time frame, each age has symbols that give form and expression to those needs and aims. For a while Bambi served that purpose. Later the Lion King did the same. Popular stories through the years have consistently represented such strivings—Luke Skywalker's attaining integration with "the Force," the reconciliation of the Prince and the Pauper in a home they both share, the odyssey of Ulysses in his voyage to rejoin his family, the many journeys in search of a spiritual home portrayed in the traditions of religion, and so on. To include metaphors drawn from popular accounts of such universal strivings enhances their therapeutic potential by drawing on the power embued by the times in which the child and therapist are functioning or to which both relate with a shared sense of history.

Principles derived from the Synergistic model have relevance as well for those who serve as caretakers for children in a variety of roles. For example, parents who admonish a child for striking a sibling simply by saying "Don't do that!" would be well advised to first seek differentiation between feeling and action and to offer a substitute means by which the impulse might be vented. An alternative admonishment might take the following form: "I know you're angry at your brother. I understand how that feels. But your brother is not for hitting. The couch (pillow, chair) can stand for whoever you want it to. It can stand for your brother, if you want. Show us how angry you feel."

Should a child then persist in striking his sibling, the resulting consequence and discipline imposed by the parent will likely be experienced by the child as contingent on behavior he or she can control. Without such prior differentiation a child might feel stymied by the unattainable requirement that he change the undifferentiated experience of anger and impulsive action by willpower alone.

Another key distinction suggested by the Synergistic approach has to do with whether a child's disruptive behavior can be understood as *acting up* or *acting out*. The former is the result of a decision to behave against rules and expectations to, for example, amuse classmates. Acting out, on the other hand, represents an effort to reduce tension associated with some conflict by allowing it behavioral expression.

When the pressure of conflict is intensified by some event or circumstance, dedifferentiation and regression may take place in seemingly spontaneous fashion. Whether the setting is the nuclear family, a foster home, or even a residential group home, the resulting behavior may take a form that lends itself to the mistaken interpretation of simple oppositionality or defiance that requires only increased limit setting.

Although acting up frequently takes the form of willfully disruptive behavior that calls for a disciplinary response, motoric discharge can, as in Mickey's case, be a form of expression activated by inordinate anxiety and internal conflict. Such behavior is best understood as part of a continuum that also includes the potential for metaphoric as well as direct verbal statement of the underlying issues. It thus becomes imperative for the parent, foster parent, residential staff member, and classroom teacher to provide an opportunity for the acting-out child to move from motoric discharge states to verbal expression. A transition of that sort—from dedifferentiated states to differentiated and integrated ones—may well include metaphoric as well as direct verbal representation of internal states.

The instrumentalities available to caretakers seeking to facilitate that transition may take various forms. Throughout Mickey's play therapy treatment it was apparent that a child can be invited to draw, paint, or clay-model his concerns. Even in a classroom setting where a teacher must attend to a number of children at once, a child who has been swept away in impulsive action might be invited to go to an assigned area of the room and "draw how you're feeling and you and I can talk about it afterwards."

Establishing specific times in the home or classroom for a child, with other children, to playact a story for the adult(s) can be a particularly powerful way to attain metaphoric expression. The impact is likely to be enhanced when even makeshift props are provided and the adult assumes the attitude of a highly interested and appreciative audience. A postplay discussion period can further enhance the process.

Whatever modality of expression is chosen, it is important for the parent, residential staff member, or teacher to respect the disguise that the metaphor provides. Even when focal issues appear extremely transparent in their metaphorical wrappings, the Synergistic approach would suggest that references to the underlying meaning of the child's productions should not be made directly. Questions about such productions should also be cast tentatively and indirectly (e.g., in response to a dramatic playacted scene a teacher might ask, "I wonder what it means for a guy to have had that happen to him"). It is important to keep in mind that metaphorical expression alone may allow differentiation and hierarchic integration of core feelings and thoughts. Metaphor thus allows developmental advance without the interference that might otherwise be introduced by the intensity of affect associated with stark and direct expression.

Should a child abandon metaphor, however, and move to direct verbal expression of core conflicts, the adult entrusted with such expression must listen nonjudgmentally and resist the temptation to explain away the child's perception. References can be framed in terms that make clear that the perceptions are those of the child and not necessarily shared by the adult (e.g., "I understand how you feel . . . it must be really scary to think that . . ."). In short, whether in play therapy or simple interaction with a child who is sharing a concern, the goal is to convey empathic appreciation of her or his perspective without endorsing a shared view of the circumstances upon which that perspective is based or the interpretation that the child has placed upon them. When the intensity accompanying initial disclosure of conflict or concern subsides, carefully phrased and tentatively posed questions can provide a vehicle that will help a child reframe his or her interpretation of available data (e.g., "I wonder if maybe the teacher might have been laughing at something else even before you came into the room and maybe not at you").

In effect, the Synergistic model holds that feelings can function as mirrors of the external world. Some are like true mirrors that reflect the world as it is. Others, however, like the mirrors of a carnival house, distort what they reflect. In the latter instance it is important to recognize that, when feelings misrepresent the world, the images are nonetheless real for the person and their impact calls for an empathic response. At the same time, however, it is important to help the individual recognize that those images, however compelling and/or unsettling, do not necessarily reflect the external reality.

A critical dimension of any psychological treatment approach is its teachability. Unless an approach can be shared so that its theoretical under-pinnings and the internal consistency of techniques derived from its con-structs are made clear, treatment becomes little more than a well-meaning but vaguely defined effort. In such instances the process is guided at best by the therapist's intuition. Such an idiosyncratic function of the therapist's individuality does not, however, lend itself readily to reliable clinical instruction.

The Synergistic approach addresses this problem in at least two ways. First, a beginning effort has been made to codify principles and derivative techniques. More needs to be accomplished in this regard, but a format for doing so has been established. Second, the application of the approach in the treatment of Mickey demonstrated that a one-way mirror and video-tapes can be used as an effective teaching modality, even when presenting issues include sexual victimization with boundary intrusion and voyeurism.

To codify principles and applications minimizes the fuzzy thinking that too often characterizes clinical teaching. "That's one way to do it" is a frequently heard comment, along with "That's another way." Like quick-silver, the therapeutically appropriate intervention is hard to grasp when codification is lacking. The appropriateness of an intervention, or even of an overall treatment plan, is, of course, relative to the model to which ref-erence is made and definable only in terms of such reference. To argue that only one approach yields benefit would be foolhardy, but to proceed without the internal consistency allowed by a well-defined approach averts incompetence of effort guided only by virtue of the therapist's intuition. One purpose in presenting Synergistic Play Therapy as a defined approach is therefore to provide a matrix within which appropriateness and, ulti-mately, effectiveness of effort can be measured and through which it can be taught. As such, the Synergistic approach represents only a beginning point subject to revision and refinement, but, unlike the elusive quicksilver of clinical intuition alone, it is anchored in articulated principles.

Ultimately treatment ends. When it does, the therapist may be left asking "What will become of this patient?" and "Will the advances made in this treatment endure in the face of future challenges?" When the patient is a child, the concern is even more poignant. For the therapist, of course, there can be no certain answer to these questions. There can be hope, however, derived from the knowledge that therapist and child have traversed a very significant journey, a journey that has taken both, in the setting of the playroom, from global, diffuse states of self–world experience to progressively more differentiated and integrated ones. Through that journey, which is both immediate and archetypal in its dimensions, both therapist and child have, in a sense, like E.T., been able to "go home again."

References

Acunzo, M., Siegel, E., and Ciottone, R. (1991). *The talk show technique: bridging the transition from play to dialog in play therapy*. Paper presented at the 42nd annual meeting of the American Association of Psychiatric Services for Children, Miami, FL, November.

Anderson, S. C., and Berliner, L. (1983). Evaluation of child sexual assault in the health care setting, In *American Training Manual*. Seattle: Sexual Assault Center.

Axline, V. (1947). *Play therapy: The Inner Dynamics of Childhood*. Boston: Houghton Mifflin.

Azrin, N. H., and Nunn, R. G. (1977). *Habit Control: Stuttering, Nail Biting and Other Nervous Habits*. New York: Simon & Schuster.

Bandura, A. (1977). Self-efficacy: toward a unifying theory of behavioral change. *Psychological Review* 84:191–215.

Bandura, A., and Walters, R. H. (1963). *Social Learning and Personality Development*. New York: Holt, Rinehart & Winston.

Brassard, M. R., Tyler, A., and Kehle, T. J. (1983). Sexually abused children: identification and suggestions for intervention. *School Psychology Review* 12:93–97.

Burke, K. E. (1954). *Permanence and Change*. Los Altos, CA: Hermes.

——— (1972). *Dramatism and Development.* Barre, MA: Clark University Press with Barre Publishers.

——— (1973). *The Philosphy of Literary Form.* Berkeley, CA: University of California Press.

Ciottone, R., and Madonna, J. (1984). The treatment of elective mutism: the economics of an integrated approach. Techniques: *A Journal for Remedial Education and Counselling* 1:23–29

——— (1992). *Crucial issues in the play therapy treatment of a latency aged boy.* Paper presented at the 43rd annual meeting of the American Association of Psychiatric Services for Children, New Orleans, LA, November.

——— (1993). Crucial issues in the treatment of a sexually abused latency-aged boy. *Issues in Comprehensive Nursing* 16:31–40.

Ciottone, R., Madonna, J., and Acunzo, M. (1992). *Crucial Issues in the play therapy treatment of a latency-aged boy.* Workshop presented at the 9th Annual International Play Therapy Conference, Nashua, NH.

Cirillo, L., and Kaplan, B. (1983). Figurative action from the perspective of genetic dramatism. In *Toward a Holistic Developmental Psychology*, ed. S. Wapner and B. Kaplan, pp. 235–252. Hillsdale, NJ: Erlbaum.

Corder, B. (1990). A pilot study for a structured, time-limited therapy group for sexually abused pre-adolescent children. *Child Abuse and Neglect: The International Journal* 14:243–251.

Erikson, E. H. (1963). *Childhood and Society.* New York: McGraw-Hill.

Feldman, S. (1968). Personal communication. University of Rochester School of Medicine, Department of Psychiatry, Residency training seminar, Rochester, New York.

Finkelhor, D. (1979). *Sexually Victimized Children.* New York: Free Press.

——— (1982). Sexual abuse: A sociological perspective. *Child Abuse and Neglect* 4:265–273.

Finkelhor, D., and Araji, S. (1983). *Explanations of Pedophilia: A Form Factor Model.* Durham, NH: University of New Hampshire Press.

Freud, A. (1926). *Four Lectures on Child Analysis.* New York: Nervous and Mental Disease Publishing Company.

——— (1928). *Introduction of the Technic of Child Analysis.* New York: Nervous and Mental Disease Publishing Company.

——— (1929). On the theory of the analysis of children. *International Journal of Psycho-Analysis* 10:29–38.

———— (1964). *Pyschoanalytic Treatment of Children*. New York: Schoken.

———— (1965). *Normality and Pathology in Childhood*. New York: International Universities Press.

Freud, S. (1909). Analysis of a phobia in a five year old boy. *Standard Edition* 10:1–49. London: Hogarth, 1955.

Gardner, R. (1994). *Child Psychotherapy: The Initial Screening and the Intensive Diagnostic Evaluation*. Northvale, NJ: Jason Aronson.

Ginott, H. (1957). Differential treatment groups in guidance, counseling, psychotherapy and psychoanalysis. *International Journal of Social Psychiatry* 3:231–235.

———— (1958). Play group therapy: a theoretical framework. *International Journal of Group Psychotherapy* 8:410–418.

———— (1959). Theory and practice of therapeutic intervention in child treatment. *Journal of Consulting Psychology* 23:160–166.

———— (1960). Rationale for selecting toys in play therapy. *Journal of Consulting Psychology* 24:243–246.

———— (1961a). Play therapy: the initial session. *The American Journal of Psychotherapy* 15:73–88.

———— (1961b). *Group Psychotherapy with Children*. New York: Norton.

———— (1975). Group play therapy with children. In *Basic Approaches to Group Psychotherapy and Group Counseling*, ed. G. Gazda, 2nd ed., pp.327–341. Springfield, IL: Thomas.

Ginott, H., and Lebo, D. (1961). Play therapy limits and theoretical orientation. *Journal of Consulting Psychology* 25:337–340.

———— (1963). Most and least used play therapy limits. *Journal of Genetic Psychology* 103:153–159.

Goldfried, M. R., and Davison, G. C. (1976). *Clinical Behavioral Therapy*. New York: Holt.

Guerney, L. (1976). The treatment of child abuse: play therapy with a four year old child. *Journal of the American Academy of Child Psychiatry* 15:430–440.

———— (1983). Client-centered (non-directive) play therapy. In *Handbook of Play Therapy*, ed. C. Schaefer and K. O'Connor, pp. 21–64. New York: Wiley.

Haworth, M. (1964). *Child Psychotherapy: Practice and Theory*. New York: Basic Books.

———— (1990). *A Child's Therapy: Hour by Hour*. Madison, CT: International Universities Press.

Haworth, M., and Menolascino, F. (1967). Video-tape observations of disturbed young children. *Journal of Clinical Psychology* 23:135–140.

Hinshelwood, R. D. (1994). *Clinical Klein: From Theory to Practice.* New York: Basic Books.

Hug-Hellmuth, H. (1920). *A Study of the Mental Life of the Child.* Washington, DC: Nervous and Mental Disease Publishing Company.

———— (1921). On the technique of child analysis. *International Journal of Psycho-Analysis* 2:287–305.

Kaplan, B., Wapner, S., and Cohen, S. B. (1976). Exploratory applications of the organismic developmental approach to man-in-environment transactions. In *Experiencing the Environment*, eds. S. Wapner, S. B. Cohen, and B. Kaplan. New York: Plenum.

Klein, M. (1927). The psychological principle of infant analysis. *International Journal of Psycho-Analysis* 8:25–37.

———— (1955). The psychoanalytic play technique. *The American Journal of Orthopsychiatry* 25:223–237.

———— (1959). *The Psychoanalysis of Children.* London: Hogarth.

———— (1960). Psychoanalytic play technique. *American Journal of Orthopsychiatry* 30:483–493.

———— (1975a). *The Narrative of a Child Analysis.* New York: Dell.

———— (1975b). *The Psychoanalysis of Children.* London: Hogarth and The Institute of Psychoanalysis.

Landreth, G. (1991). *Play Therapy: The Art of the Relationship.* Muncie, IN: Accelerated Development Press.

Landreth, G., and Barkley, H. (1982). The uniqueness of the play therapist in a child's life. *Texas Personnel and Guidance Journal* 10:77–81.

Lindholm, K. (1984). *Trends in child sexual abuse: a study of 611 reported cases in Los Angeles County.* Paper presented at the 64th annual convention of the Western Psychological Association, Los Angeles, CA, March.

MacFarlane, K., et al. (1986). *Sexual Abuse of Young Children: Evaluation and Treatment.* New York: Guilford.

Madonna, J. (1990). An integrated approach to the treatment of a specific phobia in a nine year old boy. *Journal for Phobia Research* 3:95–105.

Madonna, J., and Chandler, R. (1986). Aggressive play and bereavement in group therapy with latency-aged boys. *Journal of Child and Adolescent Psychotherapy* 3:109–114.

Madonna, J., and Ciottone, R. (1984). A family systems orientation to the problem of fire setting. In *Family Therapy Techniques for Problem*

Behaviors in Children and Teenagers, eds. C. Schaefer, J. Briemeister, and M. Fitton, San Francisco: Jossey Bass.

Marlatt, G. A., and Gordon, J. R. (1980). Determinants of relapse: implications for the maintenance of behavior change. In *Behavioral Medicine: Changing Healthy Life Styles*, eds. P. O. Davidson and S. M. Davidson, pp. 410–452. New York: Bruner/Mazel.

————— (1985). *Relapse Prevention*. New York: Guilford.

Maslow, A. H. (1954). *Motivation and Personality*. New York: Harper.

Meadow, P. (1981). Drive theory in diagnosis and treatment. *Modern Psychoanalysis* 86:141–176.

Moustakis, C. (1953). *Children in Play Therapy: A Key to Understanding Normal and Disturbed Emotions*. New York: McGraw-Hill.

————— (1955). Emotional adjustment and the play therapy process. *Journal of Genetic Psychology* 86:79–99.

————— (1959). *Psychotherapy with Children: The Living Relationships*. New York: Harper & Row.

————— (1966). *Existential Child Therapy: The Child's Discovery of Himself*. New York: Basic Books.

————— (1973). *The Child's Discovery of Himself*. New York: Jason Aronson.

Piaget, J. (1951). *Play, Dreams and Imitation in Childhood*. New York: Norton.

Rogers, C. (1948). *Dealing with Social Tension: A Presentation of Client-Centered Counseling as a Means of Handling Interpersonal Conflict*. New York: Hinde.

————— (1951). *Client-Centered Therapy: Its Current Practice, Indications and Theory*. Boston: Houghton Mifflin.

————— (1961). *On Becoming a Person*. Boston: Houghton Mifflin.

Schaefer, C., ed. (1976). *Therapeutic Use of Children's Play*. New York: Jason Aronson.

Schaefer, C. (1988). *Innovative Interventions in Child and Adolescent Therapy*. New York: Wiley.

Schaefer, C., and O'Connor, K. (1983). *Handbook of Play Therapy*. New York: Wiley.

Sgroi, S. (1982). *Handbook of Clinical Intervention in Child Sexual Abuse*. Lexington, MA: Heath.

Spero, M. (1980). Use of the telephone in child play therapy. *Social Work* 25:57–60.

Spotnitz, H., Nagelberg, L., and Feldman, Y. (1976a). The attempt at healthy insulation in a withdrawn child. In *Psychotherapy of Pre-oedipal Conditions*, ed. H. Spotnitz, pp. 175–187. New York: Jason Aronson.

———— (1976b). Ego reinforcement. In *Psychotherapy of Pre-oedipal Conditions*, ed. H. Spotnitz, pp. 175–187. New York: Jason Aronson.

Sullivan. H. S. (1953). *The Interpersonal Theory of Psychiatry*. New York: Norton.

Wapner, S. (1981). Transactions of persons-in-environments: Some critical transitions. *Journal of Environmental Psychology* 1:223–239.

Wapner, S., Kaplan, B., and Ciottone, R. (1981). Self–world relationships in critical environment transitions: childhood and beyond. In *Spatial Representation and Behavior Across the Life Span*, eds. L. Liben, A. Patterson, and N. Newcombe, New York: Academic.

Wapner, S., Kaplan, B., and Cohen, S. (1973). An organismic-developmental perspective for understanding transactions of men-in-environments. *Environment and Behavior* 5:255–289.

Wapner, S., and Werner, H. (1957). *Perceptual Development*. Worcester, MA: Clark University Press.

Werner, H. (1948). *The Comparative Psychology of Mental Development*. New York: International Universities Press.

———— (1957). The concept of development from a comparative and organismic point of view. In *Concept of Development*, ed. D. B. Harris, pp. 125–148. Minneapolis: University of Minnesota Press.

Werner, H., and Kaplan, B. (1963). *Symbol Formation*. New York: Wiley.

Winnicott, D. W. (1952). *Through Paediatrics and Psychoanalysis*. New York: Basic Books.

Yates, A. J. (1970). *Behavior Therapy*. New York: Wiley.

Young, M. H. (1989). *Self-management training in children with tic disorders: clinical experience with hypno-behavioral treatment*. Paper presented at the 31st annual scientific meeting of the American Society of Clinical Hypnosis, Nashville, TN.

———— (1991). Tics. In *Clinical Hypnosis with Children*, eds. W. C. Wester and D. J. O'Grady, New York: Bruner/Mazel.

Index

Abuse. *See* Sexual abuse
Acting out, Synergistic Play
    Therapy, 48–49
Action
    agent–act distinction, play
        therapy and, 31
    rage and, 157–160
    Synergistic Play Therapy, 48
Acunzo, M., 33
Adult psychoanalysis. *See*
    Psychoanalysis
Agent–act distinction, play therapy
    and, 31
Anatomically correct dolls, 85, 90, 91
Anderson, S. C., 23
Anger. *See* Rage
Anxiety
    full disclosure, 140
    trauma recall, 131

Araji, S., 23
Aristotle, 27
Assessment and planning phase,
    Synergistic Play Therapy, 8–
    11
Axline, V. M., 30, 31, 32
Azrin, N. H., 32

Bandura, A., 32, 33
Berliner, L., 23
Body image, sexual abuse and,
    19–20
Boundaries
    play therapy and, 33–36
    Synergistic Play Therapy,
        80
    trauma recall, 132
Brassard, M. R., 23
Burke, K. E., 208

Chandler, R., 152
Child–adult distinction,
    Synergistic Play Therapy, 43–
    44, 204
Ciottone, R., xii, 2, 11, 33
Cirillo, L., ix, 54, 208
Clothing, Synergistic Play
    Therapy, 56
Cognitive development,
    Synergistic Play Therapy, 37
Cohen, S. B., ix
Color, Synergistic Play Therapy,
    77
Communication, Synergistic Play
    Therapy, 41–42
Compassion. *See* Empathy
Confidentiality, Synergistic Play
    Therapy, 54–55
Conflict, Synergistic Play Therapy,
    37
Corder, B., 23
Counterphobic posture
    rage and, 151, 152
    Synergistic Play Therapy, 51,
    71, 86, 115
Countertransference, full
    disclosure, 139

Davison, G. C., 32
Dedifferentiation, closing stages,
    185–186
Defenses
    Synergistic Play Therapy, 37
    trauma recall, 134, 135
Denial
    rage and, 152
    trauma recall, 134, 135
Depersonalization, Synergistic Play
    Therapy, 38

Desensitization, play therapy and,
    32
Destructive impulses, play therapy
    and, 25
Differentiation
    closing stages, 182
    full disclosure, 142
    Synergistic Play Therapy, 38
Disclosure
    play therapy and, x
    Synergistic Play Therapy, 137–
    150
Dissociative states, Synergistic Play
    Therapy, 38
Dream
    closing stages, 197
    play and, 26
    Synergistic Play Therapy, 100
    trauma recall, 134
Dysfunctional family, dynamics of,
    6–8

Eating. *See* Food
Ego enhancement
    closing stages, 180
    retribution and, 169
    trauma recall, 120
Emotional insulation, Synergistic
    Play Therapy, 117–118
Empathy
    full disclosure, 139
    parentified child, 6
    retribution and, 175
Empowerment
    full disclosure, 138
    Synergistic Play Therapy, 54–55
Epistemology, play therapy and, 27
Erikson, E. H., 1
Extinction, play therapy and, 32

Feldman, S., 174
Finkelhor, D., 23
Food
  closing stages, 193, 196
  Synergistic Play Therapy, 52,
    164–165
Foster care
  case illustration, 7–8
  Synergistic Play Therapy and,
    11–17
Free association, play therapy and,
  24, 25, 26
Freud, A., 24, 25, 26, 27, 28, 29
Freud, S., 23, 27, 174
Full disclosure. *See* Disclosure

Gardner, R., 23
Generalization, play therapy and,
  32
Gifts
  closing stages, 184–185, 188,
    194
  Synergistic Play Therapy, 52
Ginott, H., ix, xii, 1, 33, 34, 35,
  36, 37, 38, 41, 46, 203, 205
Goldfried, M. R., 32
Gordon, J. R., 32
Groth, A. N., 23
Guerney, L., 30

Haworth, M., 23, 207
Here-and-now
  closing stages, 192
  full disclosure, 138
Hinshelwood, R. D., 24
Hug-Hellmuth, H., 24

Inferred meaning, Synergistic Play
  Therapy, 44–51

Interpretation
  play therapy and, 28, 29
  retribution and, 176–177
  trauma recall, 123
Intervention
  metaphor, 106–107, 114
  Synergistic Play Therapy, 37,
    40–41
  trauma recall, 134, 136
Intimacy, Synergistic Play
  Therapy, 51–52, 205

Kaplan, B., ix, 2, 54, 208
Klein, M., 20, 24, 25, 26, 27, 28

Landreth, G., 150
Language
  inferred meaning, Synergistic
    Play Therapy, 44–51
  mastery and, 54
Learning theory
  play therapy and, 32–33
  retribution and, 163
  Synergistic Play Therapy, 37
Lebo, D., 46
Limit setting, boundaries, play
  therapy and, 35–36, 46
Lindholm, K., 23
Little Hans case (Freud), 23–24

MacFarlane, K., 23
Madonna, J., xii, 32, 33, 152
Marlatt, G. A., 32
Maslow, A. H., 30
Mastery
  full disclosure, 142
  language and, 54
  Synergistic Play Therapy, 37
Menolascino, F., 207

Metaphor
    closing stages, 183, 186
    full disclosure, 142
    play therapy and, 31–32
    rage and, 152–153, 158
    retribution through, 163–178
    Synergistic Play Therapy, 40–
        41, 85–115
    trauma recall, 122, 125, 132
Modeling, play therapy and, 33
Moustakas, C., 23, 30

Nondirective therapy, play therapy
    and, 30–31
Nunn, R. G., 32

Object constancy
    play therapy and, 21
    trauma recall, 120
O'Connor, K., 23
Olfactory stimulation, Synergistic
    Play Therapy, 73–74
Ordeal therapy, play therapy and,
    33
Organismic developmental
    metatheory, Synergistic Play
    Therapy and, 2–3, 38–39
Orthogenetic principle, Synergistic
    Play Therapy, 37, 91

Paradoxical prescription, play
    therapy and, 33
Parentified child, empathy, 6
Peeking, Synergistic Play Therapy,
    65–67
Phobias, play therapy and, 32
Physical restraint, Synergistic Play
    Therapy, 49–50
Piaget, J., 37, 205

Plato, 27
Play, dream and, 26
Play therapy. *See also* Synergistic
        Play Therapy
    boundaries and, 33–36
    epistemology and, 27
    free association and, 24, 25, 26
    interpretation and, 28, 29
    learning theory and, 32–33
    metaphor and, 31–32
    nondirective therapy and, 30–31
    object constancy and, 21
    overview of, ix–xi
    principles of, 32
    rapport and, xi–xii, 35
    self actualization and, 30
    social learning theory and, 33
    symbolism, 26, 28, 29
    transference and, 27–28
    transference neurosis and, 28
Power dimension, Synergistic Play
        Therapy, 44–51, 204
Primal scene, case illustration, 7
Process, play therapy and, 29
Psychoanalysis, play therapy and,
    24, 25
Psychodynamics, Synergistic Play
        Therapy, 37

Rage
    accessing of, 151–161
    retribution and, 163, 167, 175–
        176, 177–178
    trauma recall, 124, 125, 128, 132
Rape, trauma recall, 127
Rapport
    play therapy and, xi–xii, 35
    Synergistic Play Therapy, 42–
        43, 203–204

Reframing, closing stages, 181
Regression, full disclosure, 147
Religion, family dynamics and, 10
Resistance
    closing stages, 180, 181
    Synergistic Play Therapy, 75–
        76
Retribution, Synergistic Play
        Therapy, 163–178
Rogers, C., 30, 205
Romano, J., 20

Schaefer, C., 23
Self actualization, play therapy
        and, 30
Self-aggrandizement, trauma
        recall, 130
Self-esteem, full disclosure, 138
Self theory, Synergistic Play
        Therapy, 37
Self–world relationship
    full disclosure, 144
    rage and, 151, 156
    Synergistic Play Therapy, 39–
        40, 88
Sex of therapist, child sex abuse
        therapy and, 10–11
Sexual abuse
    body image and, 19–20
    boundaries, play therapy and,
        33–36
    play therapy and, x–xi
    Synergistic Play Therapy
        physical setting, 54
        power dimension, 50, 51
Sexuality. See Primal scene
Sgroi, S., 23
Siblings, parentified child, 6
Silence, trauma recall, 135

Social learning theory, play
        therapy and, 33
Space, Synergistic Play Therapy,
        51
Spero, M., 171
Spotnitz, H., 42, 117
Strivings, Synergistic Play
        Therapy, 37
Substitution, play therapy and, 36
Suicide
    case illustration, 5, 6, 7, 18, 59,
        68
    full disclosure, 147
    retribution and, 176
    trauma recall, 124
Sullivan, H. S., 43, 129
Symbolism
    dream/play, 26
    full disclosure, 138
    play therapy and, 28, 29
    rage and, 157
    Synergistic Play Therapy, 48
Synergistic Play Therapy, xii. See
        also Play therapy
    assessment and planning phase,
        8–11
    case example
        family dynamics, 5–8
        initiation of therapy, 53–84
    clinical antecedents of, 23–36
    closing stages, 179–202
    conceptual framework of, 37–
        52
    foster care interface, 11–17
    full disclosure, 137–150
    implications of, 203–213
    metaphor, 85–115. See also
        Metaphor
    overview of, 1–3

Synergistic Play Therapy (*continued*)
    problems and goals, overview
        of, 17–21
    rage, 151–161
    retribution, 163–178
    sources of, ix
    trauma recall, 117–136

Termination
    of session
        full disclosure, 146, 148
        Synergistic Play Therapy, 81–
            83
    of Synergistic Play Therapy,
        closing stages, 179–202
Timing, Synergistic Play Therapy,
    43
Toys, play therapy and, 24, 25,
    41
Transference
    play therapy and, 27–28
    rage and, 153, 154, 160–161

Synergistic Play Therapy, 37, 48
    trauma recall, 132
Transference neurosis, play
    therapy and, 28
Transitional object
    closing stages, 193
    full disclosure, 149
Trauma, play therapy and, x–xi
Trauma recall, Synergistic Play
    Therapy, 117–136

Unconscious, play therapy and, 28

Walters, R. H., 33
Wapner, S., ix, 2
Werner, H., ix, xii, 2, 54
Winnicott, D. W., 165
Working through, play therapy
    and, x

Yates, A. J., 32
Young, M. H., 32, 33